COMPLETE BOOK ON CONSTITUTIONAL CONVENTION

COMPLETE BOOK ON CONSTITUTIONAL CONVENTION

G.K. Pagare

CYBER TECH PUBLICATIONS
4264/3, Ansari Road, Daryaganj, New Delhi-110002 (India)
Ph.: 011-23244078, 011-43559448 Fax: 011-23280028
E-Mail: cyberpublicationsdelhi@yahoo.com
Website: www.cybertechpublications.com

COMPLETE BOOK ON CONSTITUTIONAL CONVENTION

G.K. Pagare

First Edition 2010

Published by :

G.S. Rawat for **Cyber Tech Publications**
4264/3, Ansari Road, Daryaganj, New Delhi-110002 (India)
Ph.: 011-23244078, 011-43559448 Fax: 011-23280028
E-Mail: cyberpublicationsdelhi@yahoo.com
Website: www.cybertechpublications.com

Printed at: Asian Offset Printers, Delhi-53

Preface

This study explores both the empirical and the substantive validity of the traditional historical and philosophical interpretations of the cre-ation of the American Constitution. Advocates of differing interpreta-tions of the Constitution's drafting have taken two distinct views, some arguing that the Convention created the Constitution out of a commit-ment to ideas and political principles, others arguing that the partici-pants designed the Constitution to aid and protect their social, political, and economic interests. This study looks more closely at the roll-call voting record of the Constitutional Convention than any previous study and concludes that an accurate understanding of the constitution-mak-ing process must acknowledge that both philosophical and material concerns were at work in the Federal Convention.

I will demonstrate that constitution making is an elaborate and delicate, yet elegantly simple, process in which the participants refer to distinctly different sources of knowledge and information to reach judgments about two fundamental aspects of constitutional design. Thus, I will show that the Founding Fathers acted out of broad, though distinct and competing, philosophical perspectives concerning the work-ing relationships between human nature, particular political institutions, and the resulting social order, when they struggled to design the general institutional structure for the new national government. On these issues of basic governmental organization and design, the nationalist delegates from the Middle Atlantic states, generally supporting Madison's vision of an "extended" republic, opposed the delegates from New England and the lower South, who held tenaciously to Montesquieu's warning that free institutions could survive only in "small" republics.

The delegates, on the other hand, pursued narrow material interests when they voted on specific mechanisms for implementing various aspects of the constitutional design. When debate touched upon the distribution of power and influence within the institutions of the new government, coalitions based upon interest posed the large states against the small, the northern states against the southern, and the states with large claims to the lands in the West against the states that had no such claims to future wealth and power.

—*Author*

CONTENTS

CONTENTS

1

Introduction

CONSTITUTIONAL CONVENTION (POLITICAL CUSTOM)

A **constitutional convention** is an informal and uncodified procedural agreement that is followed by the institutions of a state. In some states, notably those Commonwealth of Nations states which follow the Westminster system and whose political systems are derived from British constitutional law, most of the functions of government are guided by constitutional convention rather than by a formal written constitution. In these states, the actual distribution of power may be markedly different from those which are described in the formal constitutional documents. In particular, the formal constitution often confers wide discretionary powers to the head of state which in practice are used only on the advice of the head of government. Some constitutional conventions operate separate from or alongside written constitutions. Others, notably in Britain, which has much of its constitution unwritten, have a form of constitutional status. Many old conventions have been replaced or superseded by laws.

Definitions

Conventions can be analysed from either a *descriptive* or *prescriptive* viewpoint. A descriptive view is that a convention is:

... a generally accepted political practice, usually with a record of successful applications or precedents.

An alternative, prescriptive, view sees conventions as:

... rules of constitutional behaviour which are considered to be binding by and upon those who operate the Constitution but which are not enforced by the law courts ... nor by the presiding officers in the [legislature].

Origins

Constitutional conventions generally arise from precedent. For example, the constitutional convention that the Prime Minister of the United Kingdom must govern with the support of the House of Commons derived from the unsuccessful attempt of Robert Peel to govern without it in 1834-1835.

Constitutional conventions are the same as formal constitutional amendments in that they are created over time, and it may be difficult or impossible to identify when a constitutional convention has come into effect or sometimes even what the constitutional conventions are.

Unenforceability

Constitutional conventions are not obligatory, but are in effect procedural agreements to which all sides adhere. Some conventions evolve or change over time; for example, before 1918 the British cabinet requested a parliamentary dissolution from the monarch, with the Prime Minister conveying the request. Since 1918, prime ministers on their own initiative request dissolutions, and need not consult members of the cabinet. However conventions are rarely ever broken. Unless there is general agreement on the breach, the person who breaches a convention is often heavily criticised, on occasions leading to a loss of respect or popular support. It is often said that "conventions are not worth the paper they are not written on", i.e., they are unenforceable in law because they are not written down. Whatever enforceability they have comes from history, tradition, symbolism and their cross-party support.

In the Patriation Reference made over negotiations on the Constitution of Canada, the Supreme Court of Canada ruled that a convention, even through long and rigorous usage, could not "crystallize" into law. This principle is regarded as authoritative in a number of other jurisdictions, including the UK.

CONSTITUTIONAL CONVENTIONS IN THE UNITED KINGDOM

While Britain does not have a written constitution that is a single document, the collection of legal instruments that have developed into a body of law known as constitutional law has existed for hundreds of years. As part of this uncodified British constitution, **constitutional conventions** of British constitutional law play a key role. They are rules that are observed by the various constituted parts though they are not written in any document having legal authority; there are often underlying enforcing principles that are themselves not formal and codified. Nonetheless it is very unlikely that there would be a departure of such conventions without good reason, even if an underlying enforcing principle has been overtaken by history, as these conventions also acquire the force of custom.

EXAMPLES OF CONSTITUTIONAL CONVENTIONS

Australia

- The Senate will not deny supply to the government. (Broken in 1975. The Senate argued that its breaking of convention was in response to alleged breaking of numerous conventions by then Prime Minister Gough Whitlam. Whitlam did not agree. See Australian constitutional crisis of 1975.)
- A Loss of Supply requires either the resignation of the Prime Minister or a parliamentary dissolution. (Broken in 1975 by Whitlam, who argued that the Senate's breach of convention in delaying supply indefinitely did not require a dissolution or resignation. The result was a stalemate and the intervention of the Governor-General mentioned below. Each party to the dispute blamed someone else for breaching a convention, requiring *their* own breaching of another one in response.)

Bosnia and Herzegovina

- The six members of the Constitutional Court of Bosnia and Herzegovina, that are chosen by the Parliaments of entities of Bosnia and Herzegovina, should be chosen in a way as to establish the national balance, of "constituent peoples", in the Court (two Bosniaks, two Croatians and two Serbs), although the Constitution does not have this requirement.
- The Chairman of the Council of Ministers of Bosnia and Herzegovina should be of different nationality in every new term (establishing the "rotation"), although this is not formally regulated.
- The government of Republika Srpska should inform the government of Bosnia and Herzegovina of its intention to establish special parallel relationships with neighboring states, including negotiations. Also, High Representative should be notified of any such intent, especially if there is a document that should be signed between parties, although the Constitution does not have this requirement (also for first example).

Canada

- Previously the Senate would not defeat a bill passed by the House of Commons, it was broken in 1989 when the Senate defeated a bill regulating abortions. Broken again for a bill that would have ratified a free trade agreement between Canada and the United States. Currently the convention is that the Senate will not defeat a bill considered to be a matter of confidence, because the Government by convention is accountable to the House of Commons.
- The Prime Minister will request the Governor General to call an election upon the defeat of the government in a confidence or money vote. This convention was broken in 1968 when the ruling minority government unexpectedly lost a money vote. All the parties in Parliament, who were not prepared for a snap election, agreed to pass a resolution

retroactively declaring the lost money vote was not a matter of confidence.

- Though it is mentioned in various constitutional documents, the precise nature of the office of the Prime Minister operates mostly according to understood, uncodified British conventions.

Commonwealth Realms

- The Governor-General is appointed on the advice of the Prime Minister of the day, is a resident of the country he will represent, and can be dismissed immediately on the advice of the Prime Minister (exceptions are Papua New Guinea and the Solomon Islands, where the Governor-General is elected by Parliament and then formally appointed by the Queen, and the United Kingdom which has no vice-regal office). Similarly, state Governors or Lieutenant-Governors are appointed on the advice of the relevant state ministers.
- Neither the Monarch or Governors-General will participate in the political process unless there is an extreme circumstance that merits the use of reserve powers (the last case being in Australia in 1975, when Sir John Kerr controversially dismissed the Prime Minister over the stalemate mentioned above).
- Neither the Monarch or Governors-General will make partisan speeches or state partisan opinions. This convention was broken in 1975 by Sir Colin Hannah, the Governor of Queensland, who called for the defeat of the Whitlam Government. The Queen, on Whitlam's advice, revoked Hannah's dormant commission to act as Administrator of the Commonwealth of Australia and the Foreign and Commonwealth Office later refused the Premier of Queensland's request that they advise the Queen to appoint Hannah to a second term as Governor (in 1975, Australian State Governors were still appointed on the advice of UK ministers)

- All executive decisions are taken by a formal meeting of the Executive Council, i.e. the Governor-General-in-Council (allegedly broken in the mid 1970s, but followed since)

Denmark

- The Danish Constitution makes reference to the King in great detail. Apart from the fact that this is understood to include a Queen regnant as well, references to the King acting in a political capacity are understood to mean the Prime Minister, as the Constitution stipulates that the King exercises his powers through the Cabinet.
- According to the Constitution, any public expenditure must be provided for in the annual money bill or provisional money bills. However, although not provided for in the Constitution, according to constitutional custom, the Parliamentary Budgetary Committee has the power to authorise provisional expenditure, regardless of the fact that such expenditure is not formally included in the budget (such grants are however then marked for adoption in the next forthcoming money bill).

France

- If the President of the Republic and the Prime Minister are not from the same party, foreign affairs and defense are conducted by the President.
- If the president of the National Assembly, the president of the Senate or 60 deputies or 60 senators claim that a just-voted statute is unconstitutional, the President of the Republic does not sign the law and instead waits for a petition to be sent to the Constitutional Council.
- When the death penalty was in effect, sentenced prisoners were not executed until they had asked the President of the Republic to grant clemency and the president had declined to do so, unless they did not seek clemency.

Ireland

- Although the President of Ireland is empowered to refuse a request by the Taoiseach to dissolve the Dail if he no longer has a majority, he or she has never done so. Brian Lenihan made several attempts to contact President Patrick Hillery when the government of Garret FitzGerald fell in 1982 to try to convince him to do so, but President Hillery refused to take any calls.

Lebanon

- The Lebanese constitution states that the President of Lebanon is elected by a simple majority of the Parliament of Lebanon. However, due to the country's delicate ethnic balance, the Parliament's various factions usually try to agree on a consensus candidate.
- Under the unwritten National Pact, the president must always be a Maronite Christian; the prime minister a Sunni Muslim; the speaker of Parliament a Shia Muslim; and the deputy speaker Greek Orthodox.

New Zealand

- The Prime Minister of New Zealand will not ask for an early election unless he or she is unable to govern, or needs to seek the opinion of the electorate on an issue of major importance.

Norway

Because of its pivotal role in providing independence and establishing democracy in the 19th century, the Norwegian parliament has been very reluctant in changing the written constitution of 1814. Few of the developments in the political system that have been taking place since then have been codified as amendments. This reluctance has been labelled "Constitutional conservatism". The two most important examples of Constitutional conventions in the Norweigan political system are parliamentarism and the declining power of the King.

- Parliamentarism has evolved since 1884 and entails that the cabinet must maintain the support of parliament (an absence of mistrust, but it need not have its express support).
- All new laws are passed and all new governments are therefore formed in a de jure fashion by the King, although not necessarily in a de facto sense.
- According to the written constitution, new governments are appointed by the King. The appointment of new governments by the King is a formality, and the king has not directly exercised executive powers since 1905.

United Kingdom

- The texts of most international treaties are laid before Parliament at least twenty one days before ratification (the 'Ponsonby Rule' of 1924).
- Treaties, although ratified using Royal Prerogative, will not be ratified until the passing of a suitable statute law by Parliament. This is necessary if the treaty requires an amendment to domestic law, affects the rights of private individuals, requires public expenditure, grants the Crown additional powers, or cedes territory. Examples include extradition treaties, double taxation treaties, and reciprocal social-security treaties.
- The monarch will accept and act on the advice of their ministers, who are responsible to Parliament for that advice; the monarch does not ignore that advice, except when exercising Reserve powers.
- The Prime Minister of the United Kingdom is the leader of the party (or coalition of parties) with an absolute majority of seats in the House of Commons and therefore most likely to command the support of the House of Commons.
- All money bills must originate in the House of Commons.
- The Prime Minister alone advises the monarch on a dissolution of Parliament (since 1918).
- The monarch will grant a dissolution if requested (since 1832 – the Lascelles Principles in 1951 informally outlined

the principles and issues that might lead to a refusal of a dissolution).

- The monarch grants the Royal Assent to all legislation – sometimes characterised as all legislation passed in good faith. It is possible that ministers could advise against giving consent, as happens with the Crown dependencies (convention since the early 1700s – previously monarchs did refuse or withhold the Royal Assent).
- Parliament will not debate the monarchy without the monarch's prior consent (given on the advice of ministers) – known as Queen's Consent.
- The Prime Minister should be a member of either House of Parliament (between the 1700s-1963).
    - o In 1963 it was amended to the effect that no Prime Minister should come from the House of Lords. When the last Prime Minister peer, the Earl of Home, took office he renounced his peerage, and as Sir Alec Douglas-Home became an MP.
    - o The Prime Minister can hold office temporarily whilst not a Member of Parliament, for example during a General Election or in the case of Douglas-Home, between resigning from the Lords and being elected to the Commons in a by-election.
- All Cabinet members must be members of the Privy Council.
- The House of Lords should not reject a budget passed by the House of Commons. This was broken controversially in 1909 by the House of Lords, which argued that the Convention was linked to another Convention that the Commons would not introduce a Bill that 'attacked' peers and their wealth. The Lords claimed that the Commons broke this Convention in Chancellor of the Exchequer David Lloyd George's budget, justifying the Lords' rejection of the budget. The Commons disputed the existence of a linked convention. As a consequence, the Lords' powers over budgets was greatly lessened by the Parliament Act 1911.

- During a General Election, no major party shall put up an opponent against a Speaker seeking re-election. However, the Scottish National Party (SNP) does stand against the Speaker if he or she represents a Scottish constituency, as is the case with Michael Martin, the current Speaker.
- The Westminster Parliament will only legislate on reserved matters. It will not legislate on non-reserved matters ('devolved matters') without first seeking the consent of the Scottish Parliament (since 1999, the Sewel convention, later renamed to Legislative Consent Motions).
- The House of Lords shall not veto legislation from the House of Commons that was a part of the government's manifesto (the Salisbury Convention).

United States

- The President of the United States will give his State of the Union Speech in person, before a joint session of Congress. The constitution requires the President give an update on the state of the union "from time to time", but no specifics are outlined. By custom, the President gives the SOTU annually. Only in recent years has the president given the SOTU as a public speech.
- Much of how the United States Cabinet operates is dictated by convention; its operations are only vaguely alluded to in the US constitution.
- While members of the United States House of Representatives are only required to live in the state they represent, it has long been expected that they live in the district they represent as well.

Switzerland

The following constitutional conventions are part of the political culture of Switzerland. They hold true at the federal level and mostly so at the cantonal and communal level. Mostly, they aim to reconcile the democratic principle of majority rule with the need to achieve consensus in a nation that is much more heterogeneous in many respects than other nation-states.

- The government is a body of equals composed in political proportion to the weight of the various factions in Parliament; this creates a permanent grand coalition.
- Members of a collective body, including the federal government, observe collegiality at all times, that is, they do not publicly criticise one another. They also publicly support all decisions of the collective, even against their own opinion or that of their political party. In the eye of many observers, this convention has become rather strained at the federal level, at least after the 2003 elections to the Swiss Federal Council.
- The presidency of a collective body, particularly a government, rotates yearly; the president is a primus inter pares.

CONSTITUTIONAL CONVENTION (POLITICAL MEETING)

A **constitutional convention** is a gathering for the purpose of writing a new constitution or revising an existing constitution. A **general constitutional convention** is called to create the first constitution of a political unit or to entirely replace an existing constitution.

An **unlimited constitutional convention** is called to revise an existing constitution to the extent that it deems to be proper, whereas a *limited constitutional convention* is restricted to revising only the areas of the current constitution named in the convention's *call*, the legal mandate establishing the convention. In the case of the Philadelphia Convention, delegates met for the "sole purpose of revising the Articles of Confederation."

George Washington was elected president of this convention. Once the body convened, meeting and deliberations were conducted in secrecy with James Madison serving as recorder. It was rapidly decided that the body would ignore the limitations of its call and propose the replacement of the Articles with an entirely new basic instrument of government.

Examples of constitutional conventions include the:

United States: Annapolis Convention (1786), which proposed what became the Philadelphia Convention (1787)-Drafted the United States Constitution for ratification by the states. Article V of the constitution sets forth a mechanism whereby future constitutional conventions can be held. The constitution has been amended several times since the Philadelphia Convention, but never (as of 2009) by this method.

- France: The National Convention of 1792 (commonly referred to as *The Convention*) convened during The French Revolution on September 20 with the purpose of writing a Republican Constitution following the suspension of the French Monarchy. The monarchy was officially abolished on September 21 by The Convention.
- Missouri Constitutional Convention (1861-63), established Missouri's provisional government during the American Civil War
- Canada: (1864), Quebec Conference, 1864, and London Conference of 1866 (1866).
- Australian constitutional conventions-1891, 1897, 1973 and 1998.
- Germany: Parlamentarischer Rat (Parliamentary Council) (1948)-Drafted the Basic Law of the Federal Republic for ratification by the *Länder*.
- Northern Ireland Constitutional Convention (1975-1976)-a failed attempt to find a solution to the status of Northern Ireland.
- Scottish Constitutional Convention (1989)-produced a plan for Scottish devolution.
- European Convention (2001)-Drafted the Constitution for Europe for approval by the European Council and ratification by the member states.
- Philippine Constitutional Convention
  - o 1935-to draft a constitution to create the autonomous Commonwealth of the Philippines under the U.S.

Tydings-McDuffie Act. The constitution was also used in the 3rd Republic (1946) until the passage of the 1973 constitution. Members were elected through the Philippine Constitutional Convention election, 1934

- 1971-to draft a revised constitution to replace the old U.S. customed 1935 Philippine constititution. Members were elected through the Philippine Constitutional Convention election, 1970. The system of government changed from Presidentitial to Parliamentary to Presidentital-Parliamentary (in 1984 amendment). The constitution lasted until the downfall of Ferdinand Marcos in 1986 and Corazon Aquino appointed members to draft the 1987 Constitution through a Constitutional Commission.

Constitutional conventions have also been used by constituent states of federations — such as the individual states of the United States — to create, replace, or revise their own constitutions. Though the several states have never held a national constitutional convention for the purpose of proposing amendments, the 21st Amendment to the US Constitution was ratified not by the state legislatures, but by state level conventions after it was passed by Congress, as described as an alternate method of ratification in Article V of the US Constitution.

PHILADELPHIA CONVENTION

The **Philadelphia Convention** (now also known as the **Constitutional Convention**, the **Federal Convention**, or the "**Grand Convention at Philadelphia**") took place from May 25 to September 17, 1787, in Philadelphia, Pennsylvania, to address problems in governing the United States of America, which had been operating under the Articles of Confederation following independence from Great Britain. Although the Convention was purportedly intended only to revise the Articles of Confederation, the intention of many of its proponents, chief among them James Madison and Alexander Hamilton, was from the outset to create a new government rather than "fix" the existing one. The delegates elected George Washington to preside over the convention. The result of the Convention was the United States Constitution. The Convention is one of the central events in the history of the United States.

Historical Context

Before the Constitution was drafted, the thirteen colonies operated under the Articles of Confederation, created by the Second Continental Congress which eventually caused deep divides between the states that the national government could not resolve.

On January 21, 1786, the Virginia Legislature, following James Madison's recommendation, invited all the states to send delegates to Annapolis, Maryland to discuss ways to reduce these interstate conflicts. At what came to be known as the Annapolis Convention, the few state delegates in attendance endorsed a motion that called for all states to meet in Philadelphia in May, 1787 to discuss ways to improve the Articles of Confederation in a "Grand Convention."

Delegates

The 55 delegates who drafted the Constitution included most of the outstanding leaders, or Founding Fathers, of the new nation. Thomas Jefferson, who was Minister to France during the convention, characterized the delegates as an assembly of "demi-gods." John Adams also did not attend, being abroad in Europe as Minister to Great Britain, but he wrote home to encourage the delegates. Patrick Henry was also absent; he refused to go because he "smelt a rat in Philadelphia, tending toward the monarchy." Rhode Island refused to send delegates to the convention.

The Convention

Due to the difficulty of travel in the late 1700s, very few of the selected delegates were present on the designated day of May 14, 1787, and it was not until May 25 that a quorum of seven states was secured. The convention convened in the Pennsylvania State House, and George Washington was unanimously elected as president of the convention. Although William Jackson was elected as secretary,

Madison's Notes of Debates in the Federal Convention of 1787 remain the most complete record of the convention.

DELIBERATIONS

Virginia Plan

Prior to the start of the convention, the Virginian delegates met, and using Madison's thoughts, work, and notes; came up with what came to be known as the Virginia Plan, also known as the "Large State" Plan. For this reason, James Madison is sometimes called the Father of the Constitution. Presented by Virginia governor Edmund Randolph on May 29, 1787, the Virginia Plan proposed a very powerful bicameral legislature. Both houses of the legislature would be determined proportionately. The lower house would be elected by the people, and the upper house would be elected by the lower house. The executive would exist solely to ensure that the will of the legislature was carried out and would therefore be selected by the legislature. The Virginia Plan also created a judiciary, and gave both the executive and some of the judiciary the power to veto, subject to override.

Plan of Charles Pinckney

Immediately after Randolph finished laying out the Virginia Plan, Charles Pinckney of South Carolina presented his own plan to the Convention. As Pinckney did not supply a hard copy, the only evidence we have are Madison's notes, so the details are somewhat sketchy. It was a confederation, or treaty, among the 13 states. There was to be a bicameral legislature made up of a Senate and a House of Delegates. The House would have one member for every one thousand inhabitants. The House would elect Senators who would serve by rotation for four years and represent one of four regions. Congress would meet in a joint session to elect a President, and would also appoint members of the cabinet. Congress, in joint session, would serve as the court of appeal of *dernier resort* in disputes between states. Pinckney did also provide for a supreme Federal Judicial Court. The Pinckney plan was not debated, but it may have been referred to by the Committee of Detail.

New Jersey Plan

After the Virginia Plan was introduced, New Jersey delegate William Paterson, asked for an adjournment to contemplate the Plan. Under the Articles of Confederation, each state was perfectly equal — each had one vote in Congress. The Virginia Plan threatened to limit the smaller states' power by making both houses of the legislature proportionate to population. On 14/15 June, 1787, a small-state caucus met to create a response to the Virginia Plan. The result was the New Jersey Plan, otherwise known as the "Small State Plan."

Paterson's New Jersey Plan was ultimately a rebuttal to the Virginia Plan, and was much closer to the original plan for the Convention-draft amendments to the Articles of Confederation to fix the problems in it. Under the New Jersey Plan, the current Congress would remain, but it would be granted new powers, such as the power to levy taxes and force their collection. An executive branch was created, to be elected by Congress (the plan allowed for a multi-person executive). The executives would serve a single term and were subject to recall on the request of state governors. The plan also created a judiciary that would serve for life, to be appointed by the executives. Lastly, any laws set by Congress would take precedence over state laws. When Paterson reported the plan to the convention on June 15, 1787, it was ultimately rejected, but it gave the smaller states a rallying point for their beliefs.

Hamilton's Plan

Unsatisfied with the New Jersey Plan and the Virginia Plan, Alexander Hamilton proposed his own plan. It also was known as the British Plan, because of its resemblance to the British system of government. In his plan, Hamilton advocated getting rid of state sovereignty to consolidate the states into a single nation. The plan featured a bicameral legislature, the lower house elected by the people for three years. The upper house would be elected by electors chosen by the people and would serve for life. The plan also gave the Governor, an executive elected by electors for a life-term of service, an absolute veto over bills. State governors would be appointed by the national legislature, and the national legislature had veto power over any state legislation.

Hamilton presented his plan to the Convention on June 18, 1787. The plan was well received as a well-thought-out plan, but it was given very little consideration because it resembled the British system too closely.

Connecticut Compromise

The Connecticut Compromise, forged by Roger Sherman from Connecticut, was proposed on June 11. Sherman proposed: "That the proportion of suffrage in the 1st. branch should be according to the respective numbers of free inhabitants; and that in the second branch or Senate, each State should have one vote and no more." Although Sherman was well liked and respected among the delegates, his plan failed at first. It was not until July 23 that representation was finally settled.

Slavery

Many questions remained unresolved. Among the most important were the controversial issues surrounding slavery. Slaves accounted for about one-fifth of the population in the American colonies. Most of them lived in the Southern colonies, where slaves made up 40 percent of the population. Whether slavery was to be permitted and continued under the new Constitution was a matter of conflict between the North and South, with several Southern states refusing to join the Union if slavery was not allowed.

One of the most contentious slavery-related issue was the question of whether slaves would be counted as part of the population in determining representation in Congress or considered property not entitled to representation. Delegates from states with a large population of slaves argued that slaves should be considered persons in determining representation but as property if the new government were to levy taxes on the states on the basis of population. Delegates from states where slavery had disappeared or almost disappeared argued that slaves should be included in taxation but not in determining representation.

Finally, delegate James Wilson proposed the Three-Fifths Compromise. This was eventually adopted by the convention.

Another issue at the Convention was what should be done about the slave trade. Ten states had already outlawed it. Many delegates heatedly denounced it, but the three states, Georgia and the two Carolinas, that allowed it threatened to leave the convention if the trade were banned. In effect they postponed the decision on the slave trade because of its contentious nature. The delegates to the Convention did not want its ratification to fail because of the conflict over slavery. Therefore, a special committee worked out another compromise: Congress would have the power to ban the slave trade, but not until at least 20 years had passed, in 1808.

Drafting and Signing

In late July, the convention appointed a Committee of Detail to draft a document based on the agreements that had been reached. After another month of discussion and refinement, a second committee, the Committee of Style and Arrangement, headed by Gouverneur Morris, and including Hamilton, William Samuel Johnson, Rufus King, and Madison, produced the final version, which was submitted for signing on September 17. Morris is credited now, as then, as the chief draftsman of the final document, including the stirring preamble.

Not all the delegates were pleased with the results; some left before the ceremony, and three of those remaining refused to sign: Edmund Randolph, George Mason of Virginia, and Elbridge Gerry of Massachusetts. George Mason demanded a Bill of Rights if he was to support the Constitution. The Bill of Rights was finally added and is considered the final compromise of the Convention-several states asked specifically for these amendments when ratifying the Constitution, and others ratified the Constitution with the understanding that a bill of rights would soon follow. Of the 39 who did sign, probably no one was completely satisfied. Their views were ably summed up by Benjamin Franklin, who said,

"There are several parts of this Constitution which I do not at present approve, but I am not sure I shall never approve them....

I doubt too whether any other Convention we can obtain, may be able to make a better Constitution.... It therefore astonishes me, Sir, to find this system approaching so near to perfection as it does; and I think it will astonish our enemies..."

CONVENTION TO PROPOSE AMENDMENTS TO THE UNITED STATES CONSTITUTION

Article Five of the United States Constitution provides for two methods to propose amendments to the Constitution. The first is a vote by two-thirds of each house of Congress. The second method is a **Convention to propose amendments to the United States Constitution**, or Article V convention. According to Article Five of the United States Constitution, an Article V convention must be called, "on the application to the Legislatures of two thirds of the several States." Once an Article V convention has proposed amendments, they must be ratified by three-fourths of the states for the amendments to become part of the Constitution. Congress has the power to choose between two methods of ratification: ratification by the state legislatures or ratification conventions called for that purpose.

History

To guard against oppressive government of any kind, the authors of the United States Constitution sought to establish institutional checks and balances. In framing the Constitution as the fundamental embodiment of such safeguards, the constitutional convention assembled in Philadelphia in 1787. One of the main reasons for the convention was that the Articles of Confederation required the unanimous consent of all 13 states for the national government to take action. This system had proved unworkable, and the constitution sought to address this problem.

The first proposal for a method of amending the constitution offered in the Constitutional Convention, contained in the Virginia Plan, sought to circumvent the national legislature, stating that "the assent of the National Legislature ought not to be required." In response, Alexander Hamilton privately circulated a proposal that gave the power to propose amendments to the national legislature, and the power to ratify the amendments to the states. The first reference in the convention records to a convention called by the states to amend the Constitution comes from drafts of the Constitution kept by the Committee of Detail. After some debate, James Madison removed reference to the convention amendment process, giving the national legislature sole authority to propose amendments whenever it thought necessary or when two-thirds of the states applied to the national legislature. As the Convention reviewed the revision the Committee of Style had made, several delegates voiced opposition to the idea of the national legislature retaining sole power to propose constitutional amendments. George Mason argued from the floor of the Convention that it "would be improper to require the consent of the Natl. Legislature, because they may abuse their power, and refuse their consent on that very account." Mason added that, "no amendments of the proper kind would ever be obtained by the people, if the Government should become oppressive." In response to these concerns, the Convention unanimously voted to add the language allowing states to petition Congress for a convention to propose amendments to the Constitution. James Madison did not oppose reintroducing language permitting the convention amendment process, but in what proved to be prescient concerns about the lack of detail in Article V about how the convention amendment process would work, stated that "difficulties might arise as to the form" a convention would take.

The text of Article V referring to the convention amendment process reads: "The Congress,... on the application of the Legislatures of two-thirds of the several States, shall call a convention for proposing Amendments." While the Article V convention process has never been used to amend the constitution, the number of states applying for a convention has nearly reached the required threshold several times. Several amendments to the constitution were proposed by Congress, at least in part, because of the threat of an Article V convention. Rather than risk a constitutional convention taking control of the amendment process, Congress acted first to propose amendments. At least four amendments (the Seventeenth, Twenty-First, Twenty-Second, and Twenty-Fifth Amendments) have been identified as being proposed by Congress partly in response to the threat of an Article V convention.

There have been two nearly-successful attempts to amend the constitution since the late 1960s. The first try was an attempt to propose an amendment that would overturn two controversial Supreme Court decisions, Wesberry v. Sanders and Reynolds v. Sims, dealing with voting districts and apportionment of votes in state elections. The attempt fell only one state short of reaching the 34 needed to force Congress to call a convention in 1969. After this peak, several states rescinded their applications, and interest in the proposed amendment subsided. The next nearly-successful attempt to call a convention was in the late 1970s and 1980s, in response to the ballooning federal deficit. States began applying to Congress for a constitutional convention to propose a balanced-budget amendment. By 1983, the number of applications had reached 32, only two states short of the 34 needed to force a convention. Enthusiasm for the amendment subsided, this time in response to concerns about whether a constitutional convention could be limited to a single subject and because Congress passed the Gramm-Rudman-Hollings Act, which required that the budget be balanced by 1991 (but was overturned by the Supreme Court in 1986).

Possible Scope

Because no Article V Convention has ever been convened, there are many unanswered questions about how a convention would function in practice. One major question is whether the scope of the convention's subject matter could be limited. The consensus is that Congress probably does not have the power to limit a convention, because the language of Article V leaves no discretion to Congress, merely stating that Congress "shall" call a convention when the proper number of state applications have been received. Comments made at the time the Constitution was adopted indicate that it was understood when the Constitution was drafted that Congress would have no discretion. In the The Federalist No. 85, Alexander Hamilton stated that when the proper number of applications had been received, Congress was "obliged" to call a convention and that "nothing is left to the discretion of Congress.".

James Madison also affirmed Hamilton's contention that Congress was obligated to call a convention when the requisite number of states requested it. In the North Carolina debates about ratifying the Constitution, James Iredell, who subsequently became one of the founding members of the Supreme Court, stated that when two-thirds of states have applied to Congress for a convention, Congress is "under the necessity of convening one" and that they have "no option."

By citing the Constitution's Necessary and Proper Clause, Congress has tried to enact a statute to regulate an Article V Convention. Sponsored by the late Senator Sam Ervin, such a bill passed the U.S. Senate unanimously in 1971 and again in 1973, but the proposed legislation remained locked up in a House committee where it died. Opponents to congressional regulation of Article V conventions argue that neither Article I nor Article V of the Constitution grants Congress this power, and the Founders intended that Congress "have no option." While the text and history of Article V seems to clearly indicate that Congress has no authority to enact such legislation, there has been no opportunity for courts to decide whether Congress has such authority because such legislation has actually never been adopted by Congress.

While Congress likely has no authority to limit the scope of an Article V Convention, the scholarly consensus is that the states *do* have that power. Congress's duty to call a convention when requested by the states means that it must call the convention that the states have requested. If the states, therefore, request a convention limited to a certain subject matter, then the convention that is called must be what the states requested. The drafting history of the Constitution at the Constitutional Convention of 1787 provides proof that it was the framers' intent that Article V conventions could be limited by the states, because it clearly indicates their intent that states could limit their applications according to subject matter.

If states have the power to limit a convention to a particular subject matter and Congress only has power to call a convention, but no further power to control or regulate it, then a potential concern becomes whether an Article V convention could become a "runaway convention" that attempts to exceed its scope. An Article V convention would merely be empowered to propose amendments. Until ratified, proposed amendments would have no constitutional effect. If a convention did attempt to exceed it scope, therefore, none of the amendments it proposed would become part of the constitution until three-fourths of the state ratified them. The states, therefore, act as a check to control a convention, by not ratifying amendments that have been inappropriately adopted. If a convention 'did' exceed its scope, and the states still chose to ratify its proposed amendments, the proposed amendments would have to enjoy widespread popularity, since ratification requires the assent of even more states (three-fourths) than are required to call a convention in the first place. Fears that an Article V convention may exceed its scope are likely unfounded, in light of the United States' experience with state constitutional convention. Over 600 state constitutional conventions have been held to amend state constitutions, with little evidence that any of them have exceeded their scope.

Subject Matter of Applications

A related question is whether Congress must tally all applications received, regardless of their subject matter, or whether Congress must tally according to the subject mater of the applications. If Congress must tally them according to subject matter, then it would only be able to call an Article V convention if it receives applications from 34 states requesting an Article V convention to address the same subject matter. States have requested that Congress call an Article V convention to propose amendments on a variety of subjects. According to the National Archives, Congress has, however, never officially totaled the applications, nor separated them by subject matter.

The drafting history of Article V indicates that states may limit the subject matter of their applications, and that Congress has a duty to tally applications separately by subject matter. During the drafting process, the Philadelphia Convention at one point adopted a version of Article V that gave power to Congress to propose amendments when two-thirds of both houses agreed, "or on the application of two thirds of the Legislatures of the several states." This version of Article V lacked any provision for a constitutional convention requested by the states. Instead, it included language almost identical to the final version of Article V, that instead gave states the power to petition Congress to propose amendments, rather than call a convention. Because the language between these two revisions is almost identical, it gives a better understanding of the meaning the framers understood Article V to have. It is obvious that applications from states petitioning Congress to propose amendments would be limited to a certain subject matter.

A general petition (IE, not limited by subject matter) asking Congress to propose amendments would serve no useful purpose, since Congress already had the general power to propose amendments. This language only makes sense if one understands it to mean that the framers understood that state petitions to Congress would be limited by subject matter.

Thus, in order to give effect to the originally understood meaning of Article V, and to give effect to states' intent when making applications to Congress for a convention, the accepted view is that state applications to Congress should be tallied individually, by subject matter to determine whether the two-thirds threshold of state applications has been met.

The legislatures of some states have submitted rescissions of applications. It is not clear from the language of Article V whether such rescissions are permissible. As discussed above, however, if the purpose of Article V is to give states power over a recalcitrant Congress, and if states may limit their applications by subject matter, it is likely that courts would hold that rescissions of applications are also valid, in order to give meaningful effect to the power Article V gives to states.

SUPREME COURT INTERPRETATIONS OF ARTICLE V

While the Supreme Court has never definitively interpreted the meaning of Article V, it has, on four separate occasions, referred to the Article V convention process:

Dodge v. Woolsey, 59 U.S. 331 (1855): "[The people] have directed that amendments should be made representatively for them, by the congress... ; or where the legislatures of two thirds of the several States shall call a convention for proposing amendments, which, in either case, become valid, to all intents and purposes, as a part of the constitution, when ratified...."

Hawke v. Smith, 253 U.S. 221 (1920): "[Article V] makes provision for the proposal of amendments either by two-thirds of both houses of Congress or on application of the Legislatures of two-thirds of the states; thus securing deliberation and consideration before any change can be proposed."

Dillon v. Gloss 256 U.S. 368 (1921): In discussing Congress's power to propose amendments, the Court affirmed that "[a] further mode of proposal—as yet never invoked—is provided, which is, that on the application of two thirds of the states Congress shall call a convention for the purpose."

United States v. Sprague, 282 U.S. 716 (1931): "[A]rticle 5 is clear in statement and in meaning, contains no ambiguity and calls for no resort to rules of construction.... It provides two methods for proposing amendments. Congress may propose them by a vote of two-thirds of both houses, or, on the application of the legislatures of two-thirds of the States, must call a convention to propose them."

Because of the political question doctrine, however, it is an open question whether federal courts could assert jurisdiction over a legal challenge to Congress, should it refuse to call a convention.

MISSOURI CONSTITUTIONAL CONVENTION (1861-63)

The **Missouri Constitutional Convention (1861-63)** was a constitutional convention in the American Civil War that decided that Missouri stay in the Union and also evicted the elected governor to create a provisional government during the war.

The exiled state legislature gathered in Neosho in October 1861 to pass an ordinance of secession. (See Missouri secession.) On the basis of this ordinance the Confederate Congress admitted Missouri as the 12th state of the Confederate States of America.

Background

Missouri has had four constitutions:

- 1820 (when the state entered the Union)
- 1865 (at the conclusion of the Civil War)
- 1875 (at the end of Reconstruction)
- 1945 (in the wake of the toppling of the Pendergast Machine).

According to Missouri law, the state constitution can only be totally rewritten via a Constitutional Convention. Since secession would have involved a new constitution, the special convention rather than the Missouri General Assembly was to decide the issue.

Missouri's official policy going into the convention was of neutrality with Missouri staying in the Union but not committing men, money or supplies to either side. The policy was first proposed in 1860 by outgoing governor Robert Marcellus Stewart (who was to eventually favor the Union) and affirmed by incoming governor Claiborne Fox Jackson (who was to eventually favor the Confederates).

Those who favored staying in the Union with the provision that status quo of slavery would continue were called "Conditional Union Men." Those who favored the Union regardless of whether slavery would be abolished were called "Unconditional Union Men."

The Missouri Legislature on January 17 passed a bill calling for the convention which was to have three members from each state senate district who were to be elected in a February 18 election. Charles H. Hardin introduced an amendment that passed 17-15 that required that any vote of secession would also require a majority vote of the state's qualified voters.

First Session

The first session of the Convention decided in a 98-1 vote to stay in the Union.

The convention met on February 28, 1861, in Jefferson City, Missouri and elected ex-governor Sterling Price to chair it. The convention consisted of 99 members — 82 of whom were born in slave states including 53 from Virginia and Kentucky.

The convention adjourned and reassembled in St. Louis, Missouri on March 4 meeting at the St. Louis Mercantile Library.

Hamilton Rowan Gamble was named chairman of the Federal relations committee which recommended:

The position of Missouri in relation to the adjacent States which would continue in the Union, would necessarily expose her, if she became a member of a new confederacy, to utter destruction whenever any rupture might take place between the different republics. In a military aspect, secession and connection with a Southern confederacy is annihilation for Missouri. The true position for her to assume is that of a State whose interests are bound up in the maintenance of the Union, and whose kind feelings and strong sympathies are with the people of the Southern States with whom they are connected by ties of friendship and blood.

On March 21 the convention voted 98-1 against Secession noting: no adequate cause [existed] to impel Missouri to dissolve her connections with the Federal Union.

Second Session

The concept of Missouri neutrality came into question almost immediately after the firing on Fort Sumter. Eight days after the start of the war, on April 20, a secessionist mob in Liberty, Missouri seized the Liberty Arsenal. When the governor called up the militia and clandestinely obtained artillery for it from the Confederacy, Union troops under United States Captain Nathaniel Lyon encircled the St. Louis militia encampment in what would become known as the Camp Jackson Affair. While escorting the captured state militia to the St. Louis Arsenal a deadly riot erupted between the Union volunteers and an angry crowd. In immediate response the Missouri General Assembly passed Governor Jackson's military bill to create the Missouri State Guard. Jackson selected Sterling Price to lead the guard. Lyon's superior General William S. Harney negotiated a truce with Price, the Price-Harney Truce, that lasted until Lyon superseded Harney.

When negotiations between Lyon and governor Claiborne Fox Jackson broke down, Lyon began a pursuit of Jackson and Price across the state to evict the elected government. On June 15 Lyon captured Jefferson City and a new session of the convention was called on July 22 (although 20 of the original members were now in retreat with Jackson and Price). Robert Wilson (Missouri) who had been vice chairman of the original convention was named chairman of the convention. The convention then declared the state's top offices vacant and then named new provisional officers including:

- Governor-Hamilton Rowan Gamble
- Lt. Governor-Willard P. Hall
- Secretary of State-Mordecai Oliver
- Treasurer-George Caleb Bingham

The convention then declared all offices of the Missouri General Assembly vacant and an election was to be called in November.

The convention adjourned on July 31.

Third Session

The secessionist Missouri State Guard was to enjoy success defeating the pursuing Union army on August 10 in the Battle of Wilson's Creek. Price began an offensive to retake Missouri with its northernmost victory in the siege of Lexington on September 20. Governor Jackson called upon the exiled members of the Missouri legislature to consider secession. They met on October 21 in Neosho, Missouri called the Neosho Convention and on October 30 voted to secede.

Meanwhile, on October 10, the constitutional convention met for the third time in St. Louis. They abolished more state offices, cut the salaries of state employees by 20 percent, extended the date of the next election to August 1862, created provisions for a state militia, and created loyalty oath requirement for state officials.

Fourth Session

After the Battle of Pea Ridge on March 7-8, 1862 effectively eliminated immediate Confederate designs on the state, the convention held its fourth convention—this time in Jefferson City in June 1862. The Convention then extended its loyalty oath to voters, teachers, attorneys, bank officers and preachers ensuring strong Union votes in the elections. (Abraham Lincoln who received 10 percent of the Missouri vote in the 1860 United States presidential election was to receive 70 percent of the vote in the 1864 United States presidential election.)

Following the Fremont Emancipation which had been rescinded, the convention unsuccessfully attempted to abolish slavery in the state.

Fifth Session

After Lincoln's Emancipation Proclamation freed the slaves in revolting states but not slave states still in the Union, final session of the convention met in June 1863 with a goal of eliminating slavery in the state. The problem was the constitution had a provision that freeing of slaves required compensation and permission of the owners. The state did not have the money for this. The convention passed an ordinance for the gradual release of slaves through July 4, 1870.

MISSOURI CONSTITUTIONAL CONVENTION OF 1865

The plan to gradually release slaves infuriated Radical Republicans who were to take their grievances to Lincoln. Gamble offered to resign but the Convention refused. He died in office on January 31, 1864.

The Radicals were to oppose Lincoln in the presidential election for not acting decisively against Missouri. In 1864 the Radical Republicans elected Thomas Clement Fletcher governor of Missouri and an entirely new constitutional convention was convened in the auditorium of the St. Louis Mercantile Library on January 6, 1865 consisting of two thirds Radical Republicans. On January 11, 1865 the new convention in a 60 to 4 vote abolished slavery in the state with no compensation for owners. The convention was to go on and write a new constitution for the state. A month later the convention approved the Thirteenth Amendment to the United States Constitution which freed the slaves.

National Convention

This article is about the legislative body and constitutional convention during the French Revolution. For the presidential nominating convention in the United States, see U.S. presidential nominating convention.

"The Convention" redirects here. For "The Office" episode, see The Convention (The Office episode).

During the French Revolution, the **National Convention** or **Convention**, in France, comprised the constitutional and legislative assembly which sat from 20 September 1792 to 26 October 1795 (the 4th of Brumaire of the year IV under the French Republican Calendar adopted by the Convention). It held executive power in France during the first years of the French First Republic. It was succeeded by the Directory, commencing 2 November 1795. Prominent members of the original Convention included Maximilien Robespierre of the Jacobin Club, Jean-Paul Marat (affiliated with the Jacobins, though never a formal member), and Georges Danton of the Cordeliers. During that period, executive power was de facto exercised by the Convention's Committee of Public Safety.

Formation

During the insurrection of 10 August 1792, when the populace of Paris stormed the Tuileries and demanded the abolition of the monarchy, the Legislative Assembly decreed the provisional suspension of King Louis XVI and the convocation of a "national convention" which should draw up a constitution. At the same time it was decided that deputies to that convention should be elected by all Frenchmen 25 years old or more, domiciled for a year and living by the product of their labour.

The National Convention was therefore the first French assembly elected by universal male suffrage, without distinctions of class. The age limit of the electors was further lowered to 21, and that of eligibility was fixed at 25 years.

The first session was held 20 September 1792. The following day, royalty was abolished: this became the informal end of the French monarchy. A little over a year later, 22 September would become the base date of the new French Revolutionary Calendar, the beginning of the Year I of the French Republic.

Revolutionary Government

The Convention lasted for three years and came after the National Assembly and Legislative Assembly. The country was at war, and it seemed best to postpone the implementation of the new constitution until peace should be concluded. At the same time, as the Convention prolonged its powers, it extended them considerably in order to meet the pressing dangers which menaced the Republic.

Although it was a legislative assembly, it took over the executive power, entrusting it to its own members. This "confusion of powers", contrary to the philosophical theories — those of Montesquieu especially — which had inspired the Revolution at first, was one of the essential characteristics of the Convention. The series of exceptional measures by which that confusion of powers was created constitutes the "Revolutionary government" in the strict sense of the word, a government which was principally in vigour during the period called the "Reign of Terror". There is thus a distinction to be made, discussing the Convention, between these temporary expedients and those measures intended to be permanent.

The first years of the Convention were the height of the importance of the revolutionary political clubs such as the Jacobins and Cordeliers; the informally constituted Girondists, although past the peak of their power, were also an important factor. By the end of the Convention, most prominent members of all of these groups were dead, the bulk of them victims either of the Terror or of the Thermidorian Reaction that brought the Terror to an end.

Structure and Membership

The Convention held its first session in a hall of the Tuileries, then it sat in the Salle du Manège, and finally from 10 May 1793 in that of the Spectacles (or Machine), an immense hall in which the deputies were but loosely scattered. This last hall had tribunes for the public, who often influenced the debate by interruptions or by applause.

The members of the Convention came from all classes of society, but the most numerous were lawyers. Seventy-five members had sat in the National Constituent Assembly, 183 in the Legislative Assembly. The full number of deputies was 749, not counting 33 from the colonies, of whom only some arrived in Paris. Besides these, however, the newly-formed *départements* annexed to France from 1792 to 1795 were allowed to send deputations. Many of the original deputies died or were exiled during the Convention, but not all their places were filled by *suppléants*. Some members proscribed during the Terror returned after the legislative coup of 9 Thermidor began the Thermidorian Reaction. Finally, many members were sent away, either to the *départments* or to the armies, on missions which lasted sometimes for a considerable length of time. For all these reasons it is difficult to find out the number of deputies present at any given date, for votes by roll-call were rare. During the Terror the number of those voting averaged only 250.

According to its own ruling, the Convention elected its president every fortnight. He was eligible for re-election after the lapse of a fortnight. Ordinarily the sessions were held in the morning, but evening sessions also occurred frequently, often extending late into the night. Sometimes in exceptional circumstances the Convention declared itself in permanent session and sat for several days without interruption. For both legislative and administrative the Convention used committees, with powers more or less widely extended and regulated by successive laws. The most famous of these committees included the Committee of Public Safety (*Comité de salut public*), the Committee of General Security (*Comité de sûreté générale*), and the Committee of Education, (*Comité de l'instruction*).

Legacy

The article on the Convention in the 1911 Encyclopædia Britannica concludes, "The Convention achieved immense changes in all branches of French public affairs. To appreciate its work without prejudice, one should recall that this assembly saved France from a civil war and invasion, that it founded the system of public education (*Museum, École Polytechnique, École Normale Supérieure, École des langues orientales, Conservatoire*), created institutions of capital importance, like that of the *Grand Livre de la Dette publique*, and definitely established the social and political gains of the Revolution." By a decree of 4 February 1794 (16 pluviôse) it also ratified and expanded to the whole French colonial empire the 1793 abolition of slavery on Saint-Domingue by civil commissioners Sonthonax and Polverel, though this did not affect Martinique or Guadeloupe and was abolished by the law of 20 May 1802.

CONSTITUTIONAL CONVENTION (AUSTRALIA)

First Convention

The **first** Constitutional Convention was held in Sydney in March 1891 to consider a draft Constitution for the proposed federation of the British colonies in Australia and New Zealand. There were 46 delegates at the Convention, chosen by the seven colonial parliaments. Among the delegates was Sir Henry Parkes, known as the "Father of Federation." The Convention approved a draft largely written by Sir Samuel Griffith, but the colonial parliaments failed to act to ratify it.

Second Convention

The **second** Constitutional Convention was held in stages in 1897-98. Unlike the first Convention, the delegates were elected by popular vote. It met first in Adelaide in March 1897, secondly in Sydney in August, and thirdly in Melbourne in the sweltering heat of January 1898. The intervals between the sessions were used for intense debate in the colonial parliaments and for public discussion of the draft Constitution.

Since 1891 New Zealand had lost interest in federating with the Australian colonies, and was not represented. In Queensland, the parliament had not passed the necessary legislation, so the northern colony was also unrepresented. In the other five colonies ten delegates from each colony were elected by the people, although Western Australian attendance was sporadic. At Melbourne the Convention finally produced a draft Constitution which was eventually approved by the people at referendums in the colonies.

Third Convention

The **third** Constitutional Convention was established by the Whitlam government in 1973 to consider possible amendments to the Constitution which could be put to the people for approval at a referendum. The Convention, which was not elected but consisted of delegates chosen by the federal and state Parliaments, met through 1973-75 but was mired in the partisan atmosphere of the Whitlam years and achieved nothing.

Fourth Convention

The **fourth** Constitutional Convention met in Canberra in February 1998. The Convention was convened by Prime Minister John Howard to fulfill a promise made by his predecessor as Liberal leader, Alexander Downer. During the Convention, Prime Minister John Howard dedicated an area of parkland to the south-east of Old Parliament House as Constitution Place, Canberra.

The Convention consisted of 152 delegates, of whom half were elected by the people and half were appointed by the federal government. This latter group included senior federal, state and territory politicians appointed by virtue of their positions.

The Convention was divided into four philosophical groups: those wanting to retain Australia's existing constitutional monarchy, those wanting Australia to become a republic with a head of state chosen by the Parliament ("indirect electionists"), those wanting Australia to become a republic with a president elected by the people ("direct electionists"), and those having no fixed position or seeking a compromise between the other groups.

Republicans dominated both groups but proved far from united in their views.

"The only commonsense interpretation of this Convention is, firstly, that a majority of people have voted generically in favour of a republic... Secondly, amongst the republican models, the one that has just got 73 votes is clearly preferred. When you bind those two together, it would be a travesty in commonsense terms of Australian democracy for that proposition not to be put to the Australian people. Moreover,

it would represent a cynical dishonouring of my word as Prime Minister and the promises that my coalition made to the Australian people before the last election." – John Howard, addressing the Constitutional Convention on 13 February 1998

The Convention eventually narrowly opted for the Bi-partisan appointment model, over the bitter opposition of the direct electionists. At the Australian republic referendum, 1999 the proposed amendments to the Constitution were rejected.

CONSTITUTIONAL CONVENTION (PHILIPPINES)

Constitutional convention or "con-con" is one of the three modes in which the "Constitution of the Philippines could be amended or revised. The other two modes are via People's Initiative or "PI" and Constituent Assembly or "Con-Ass".

Under Article XVII, Sec.3 of the Constitution of the Philippines: "The Congress may, by a vote of two-thirds of all its Members, call a constitutional convention, or by a majority vote of all its Members, submit to the electorate the question of calling such a convention."

The delegates for Constitutional Convention can be either elected by the people and/or appointed by the President. The process of amending or revising the 1987 Constitution of the Philippines is popularly known to many Filipinos as Charter Change. Any proposed amendment or revision to the 1987 Constitution shall only be valid when ratified by the majority of Filipinos in a plebiscite.

History

There are three constitutional conventions in Philippine history:

- Malolos Congress (1899)
- 1935 Constitutional Convention
- 1971 Constitutional Convention

Cornish Assembly

The **Cornish Assembly** is a proposed devolved regional assembly for Cornwall in the United Kingdom along the lines of the Scottish Parliament, National Assembly for Wales and Northern

Ireland Assembly. Cornwall remains the only Celtic nation within the British Isles to have no form of effective self-government.

Overview

Post Second World War Cornwall became increasingly linked with Devon in an economic, political and statistical sense (more recently this process had become known as "Devonwall-isation". However, in the face mounting evidence that Cornwall's economic plight was deepening, Cornwall achieved NUTS2 status, allowing Cornwall's issues to become visible.

In 1998 Cornwall was recognized by the UK Government as having *"distinct cultural and historical factors reflecting a Celtic background"*, thus enhancing the case for treating Cornwall as a special case in a regional, economic and cultural sense, and separate from Devon. Also after the 1997 general election the Liberal Democrats finally withdrew their support for the 'devonwall' process as they agreed with other pressure groups and the nationalist party Mebyon Kernow that it undermined Cornwall's claims to European Objective One funding. Proposals for some form of devolved Assembly for Cornwall are in fact, long standing. As long ago as 1970, J.C. Banks wrote "Federal Britain?", which included a discussion on the Cornish position.

During the 1990's the pace of debate gathered parallel to discussions relating to National Minority status for the Cornish under the Framework Convention for the Protection of National Minorities, and recognition for the Cornish language within the European Charter for Regional or Minority Languages (the latter campaign being subsequently successful).

In July 2000 Mebyon Kernow issued the "Declaration for a Cornish Assembly", which said: *"Cornwall is a distinct region. It has a clearly defined economic, administrative and social profile. Cornwall's unique identity reflects its Celtic character, culture and environment. We declare that the people of Cornwall will be best served in their future governance by a Cornish regional assembly. We therefore commit ourselves to setting up the Cornish Constitutional Convention with the intention of achieving a devolved Cornish Assembly-Senedh Kernow."*

Three months later the Cornish Constitutional Convention (which had been meeting for some time as an informal discussion group) held its first open meeting to promote the objective of establishing a devolved Assembly. In less than two years, it had attracted the signatures of over 50,000 people on a petition calling for a referendum on a Cornish Assembly, which is a little over 10% of the total Cornish electorate. A delegation led by the West Cornwall Liberal Democrat MP Andrew George and representatives of the Convention (Richard Ford, Dick Cole, David Fieldsend and Andrew Climo) presented the declaration to 10 Downing Street on Wednesday 12 December 2001.

Currently the South West Regional Assembly and the South West Regional Development Agency have control over areas such as economic development, housing and strategic planning. The dominant Cornish political party, the Liberal Democrats, has called these "undemocratic and unaccountable".

Support

Cornwall County Council's Feb 2003 MORI poll showed 55% in favour of an elected, fully-devolved regional assembly for Cornwall and 13% against. (Previous result :46% in favour in 2002). However the same MORI poll indicated an equal number of Cornish respondents were in favour of a South West Regional Assembley, (70% in favour of a Cornish assembly, 72% in favour of a S.West Regional assembly).

The campaign has the support of all five Cornish Lib Dem MPs, Mebyon Kernow, and Cornwall Council.

Lord Whitty, as Parliamentary Under-Secretary of State at the Department of Environment, Transport and the Regions, in the House of Lords, recognised that Cornwall has a "special case" for devolution. and on a visit to Cornwall Deputy Prime Minister John Prescott said "Cornwall has the strongest regional identity in the UK."

In October 2007 Lib Dem MP Andrew George stated in a press release, *"Just because the Government has approached the whole Regional Devolution agenda in entirely the wrong way, does not mean to say that the project itself should be ditched. If Scotland is benefiting from devolution then Cornwall should learn from this and increase the intensity of its own campaign for devolution to a Cornish Assembly."*

On Tuesday 17 July 2007, Local Government Minister John Healey MP announced Government plans to abolish regional assemblies. Functions of regional assemblies are planned to pass to Regional Development Agencies in 2010. The South West Regional Assembly is due to be replaced by the South West Regional Development Agency in 2010.

On 19 July 2007 MP Dan Rogerson welcomed the government announcement that unelected Regional Assemblies are to be scrapped and he asked the government to look again at the case for a locally accountable Cornish Assembly and Cornish Development agency, "in light of the important convergence funding from the EU". Cornish MP Andrew George said in July 2007 *I'm optimistic that the Minister's announcement will give us the future prospects to build a strong consensus, demonstrate Cornwall's distinctiveness from the Government zone for the South West and then draw up plans so that we can decide matters for ourselves locally rather than being told by unelected quangos in Bristol and elsewhere."*

Government minister John Healey conceded that "Cornwall still faces some significant economic challenges" and said he would consider the need for a Cornish Development Agency alongside his decision on local government restructuring.

In December 2007 Cornwall Council Leader David Whalley stated "There is something inevitable about the journey to a Cornish Assembly. We are also moving forward in creating a Cornish Development Agency-we are confident that strategic planning powers will come back to us after the SW regional assembly goes."

In 2008 Cornish residents are being offered a new brand of local government-Cornwall's Liberal Democrat councillors have agreed plans to create a Unitary authority for the region, abolishing the six district councils. This means that where there was once one democratically elected member for every 3,000 residents, there will now be one councillor for every 7,000 people. The unitary authority "One Cornwall" Council will however not have the same powers as the proposed Cornish Assembly. Westminster has ruled out any extra powers for Cornwall and the unelected quango of the South West Regional Development Agency will remain in place. This means that Cornish Objective One money will still be managed from outside of Cornwall. There have in fact been suggestions that powers could be taken from the new Cornish unitary authority as it may struggle to cope with the extra workload inherited from the district councils. A premise for a single governing body for Cornwall was that the new Cornwall Council would have greater powers, being granted more responsibilities from Westminster.

English Constitutional Convention

The **English Constitutional Convention** is a pressure group lobbying for a devolved English Parliament.

The English Constitutional Convention aims to bring about the same constitutional changes achieved by the Scottish Constitutional Convention which ultimately secured a devolved Parliament and Executive for Scotland. However, the English Constitutional Convention faces a far greater challenge despite devolution already having been implemented everywhere else in the UK as English devolution is officially opposed by all the main British political parties. Only the Conservative Party has significant support within its ranks for an English Parliament.

Scottish Constitutional Convention

The **Scottish Constitutional Convention** (SCC) was an association of Scottish political parties, churches and other civic groups, that developed a framework for a Scottish devolution. It is credited as having paved the way for the establishment of the Scottish Parliament in 1999.

The Convention was established after prominent Scottish individuals signed the Claim of Right in 1988. The Claim of Right asserted that Scotland is a nation, is constitutionally entitled to determine the best framework of government to suit its people, and demanded that the country should have its own legislative body within the framework of the United Kingdom.

The Claim of Right and the idea of a Constitutional Convention grew out of the Campaign for a Scottish Assembly (CSA), a pressure group established in the aftermath of the failure to secure a devolved Scottish Assembly in 1979. The CSA was an organisation of individuals committed to some form of Home Rule for Scotland that by the late 1980s came to argue that a convention was the way forward to secure this.

Various organisations participated in the Convention, such as the Labour Party, the Liberal Democrats, the Scottish Green Party, the Scottish Trades Union Congress, the Small Business Federation, the Church of Scotland, as well as the other major churches, and other various bodies representing other strands of political opinion as well as civic society in general. Initially the Scottish National Party (SNP) participated, but the then party leader Gordon Wilson, along with Jim Sillars decided to withdraw the SNP from participation owing to the convention's unwillingness to discuss Scottish independence as a constitutional option.

The Conservative government of the day were very hostile to the convention and challenged the local authorities' right to finance the convention, although the courts found that they were in fact entitled to do so.

Under its executive chairman, Canon Kenyon Wright, the convention published its blueprint for devolution, *Scotland's Parliament, Scotland's Right*, on 30 November 1995, St Andrew's Day. This provided the basis for the structure of the existent Scottish Parliament, established in 1999.

2

Introduction to the Constitutional Convention

THE CALL FOR A GRAND CONVENTION

On May 15, 1776, the Second Continental Congress, meeting in Independence Hall, Philadelphia, issued "A Resolve" to the thirteen colonies: "Adopt such a government as shall, in the opinion of the representatives of the people, best conduce to the safety and happiness of their constituents in particular and America in general." Between 1776 and 1780 each of the thirteen colonies adopted a republican form of government. What emerged was the most extensive documentation of the powers of government and the rights of the people that the world had ever witnessed.

These state constitutions displayed a remarkable uniformity. Seven attached a prefatory Declaration of Rights, and all contained the same civil and criminal rights. Four states decided not to "prefix" a Bill of Rights to their constitutions, but, instead, incorporated the very same natural and traditional rights found in the prefatory declarations. New York incorporated the entire Declaration of Independence into its constitution.

The primary purpose of these declarations and bills was to outline the objectives of government: to secure the right to life, liberty, property, and the pursuit of happiness. The government that was chosen to secure these rights was declared universally to be "a republican form of government." All of the states, except Pennsylvania, embraced a two-chamber legislature, and all, except

Massachusetts, installed a weak executive and denied the Governor the power to veto bills of the legislature. All accepted the notion that the legislative branch should be preeminent, but, at the very same time, endorsed the concept that the liberty of the people was in danger from the corruption of the representatives. And this despite the fact that the representatives were installed by the election of the people. Thus, each state constitution embraced the notion of short terms of office for elected representatives along with recall, rotation, and term limits.

The Second Continental Congress also created the first continental-wide system of governance. The Articles of Confederation created a nation of pre-existing states rather than a government over individuals. Thus, the very idea of a Bill of Rights was irrelevant because the Articles did not entail a government over individuals. The states were equally represented in the union regardless of size of population, only one branch was needed, normal political activity required the support of super majorities, the union was limited to the powers expressly enumerated, and amendment was required to endow the union with powers that weren't specifically articulated. Amendments required the unanimous approval of all thirteen state legislatures. The Articles didn't come into operation until the early 1780s because of territorial disputes between two states; all of the states were required to "sign on" before the Articles became operative on any one state.

These two directives produced two opposite and rival situations: an early operating, robust and healthy state and local politics and a late arriving, weak and divisive continental arrangement. Several statesmen, especially George Washington, were concerned that the idea of an American mind that had emerged during the war with Britain was about to disappear and the Articles of Confederation were inadequate to foster the development of an American character. According to Washington, "we have errors to correct." He argued that the states refused to comply with the articles of peace, the union was unable to regulate interstate commerce, and the states met, but oh so grudgingly, just the minimum interstate standards required by the Articles. Others, especially James Madison, were concerned that the state legislatures—dominated by what he saw as oppressive, unjust, and overbearing majorities—were passing laws detrimental to the rights of individual conscience and the right to private property. And there was nothing that the union government could do about it because the Articles left matters of religion and commerce to the states. The solution, concluded Madison, was to create an extended republic, in which a variety of opinions, passions, and interests would check and balance each other, supported by a governmental framework that endorsed a separation of powers between the branches of the general government.

Between 1781 and 1785 attempts "to correct these errors" failed to secure the required unanimous consent of the state legislatures. Matters changed, however, in 1786. Following James Madison's suggestion of 21 January 1786, the Virginia Legislature invited all the States to discuss ways to reduce interstate conflicts in Annapolis, Maryland. The "commissioners" in attendance at Annapolis during September 1786, chatted about these particular concerns, but suggested that the conversation be both deepened and widened. They endorsed a motion that a "Grand Convention" of all the States meet in Philadelphia the next May 1787 to discuss how to improve the Articles of Confederation.

One might well ask, "Who or what authorized the Virginia Legislature to call the Annapolis Convention and who or what authorized the Annapolis Convention to call for a 'Grand Convention'?" The answer is to be found in the Declaration of Independence: The people have the right to choose the form of government under which they shall live and to install such government as they deem appropriate to secure their liberty, security, and happiness.

THE SELECTION OF THE DELEGATES

Madison and Washington agreed that the principles of the Revolution of 1776 were in danger due to a weak continental arrangement and overbearing, unjust, and reckless state legislatures. But how could they take advantage of the opportunity provided by the Annapolis recommendation? How was such a bold proposal to be put into effect?

Madison persuaded the Virginia Legislature to implement the challenge of the Annapolis Convention and invite all the other states to also reconsider the status of the Articles. He also persuaded the Assembly to be the first to elect delegates to the Grand Convention to consider the business "of May next."

The Virginia Assembly elected 55-year-old revolutionary hero George Washington to head the delegation. "Give me Liberty or give me Death" Patrick Henry declined because "he smelt a rat." Doctór James McClurg was selected even though he had no political experience; James Madison insisted he be present. Richard Henry Lee and Thomas Nelson, colonial heroes and Signers of the Declaration, refused to attend. 34-year-old Edmund Randolph, the Governor of Virginia, 55-year-old John Blair, an esteemed Virginia judge, 55-year-old George Wythe, the first law professor of the United States and Signer of the Declaration, 62-year-old George Mason, author of the Virginia Bill of Rights were all chosen along with five foot tall, 120 pound, 36-year-old James Madison.

Five States followed Virginia's lead.

1. New Jersey selected William Churchill Houston, Chief Justice of the New Jersey Supreme Court David Brearly, 40-year-old Irish immigrant William Paterson, Governor William Livingston, known as "the Whipping Post" because of his great height, and 27-year-old Jonathan Dayton who after the Convention went exploring and died in what is now Dayton, Ohio.
2. Pennsylvania selected eight delegates: Thomas Mifflin was elected as the leader of the delegation; he was speaker of the Pennsylvania Assembly. Other members selected were Robert Morris, financier of the Revolution, George Clymer, signer of the Declaration, Jared Ingersoll a political reformer who later bestowed on Madison the appellation, "Father of the Constitution," Irish immigrant Thomas Fitzsimons, founder of the Bank of America and one of two Catholics at the Convention, 45-year-old James "The Caledonian" Wilson from Scotland, 33-year-old peg leg and "rake" Gouverneur Morris, who spoke more than anyone at the

Convention, and 81-year-old Benjamin "the American Socrates" Franklin who was added to the delegation as a courtesy. All the delegates from Pennsylvania resided in Philadelphia.

3. Former Governor Alexander Martin was chosen to lead the North Carolina delegation, but left before the signing. 29-year-old William Davie also left the Convention early. In 1802 he was killed in a duel. 29-year-old Richard Dobbs Spaight, preacher, essayist, and mathematician Doctor Hugh Williamson, and land speculator William Blount—who later earned the dubious honor of being the first member expelled from the United States Senate—made up the core of the delegation that had a major impact on the course of the debates in July. Howard Christy gives this central signing honors in his commemoration of the Constitution.
4. 54-year-old George Read headed the Delaware delegation. Additional members included "corpulent and impetuous" Gunning Bedford Junior, prudent and educated John Dickinson, and two quiet thirty-five-year olds: Jacob Broom and Richard Bassett.
5. The head of the Georgia delegation was William Few who was joined by Abraham Baldwin, William Houstoun, and 49-year-old William Pierce, one of the poorest attendees in terms of income—thus he has no official portrait—who nevertheless left us rich sketches of the delegates.

So six of the states had taken Virginia's initiative to form a Grand Convention without waiting for any formal endorsement by the existing government under the Articles of Confederation. Other states, however, were more cautious and wanted the existing Congress to address the legitimacy of such a gathering. On 28 February 1787, the Confederation Congress endorsed the meeting of the Grand Convention on "the second Monday in May next." Exactly what the Congress authorized became a bone of contention. The recommendatory act of Congress reads thus: A Convention of delegates should meet "for the sole purpose of *revising the articles of Confederation* and reporting to Congress and the several legislatures such *alterations and provisions therein* as shall, when agreed to in Congress and confirmed by the States, render the federal Constitution *adequate to the exigencies of government and the preservation of the Union.*" (Italics in the original of the version reprinted in *Federalist* 40.) Did the Congress limit the Convention to the discussion of specific and particular matters or did the Congress empower the Convention to "run away" and propose whatever alterations the delegates considered were needed to preserve the principles of the Revolution?

New York was the first state to act after the Congressional endorsement. The Governor George Clinton faction of the New York legislature selected State Supreme Court judge Robert Yates and John Lansing to, in effect, outvote Alexander Hamilton. The New York delegation was not particularly prominent at the Convention. Yates and Lansing left in early July, just prior to the passage of the Connecticut Compromise, and the 32-year-old Hamilton, who lost his life at age 49 in a duel with Aaron Burr, was far more influential in securing the adoption of the Constitution in 1788 than in its framing in 1787.

Five States followed New York's lead.

1. In early March, South Carolina, selected John Rutledge, Charles Cotesworth Pinckney, Charles Pinckney, and Pierce Butler as their delegates; they were pro-national, pro-slavery, and very influential.
2. Massachusetts, also in March, selected Elbridge Gerry, who signed the Declaration, 32-year-old Rufus King, "backwoods lawyer" Caleb Strong, and Nathaniel Gorham, who chaired the Committee of the Whole during the Convention.
3. Four days before the Convention began, Connecticut elected three delegates: William Samuel Johnson, who learned of his appointment to the Presidency of Columbia College on his way to Philadelphia, Roger Sherman, who signed both the Declaration and the Articles, and 42-year-old Oliver Ellsworth who had the reputation of talking to himself and being a chain chewer of snuff.
4. Irish immigrant Doctor James McHenry, after whom Fort McHenry is named, was a leader of the Maryland delegation.

He was joined by 60-year-old bachelor, Daniel of St. Thomas Jenifer, 30-year-old Daniel Carroll—one of two Catholics at the Convention—29-year-old John F. Mercer, who blew into and out of town during the first week of August, and Luther Martin, who apparently had a great capacity to consume immense amounts of alcohol, and sober up at a moment's notice.

5. New Hampshire was short of cash so John Langdon funded the expenses for himself and Nicholas Gilman; they arrived at the Convention on July 23, after the main debate over the Connecticut Compromise was completed and yet just in time for a one-week recess.

Rhode Island, the thirteenth state, declined to send delegates.

Thomas Jefferson characterized the 55 men who showed up in Philadelphia as "demi-gods," who created a Constitution that would last into remote futurity. Alexis de Tocqueville marveled at the work of the American Founders: never before in the history of the world had the leaders of a country declared the existing government to be bankrupt, and the people, after debate, calmly elected delegates who proposed a solution, which, in turn, was debated up and down the country for nearly a year, and not a drop of blood was spilled. Madison, in *Federalist* 37, indicates the uniqueness of the Founding: never before had there been a democratic founding; all previous foundings had been the work of a single founder like Romulus. And Hamilton, in *Federalist* 1, suggested that this was a unique event in the history of the world; finally government was going to be established by reflection and choice rather than force and fraud. And what is also unique is the fact that the framers were relatively young, well educated, and politically experienced. Like the Declaration of Independence, the Constitution was written by delegates immersed in 1) the writings of Aristotle, Cicero, Locke, and Montesquieu, and 2) a world of political experience at both the state and continental level. Both basic documents were written in Independence Hall, Philadelphia, and thirty signers of the Declaration in 1776 played a vital part in the creation and adoption of the Constitution, 1787-1789.

How to Read the Convention

Very few of the delegates selected were present at the appointed time for the meeting of the Grand Convention in Philadelphia on May 14, 1787. All the Virginia delegates were present, however, and fully settled into their accommodations. Washington stayed at Robert Morris's Town House, and Madison secured lodgings across the street at Mrs. House's Boarding House. During this waiting period, the Virginia delegates caucused with each other in an attempt to set the tone for the deliberations of the Convention and paid courtesy calls on prominent members of Philadelphia society. Some entered a Catholic church for the first time.

On May 25, a quorum of seven states was secured. The first order of business was to elect a President, and George Washington was the obvious choice. William Jackson, yet another immigrant at the Convention, was elected Secretary of the Convention and he recorded the propositions and amendments as well as the vote tabulation.

James Madison took extensive *Notes* of the proceedings and although some scholars have questioned their authenticity and completeness, they remain the primary source for reproducing the conversations at the Convention. Other delegates kept specific notes on certain days, there are letters back home to friends and loved ones, there are urgent bills sent for immediate payment that augment, and there are personal diaries, some more complete than others. Nothing, however, can compete with, or ever replace, Madison's *Notes*.

The delegates also agreed that the deliberations would be kept secret. The case in favor of secrecy was that the issues at hand were so important that honest discourse needed to be encouraged and delegates ought to feel free to speak their mind, and change their mind, as they saw fit. Thus, despite the hot summer weather in Philadelphia, and delegates who, on the whole, were rather overweight and hardly "dressed down" for the occasion, the windows were closed and heavy drapes drawn. The merits and demerits of the secrecy rule have been a subject of considerable debate throughout American history.

In Act One of the Convention, Governor Randolph introduces the fifteen point Virginia Plan at the end of May to "revise the Articles of Confederation." The decisive features of this plan are 1) the complete structural exclusion of the states in terms of both election and representation; 2) the complete diminution of the powers of the states and the virtual freedom of Congress to act in those areas for which the states are incompetent; 3) the establishment of an extended national republic with institutional separation of powers and the introduction of the possibility that short terms of office and term limits—standard features of traditional republicanism—will be abandoned. Under the wholly federal Articles of Confederation, only the states are represented and the central government was restrained to the exercise of expressly delegated powers. And under the state republican constitutions, the governor had very little authority, and the elected representatives were kept under close scrutiny. Madison's Virginia Plan introduces a new understanding of federalism and republicanism. This wholly national republican plan is debated, and amended, over the next two weeks, and the main features are adopted by the delegates in mid June over two alternatives: the wholly federal, or state based, New Jersey Plan, that argues that the Virginia Plan goes too far, and the Hamilton Plan that claims the Virginia Plan does not go far enough. Hamilton, among other things, envisioned a President for life.

Act Two portrays the Convention in crisis, in the sense that the delegates were at a stalemate. Far from the wholly national republican Virginia Plan being accepted, as we might very well anticipate when the curtain fell at the end of Act One, the delegates from Connecticut, New Jersey, Delaware, New York, and Mr. Martin from Maryland—the defenders of the New Jersey Plan, the old style federalism of the Articles, and the old fashioned republicanism of the state constitutions—insisted on questioning the validity of the Virginia Plan. They argued that the Convention had exceeded the Congressional mandate because the Articles had in fact been scrapped rather than revised. Thus the Convention had violated the rule of law. Moreover, the Convention was about to propose a novelty—a large country under one republican form of government—that would never be accepted by the electorate. These delegates knew their Locke and Montesquieu and they relied on their own political experience which was remarkably extensive: republican government could only exist in areas of small extent where the people kept close watch over their representatives.

A breakthrough occurs at the end of June when Oliver Ellsworth of Connecticut suggests that we are neither wholly national nor wholly federal but a mixture of both. Several delegates echo this theme and the Convention decides to move beyond the exclusively national or federal paradigms. The Gerry Committee is created to explore the ramifications of this suggestion that the people be represented in the House and the states be represented in the Senate. This recommendation—the Connecticut Compromise—is accepted over Madison's objections in mid-July.

Act Three focuses on the debates during August over the Committee of Detail Report, especially concerning the itemization of Congressional powers. With the Connecticut Compromise in place, the delegates turned from the question of structure to the question of national and state powers. Under the Virginia Plan, Congress was empowered to do anything the States were incompetent to do. By July, that was no longer acceptable to the delegates. A Committee was created to draft a Constitution—the Committee of Detail—that would address the division of powers between the central and state governments and also the separation of powers between Congress, the President, and the Supreme Court.

Another issue that emerged in Act Three is the slavery question. What could Congress do and not do to regulate and/or abolish slavery? This is a vital question and deserves special coverage. It is instructive to compare the clause in the Committee of Detail Report of August 6 with the Signed Constitution of September 17. The former forbids Congress from ever regulating the slave trade and prohibits Congress from discouraging the trade by means of a tax or tariff. By contrast the final Constitution, limits the prohibition on Congress until 1808 and permits Congress to discourage the slave trade. In March, 1807, President Jefferson signed into law an Act of Congress prohibiting the slave trade effective January 1, 1808, and during the 1790s Congress took specific steps to discourage the importation of Africans for the purpose of being sold into slavery. Act Four covers the final three weeks of the Convention during the month of September. Despite all the progress that had been made on the structural role of the states and enumerating the powers of Congress, there was much work still to be done on the Presidency. The Brearley Committee came up with the idea of an Electoral College as a sensible compromise to the long and largely fruitless debates on how to elect the President. It had been clear for four months that until the mode of election was settled, no progress could be made on 1) length of term, 2) the issue of re-eligibility, and 3) the powers of the President. The Electoral College was modeled on the Connecticut Compromise: the President would be elected by a combination of people and states.

The Committee of Style wrote the final draft of the Constitution. It included a Preamble and an obligation of contracts clause, both written by Gouverneur Morris, and an enumeration of the powers of Congress in Article I, Section 8. During the last week of the Convention the delegates added a few refinements, raised some serious concerns, and discussed what they agreed to over the four months of deliberations. Mason expressed the wish that "the plan had been prefaced by a Bill of Rights." Elbridge Gerry supported Mason's unsuccessful attempt to attach a Bill of Rights. Randolph joined Mason and Gerry and declared that he too wouldn't sign the Constitution. And the delegates wondered whether or not the power to create a national university was implied within the meaning of the necessary and proper clause.

On the last day of the Convention, September 17, Benjamin Franklin looked at the chair occupied by Washington and declared the sun enshrined on the chair to be a rising sun. Many delegates over the four months of deliberation often thought that it was a setting sun.

3

The Constitutional Convention: Day by Day Summary

Monday, May 14

Date fixed for start of Convention. Only eight delegates are present.

Friday, May 25

Convened and elected officers. (Washington as President, William Jackson as Secretary).

Chose a committee (Wythe, Hamilton, and C. Pinckney) to prepare rules.

Monday, May 28

Committee on Rules reported.

16 rules were adopted and additional suggested rules referred to the committee.

Tuesday, May 29

Committee on Rules reported and 5 additional rules, including secrecy, were adopted.

Randolph submitted and defended a set of Fifteen Resolutions, known as The Virginia Plan.

The Convention agreed to meet the following day as a Committee of The Whole.

Wednesday, May 30

The Convention resolves itself into Committee of The Whole, Gorham in the Chair.

Resolution 1 : After discussion, agreed (6-1-1) that a national government consisting of a supreme legislature, judiciary, and executive should be formed (Connecticut voting against, New York divided).

Resolution 2 : Discussed whether representation should be based on population or the amount of each State's financial contribution.

Thursday, May 31

Resolution 3: Decided on a bicameral legislature.

Resolution 4a: Agreed (6-2-2) on election of First House by the people.

Resolution 5a : Defeated (7-3) Second House elected by the First House.

Madison's reaction: "a chasm (was) left in this part of the plan."

Sherman's suggestion: "election of one member by each of the State Legislatures."

Resolution 6 :Agreed that either house could initiate legislation.

Agreed to incompetence clause and negative on State laws.

Friday, June 1

Resolution 7: Agreed to institute a national Executive with power to carry into effect the national laws and to appoint officers not otherwise provided for.

Agreed (5-4-1) on a seven-year term for Executive.

Postponed consideration of single or plural Executive.

Saturday, June 2

Resolution 7 : Confusing day on the Executive.

Agreed to selection of Executive by Legislature.

Agreed (8-2) on seven-year term, and ineligibility after one term (7-2-1).

Defeated (9-1) Dickinson's motion that Executive be subject to impeachment.

Franklin: Executive should receive no salary. (Motion postponed)

Monday, June 4

Resolution 7 : Another confusing day on the Executive.

Agreed (7-3) on single Executive.

Resolution 8 : Council of Revision postponed.

Agreed (8-2) to give Executive a veto over legislation subject to override by 2/3 of each branch of Legislature.

Resolution 9 : Agreed to establish a National Judiciary consisting of a Supreme Court and one or more inferior tribunals. (Compare with July 21 and August 15.)

Tuesday, June 5

Resolution 9 : Agreed to delete "one or more" and change to "a Supreme Court and inferior tribunals."

Resolution 9 : Debated judicial selection and postponed decision, but agreed (8-2) to reject approval of judicial appointments by Legislature.

Resolution 9 : Agreed on judicial tenure during good behavior.

Agreed on a salary provision.

Resolution 9 : Reconsidered inferior tribunals and agreed to eliminate reference to them, then agreed to empower the Legislature to establish such courts.

Resolution 10 : Agreed (8-2) on admitting new states (on equal footing with original states).

Resolution 11 : Postponed republican guarantee clause until representation is settled.

Resolution 12 : Passed (8-2) an Interim Government provision.

Resolution 13 : Postponed (7-3).

Resolution 14 : Postponed (6-4-1) (New Jersey not voting).

Resolution 15 : Postponed.

Wednesday, June 6

Resolution 4a : Defeated (8-3) motion to have State Legislature elect First House of National Legislature.

Sherman: "The people are more happy in small than large states." His argument invokes the traditional understanding of republicanism.

Madison: We need to "enlarge the sphere." His argument points back to "vices" and forward to Federalist 10.

Thursday, June 7

Resolution 5a : Agreed (11-0) to a proposal by Dickinson and Sherman that the State Legislatures elect the Second House of the National Legislature.

Madison and Dickinson differ on the purpose of the Senate.

Friday, June 8

Resolution 6 : Defeated (7-3-1) a motion by Madison and C. Pinckney to extend the Congressional negative to all state laws.

Saturday, June 9

Resolution 7 : Defeated (10-1) a motion by Gerry that State Executives elect the National Executive.

Resolution 4a : Debated voting procedures within the National Legislature.

Monday, June 11

Resolution 4a : Return to National Representation.

3/5 clause introduced.

Decided (9-2) that representation in Lower House of the National Legislature should be based on free population plus 3/5 of all other persons. Sherman and Ellsworth (both from Connecticut) propose one State one vote in Senate.

Disagreed (6-5) that each state should be equally represented in Senate.

Resolution 5a : Agreed (6-5) that representation in the Second House should also be proportional plus 3/5 of all others persons.

Resolution 13 : Discussed.

Resolution 14 : Agreed (6-5) to require oaths to observe the National Constitution and National laws by State officers.

Tuesday, June 12

Resolution 15 : Agreed (5-3-2) to refer Constitution to the people of the several states for ratification. (Pennsylvania not voting)

Resolution 4b : Agreed (7-4) on three-year terms for First House of National Legislature

Resolution 4c : Struck out, without discussion, rotation and recall provisions, ending a republican tradition.

Resolution 4d : Agreed (8-3) to provide "Liberal compensation for members of the First House to be paid from the National Treasury."

Resolution 4e : Agreed (8-1-2) to make members of the First House ineligible for offices under the National Government for one year after leaving the House.

Resolution 5b,c : Agreed to require a minimum age of 30 (7-4) and a seven-year term for Senators (8-1-2).

Resolution 5d : Defeated (7-3-1) no pay for Senators.

Resolution 9 : Discussed and postponed the jurisdiction to be given the Supreme Court.

Wednesday, June 13

Resolution 9 : Agreed that the jurisdiction of the National Judiciary should extend to cases that respect the collection of the national revenue, impeachment of any national officers, and questions involving the national peace and harmony.

Resolution 9 : Agreed that the Supreme Court should be appointed by the Senate.

Resolution 6 : Rejected (8-3) a motion requiring money bills to originate in the first branch of the Legislature.

Agreed to vote on Amended Virginia Plan with 19 Resolutions.

Thursday, June 14

New Jersey requested postponement of the Amended Virginia Plan to present an alternative plan.

Friday, June 15

Patterson from New Jersey submitted 9 Resolutions.

Saturday, June 16

New Jersey Plan debated.

Monday, June 18

Hamilton's Plan introduced.

Sketch of a very strong central government.

Tuesday, June 19

In Committee of The Whole:

Defeated (6-4-1) Dickinson's motion to defer consideration of New Jersey Plan.

Heard Madison's 8 Arguments against New Jersey Plan.

Defeated New Jersey Plan (7-3-1).

Wednesday, June 20

Revised Resolution 1 & 2 : Debated the issue of a two-house legislature.

Revised Resolution 2 : Defeated (6-4-1) a motion to consider vesting the powers of legislation in a one-house Congress.

Thursday, June 21

Revised Resolution 2 : Resumed discussion of the legislature and resolved (7-3-1) that it should have two branches.

Revised Resolution 3 : Considered method of electing First House

Defeated (6-4-1) a motion for election as stated by State Legislatures and agreed (9-1-1) to popular election.

Revised Resolution 3b : Discussed length of term of First House.

Agreed (7-3-1) to strike "three years" and agreed *nem con* on two years.

Friday, June 22

Revised Resolution 3c : Defeated (7-2-2) a motion to permit the First House to determine its pay.

Revised Resolution 3d : Defeated (5-4-2) a motion to strike the National Treasury as the source of pay.

Revised Resolution 3 : Agreed (7-3-1) on minimum age of 25 for members of the House.

Revised Resolution 3 : Discussed making members ineligible for other state or national office during their own term of office plus one year after leaving office.

Defeated (4-4-3) a motion to strike.

Saturday, June 23

Revised Resolution 3 : Defeated (5-5-1) a motion by Butler to provide House members with adequate compensation from the National Treasury.

Revised Resolution 3 : Agreed (8-3) to strike ineligibility of House members for other Federal Offices.

Monday, June 25

Revised Resolution 4 : Agreed (5-5-1) to change "Second Branch of the National Legislature" to "Second Branch of the United States Legislature."

Revised Resolution 5 : Agreed (9-2) to election of the Second Branch by State Legislatures.

Revised Resolution 4b : Agreed unanimously to minimum age of 30 for Senators.

Tuesday, June 26

Revised Resolution 4 : Resumed discussion of Senate terms.

Defeated (8-3) 9-year terms with triennial rotation.

Approved (7-4) 6 years with biennial rotation.

Revised Resolution 4 : Agreed (10-1) that members should "receive a compensation for the devotion of their time to the Public service."

Revised Resolution 4 : Disagreed (6-5) that State Treasuries should pay Senators.

Revised Resolution 4 : Discussed and agreed unanimously on eligibility for other Federal and State offices.

Madison outlines two theories of the Senate. See Federalist 63.

Wednesday, June 27

Revised Resolution 6 : Postponed.

Revised Resolution 7 : Discussed "the right of suffrage in the first branch."

Revised Resolution 8 : Discussed "the right of suffrage in the second branch" to be the same as the first branch.

L. Martin delivers a three-hour "desultory" speech, the substance of which was "that an equal vote in each State was essential to the federal idea, and was founded in justice & freedom, not merely in policy"

Thursday, June 28

Revised Resolution 7 : Resumed discussion on representation in the First Branch.

Revised Resolution 8 : Resumed discussion on representation in the Second Branch.

L. Martin continued his speech from the previous day, "contending that the General Government ought to be formed for the States, not individuals."

Madison and Wilson oppose Martin's argument.

Franklin, disturbed by "the small progress we have made after 4 or 5 weeks," calls for "prayers imploring the assistance of heaven."

Friday, June 29

Revised Resolution 7 : Approved (6-4-1) proportional representation in the House.

Revised Resolution 7 : Approved (9-2) a motion to postpone consideration of the rest of Resolution 7, representation by States in Second Branch.

Revised Resolution 8 : Ellsworth introduces "Connecticut Compromise Motion": Equal representation in Second Branch with proportional representation in First House.

Saturday, June 30

Defeated (5-2-1) resolution to ask New Hampshire to send its delegates.

Revised Resolution 8 : Madison claims the great divide in American politics is "having or not having slaves" rather than large and small states.

Davie suggested, "we were partly federal, partly national in our Union."

Monday, July 2

Revised Resolution 8 : Tied (5-5-1) on Ellsworth's motion giving each state one vote in Senate and proportional representation in House

Revised Resolution 8 : Voted (9-2) to commit the question.

Revised Resolution 8 : Voted (10-1) to commit to committee of one member from each state.

Gerry chaired committee made up of Gerry, Ellsworth, Yates, Patterson, Franklin, Bedford, L. Martin, Mason, Davie, Rutledge, and Baldwin.

"That time may be given to the committee, and to such as chuse to attend to the celebrations of the Anniversary of Independence," the Convention adjourned till Thursday.

Tuesday, July 3

Gerry Committee met to work on the questions of the previous day.

Wednesday, July 4

Independence Day observed

Delegates attend Race Street Church (also known as First Reformed Church) on Fourth and Race Streets to hear annual oration on the anniversary of the Declaration of Independence given by Mr. Mitchell, a student of law.

Thursday, July 5

Received a Report from the Gerry Committee:

1. Representation in First House by population (1:40,000).

2. Representation in Second House to give each State an equal vote.

3. Money Bills to originate in First House and not subject to amendment in Second House.

Friday, July 6

Gerry justifies Report: "We were neither the same nation nor different nations."

Gerry Committee Report:

Agreed (7-3-1) to commit the question of 1:40,000 representation in the First House to the Morris Committee made up of G. Morris, Gorham, Randolph, Rutledge and King.

Agreed (5-3-3) to retain money bills provision.

Saturday, July 7

Gerry Committee Report:

Took up question of equal vote for each state in Second House and Agreed (6-3-2) to retain this provision.

Gerry: "The new Government would be partly national, partly federal."

Monday, July 9

Gerry Committee Report:

Morris Committee suggested approval of the population formula (1:40,000).

Second paragraph of Gerry Committee Report was approved (9-2).

The first paragraph was referred to an eleven-man committee (9-2).

Tuesday, July 10

Received report from the Eleven Member Committee allocating 65 representatives among the 13 States for the House.

Delegates Yates and Lansing from New York left the Convention and explained their reasons to Governor Clinton of New York.

Wednesday, July 11

Inconclusive discussion on periodical censuses.

Defeated (7-3) motion to strike out "3/5" for "all."

G. Morris "could never agree to give such encouragement to the slave trade."

Defeated (6-4) a motion "to include 3/5 of the blacks."

Thursday, July 12

Approved (5-4-1) a motion to have a census within 6 years of the First Congress.

Defeated (7-3) a motion for succeeding censuses every 20 years.

Agreed (8-2) on a census every 10 years.

Defeated (8-2) a motion "for rating blacks as equal to whites as of 3/5."

Approved (6-2-2) a motion to proportion direct taxes, including 3/5, to representation.

Friday, July 13

Approved (5-4-1) a motion to proportion direct taxes to the number of representatives until the first census.

Agreed (9-0-1) that the Legislature can regulate the number of representatives in accordance with the number of inhabitants.

G. Morris and Butler have a pointed exchange over slavery.

Confederation Congress passes Northwest Ordinance.

Saturday, July 14

Defeated (5-4-1) a motion to limit representation of new western states.

Discussed equal vote for each State in Second House with money bills originating in First House.

Madison argues against the "partly federal, partly national" accommodation.

C. Pinckney moved "that instead of an equality of votes" there should be proportional representation in Senate. Defeated (4-6).

Monday, July 16

Agreed (5-4-1) to Gerry Committee Report (House proportional, Senate equal representation for each State, and money bills originating in the First House and unamendable by the Second House. This is also known as the Connecticut Compromise.)

Revised Resolution 6b : Began consideration of the proposal to give Congress the authority in all cases to which the separate states are incompetent.

Tuesday, July 17

The delegates from large States caucused to decide whether to challenge equal representation in the Senate. They decided not to challenge the compromise.

Revised Resolution 6b : Resumed consideration of the powers to be given Congress. Agreed (6-4) to a motion to include the power to legislate in all cases for the general interests of the Union and in those cases where States are separately incompetent.

Revised Resolution 6c : Defeated (7-3) negative of State Laws. Madison thought the negative "essential," L. Martin considered it "improper."

Revised Resolution 6c : Motion by L. Martin to make laws and treaties supreme law of the respective States approved, nem con.

Revised Resolution 9 : Began consideration of an independent Executive.

Agreed (10-0) on single Executive.

Defeated (9-1) election by citizens of the United States.

Defeated (8-2) election by electors appointed by State Legislatures.

Approved (10-0) election by Legislature.

Postponed decision on 7-year term.

Defeated (6-4) ineligibility requirement.

Defeated (6-4) a motion to substitute hold office "during good behavior" rather than 7 years.

Defeated (6-4) a motion to strike seven years.

Wednesday, July 18

Revised Resolution 9 : Agreed to reconsider ineligibility of executive (8-0) (New Jersey and Georgia not voting).

Agreed to Executive Veto with 2/3 override.

Revised Resolution 11 : Began consideration of Judiciary.

Defeated (6-2) motion for appointment by Executive.

Defeated (4-4) motion for Executive nomination and appointment on advice and consent of Second House.

Revised Resolution 12 : Agreed (9-0) to let Legislature create inferior tribunals (New Jersey voting).

Agreed "that the jurisdiction shall extend to all cases arising under the national laws and to such other questions as may involve the national peace and harmony," nem con.

Revised Resolutions12-16 : Agreed to admit new States with the consent of less than the whole of the National Legislature.

Began consideration of continuing the Confederation during the transitional period.

Took up Guarantee of Republican Government for States.

Thursday, July 19

Revised Resolution 9 : Agreed (10-0) to a motion by G. Morris to reconsider the appointment, duration, and eligibility of the Executive.

Agreed to Ellsworth's motions to appointment of Executive by electors (6-3-1) chosen by state legislatures (8-2).

Defeated (8-2) ineligibility for re-election.

Defeated (5-3-2) 7-year term.

Agreed (9-1) to 6-year term.

Friday, July 20

Revised Resolution 9 : Took up apportionment of electors among the states with a minimum of 1 and a maximum of 3 per state.

Defeated (7-3) motion to add an elector for New Hampshire and Georgia.

Agreed (6-4) to Gerry's allocation of 1 to 3 per State.

Revised Resolution 9 : Agreed (8-2) to make Executive removable by impeachment.

Franklin saw impeachment as the republican peaceful alternative to assassination under despotism.

Revised Resolution 9 : Agreed on fixed compensation, nem con.

Agreed (9-1) to be paid out of National Treasury.

Saturday, July 21

Revised Resolutions 10, 11 : Wilson and Madison argued unsuccessfully on behalf of reinstating original Council of Revision.

Rejected (4-3-2) motion to join Judiciary with Executive in the exercise of veto power (New Jersey not voting, Pennsylvania and Georgia divided).

Agreed (9-0) on qualified Executive Veto.

Resumed consideration of Judicial appointment.

Defeated (6-3) Executive appointment unless Senate disagrees

Approved (6-3) selection by Senate alone.

Monday, July 23

New Hampshire Delegates, John Langdon and Nicholas Gilman arrive.

Revised Resolution 17, 18, 19 : Agreed unanimously on requiring oaths by both national and state officials to support the Articles of Union.

Began discussion of ratification.

Discussed Resolution 19 of the Amended Virginia Plan of June 13: "The amendments which shall be offered to the Confederation by the Convention ought at a proper time or times, after the approbation of Congress to be submitted to an assembly or assemblies of representatives, recommended by the several Legislatures, to be expressly chosen by the People to consider and decide thereon."

Defeated (7-3) motion by Ellsworth and Paterson to amend Resolution 19 to have new Constitution referred to State Legislatures for ratification.

Agreed (9-1) to referral to conventions of the people.

Agreed (7-3) to reconsider election of Executive.

Agreed to refer Revised Resolutions to a Committee of 5 members to be named tomorrow.

Tuesday, July 24

Chose Rutledge, Randolph, Gorham, Ellsworth and Wilson to the Committee of Detail.

Revised Resolution 9 : Reconsidered choice of Executive by electors.

Approved (7-4) appointment by national legislature.

Wednesday, July 25

Defeated (6-5) resolution to let members have copies of the Revised Resolutions of the Virginia Plan during the break.

Revised Resolution 9 : Resumed discussion on election of Executive.

Madison compares and contrasts the four proposals for electing the Executive.

Thursday, July 26

Revised Resolution 9 : Resumed discussion on election of Executive and approved (7-3) a 7-year term with ineligibility for re-election.

Agreed (6-3-1) to the whole resolution on Executive.

James Wilson reminds participants "We are providing a constitution for future generations, and not merely for the peculiar circumstances of the moment."

Adjourned to Monday, August 6, 1787.

July 27-August 6

The Convention in adjournment while Committee of Detail was at work.

By August 4th, the Committee draft was at the printers.

Monday, August 6

The Convention received the report of the Committee of Detail and adjourned to read the 23 Articles.

Tuesday, August 7

Began consideration of the Committee of Detail Report and covered the Preamble, Articles I, II, III, and part of IV.

Agreed (10-0) to Preamble and Articles I and II.

Took up Article III (two-house legislature)

Agreed (7-3) to delete reference to mutual veto between houses as already clear.

Discussed Congress meeting 1st Monday of December annually, and agreed (8-2) to add, "unless a different day shall be appointed by law."

Defeated (8-2) motion for May meeting instead of December.

Agreed to Article III as amended.

Took up Article IV, Section 1 (House elections)

Ellsworth and Mason object to the attempt by G. Morris and Dickinson to impose electoral restrictions.

Defeated (7-1-1) more restrictive freehold qualifications on the electors.

Wednesday, August 8

Agreed unanimously to Article IV, Section 1 concerning qualifications of the electors: "the qualifications of the electors shall be the same... as those of the electors in the several states, of the most numerous branch of their own legislatures."

Proceeded to Article IV, Section 2 (qualifications of House members).

Agreed (10-1) to 7 instead of 3e years citizenship.

Agreed to substitute "inhabitant" instead of "resident;" defeated motions to require 3 years (9-2) and 1 year (6-4-1) of residence, and approved the section (11-0).

Agreed to Article IV, Section 3: 65 members in House from the first Congress until the first census.

Took up Article IV, Section 4 (future apportionment of House).

Agreed (9-2) to insert "not exceeding" before 40,000.

Considered the last clause of Section 4: "The Legislature shall... regulate the number of representatives by the number of inhabitants... at the rate of one for every forty thousand."

Defeated (10-1) a motion by G. Morris to insert "free" before inhabitants: "Slavery... was a nefarious institution."

Agreed to add provision by Dickinson for at least one representative in the House for each state.

Moved on to Article IV, Section 5 (money bills)

Approved motion to strike (7-4), thus challenging the Connecticut Compromise Pinckney, G. Morris and Madison carry the day on this motion and Mason objects.

Thursday, August 9

Took up Article IV, Section 6 (sole power of impeachment,

choose its own speaker) and Section 7 (filling vacancies) and approved both.

Considered Article V, Section 1 (selection of Senators and provision for vacancies).

Defeated (8-1-1) motion to strike executive appointment to vacancies.

Agreed to give each Senator one vote and each state two members.

Article V, Section 2 agreed, nem con.

Article V, Section 3 (qualifications): 30 years old, citizen for 4 years, resident.

Defeated motions to require 14 years of citizenship (7-4) and 13 years of citizenship (7-4).

Defeated 10 years (7-4) and agreed to 9 years (6-4-1).

Substituted "inhabitant" for "resident."

Article V, Section 4 (Senate shall choose its own officers) approved.

Took up Article VI, Section 1 (times and places of election) amended and approved.

Again, Randolph objects to defeat of Article IV, Section 5 (Money Bills).

Friday, August 10

Reheard Article IV, Section 2 (giving Legislature authority to establish property qualification for members).

Motion by Pinckney to spell out property qualifications in the Constitution rejected on voice vote. Pinckney suggested $100,000 for President and $25,000 for Representatives.

Reconsidered (6-5) House residence requirement in Article IV, Section 2, and substituted 3 years for 7 at the request of James Wilson.

Took up Article VI, Section 3 (Quorum requirements).

Added power to compel attendance of absent members (10-0-1).

Agreed to Section 4 (each House to judge qualifications and elections of its members).

Section 5 (freedom of debate), passed nem con.

Took up Section 6 (rules, punishment for disorderly behavior, expulsion of members).

Agreed (10-0-1) to require 2/3 vote for expulsion.

Took up Article VI, Section 7 (Requiring journal and a record of each vote at request of 1/5 of members present), passed (7-3-1).

Saturday, August 11

Continued on Article VI, Section 7.

Agreed (6-4-1) to non-publication in the Journal of "such parts as may in their judgment require secrecy."

Took up Article VI, Section 8 (no more than 3-day adjournment without consent of other House nor to a location other than where they are sitting).

Amended to preclude adjournment to another place during a session (10-1).

Reconsidered Article V, Section 5 (money bills to originate in House, and not be subject to Senate amendment).

Agreed (8-2-1) to reconsider the money bills provision of the Connecticut Compromise on Monday.

Monday, August 13

Reconsidered Article IV, Section 2 (House age and citizenship).

Defeated (7-4) Hamilton's proposal to eliminate 7-year citizenship requirement.

Defeated 9 years (8-3), defeated 4 years (8-3), defeated 5 years (7-3-1), and agreed to the section as reported.

Reconsidered Article V, Section 3 (age and citizenship for Senators), and defeated (8-3) motion to reduce 9 years to 7.

Reconsidered Article IV, Section 5 (money bills).

After extensive debate, defeated (7-4) Randolph's motion to reinstate exclusive power to originate in House. Washington supported Randolph on prudential grounds.

Defeated (4-7) proposition that money bills originate in House and amended in Senate.

Dickinson suggested, "Experience must be our only guide. Reason may mislead us."

Tuesday, August 14

Took up Article VI, Section 9 (ineligibility of members of Legislature to other Federal Offices).

After extensive debate, postponed until powers of Senate were determined.

Proceeded to Article VI, Section 10 (legislative pay to be fixed and paid by their state).

Agreed (9-2) that pay should be out of the National Treasury.

Agreed that pay be ascertained by law.

Wednesday, August 15

Approved Article VI, Section 11 (enacting style for bills).

Took up Article VI, Section 12 (either House may originate bills).

Postponed (6-5) pending determination of powers to be given Senate.

Took up Article VI, Section 13 (Presidential veto) (see coverage on June 4, June 6, and July 21).

Defeated (8-3) a motion that all bills should be submitted to the Executive and Judiciary before they become law.

Madison's provision for the Committee of Revision was defeated for the fourth and final time.

Agreed (6-4-1) to 3/4 vote to override Presidential veto.

Agreed (9-2) to 10 days instead of 7 for the President to return bills.

Thursday, August 16

Took up Article VII, Section 1 (enumeration of Congressional powers).

Agreed, nem con, to power to lay and collect taxes, regulate international and interstate commerce, coin money, regulate foreign coin, and fix standards of weights and measures.

Approved (6-5) adding "and post roads" to power to "establish Post offices."

Agreed (9-2) to strike out the words "and emit bills" in the 8th clause of Article VII, Section 1.

Friday, August 17

Resumed discussion of Article VII, Section 1 (enumeration of Congressional powers).

Agreed (7-3) to elect Treasurer by joint ballot (New Jersey not voting).

Agreed to "establish inferior courts, and make rules on captures."

Agreed (7-3) to "define and punish piracies and felonies committed on the high seas."

Agreed similarly to "counterfeiting the securities and current coin of the United States, and offenses against the law of nations."

Changed the clause Congress shall "make" war to Congress shall "declare war" (8-1).

"Separate questions having been taken on the 9, 10, 11, 12, and 14 clauses of the 1st section, 7 article as amended. They passed in the affirmative."

New Jersey lacked a quorum on this day.

Saturday, August 18

Referred a list of suggested additional Congressional powers to the Committee of Detail.

Agreed (6-4-1) to a Committee of 1 per state, chaired by William Livingston, to consider assumption of state debts.

Agreed (9-2) to meet daily, except Sunday, from 10:00 until 4:00, with no earlier adjournment allowed.

Continued discussion of Article VII, Section 1 (enumeration of Congressional powers).

Agreed to add "and support" to power to raise armies and agreed to strike "build and equip" in favor of "provide and maintain" Navy.

Agreed to add power to make rules for government and regulation of land and naval forces.

Considered different motions giving authority over militia and referred them (8-2-1) to a committee.

Monday, August 20

Pinckney introduces a bill of rights and the list of 12 is sent to the Committee of Detail.

Included in this list are liberty of the press, restrictions on the removal of the Writ of Habeus Corpus, subordination of the military to the civil power, and that "no religious test or qualification shall ever be annexed to any oath of office under the authority of the U. S."

G. Morris proposes the foundations for a Presidential Cabinet:

Council of State, Domestic Affairs, Commerce and Finance, Foreign Affairs, War, and Marine

These are referred to the Committee of Detail.

Returned to Article VII, Section 1 (enumeration of Congressional powers).

Necessary and Proper Clause passed.

Defeated (8-3) Mason's proposal to give Congress power to enact sumptuary laws.

Took up Article VII, Section 2 (defining treason)

After debate and numerous amendments, Section 2 was approved.

Took up Article VII, Section 3 (direct tax, House apportionment and census).

Agreed (9-2) to have first census within 3 years.

Tuesday, August 21

Heard a report from the Committee of State Debt Assumption and Militia Regulation, and laid it on the table.

Included assuming debts incurred "for the common defense and general welfare."

Resumed discussion of Article VII, Section 3, and agreed to it (10-1).

Continued discussion of Article VI, Section 12 (origination of Bills).

Defeated (8-2-1) motion to apportion direct taxes to the number of representatives pending the first census.

Took up Article VII, Section 4 (no export taxes by States).

"The proportions of direct taxation shall be regulated by the whole number of white and other free citizens and inhabitants, of every age, sex and condition... and three-fifths of all other persons."

Defeated (7-3) move to allow export taxes for revenue only.

Defeated (6-5) motion to permit export taxes with 2/3 majority vote.

Approved Section 3 (7-4).

Took up Article VII, Section 4 (no interference with the slave trade).

Luther Martin, supported by George Mason, suggests that the slave trade be prohibited or at least taxed. He argued that the importation of slaves "was inconsistent with the principles of the revolution."

Rutledge rejoined, "Interest alone is the sovereign principle with Nations."

Ellsworth: "The morality or wisdom of slavery are considerations belonging to the states themselves."

Adjourned

Wednesday, August 22

Resumed discussion of Article VII, Section 4.

C. Pinckney stated, "if slavery be wrong, it is justified by the example of all the world." Rutledge warns that North Carolina, South Carolina and Georgia will not sign the Constitution without certain slavery protection clauses.

Dickinson considered the importation of slaves "as inadmissible on every principle of honor and safety."

Randolph added that he "could never agree to the clause as it stands" and urged that the entire section be referred to a committee to seek a compromise solution.

Voted (7-3) to commit Article VII, Sections 4 and 5 to an 11-member committee chaired by William Livingston which included Dickinson and Luther Martin and excluded C. Pinckney and Rutledge. Section 6 was also committed to this committee.

Took up Article VII, Section 2 (prohibit bills of attainder and ex post facto laws).

Agreed (7-3-1).

The report of the Committee of 5 was postponed (6-5).

The report of the Committee of 11 on Assumption of State Debts was taken up.

After brief discussion it was agreed (11-0), "The Legislature shall discharge the debts and fulfill the obligations of the United States."

Thursday, August 23

Took up Article VII, Section I (powers of Congress).

After considerable discussion and minor alterations agreed to section.

Passed Article VII, Section 7 (no titles of nobility), nem con.

Took up Article VIII.

Approved adding a prohibition against Federal officers accepting foreign titles or gifts without consent of Congress.

Also accepted a restatement of Supremacy Clause.

Took up Article IX, (Senate treaty power and appointment of Judges and ambassadors) and postponed.

Revisited Article VII, Section 1 (calling up militia to execute laws), amended and approved it.

Madison again, supported by Wilson and Pinckney, proposed a motion to restore Congressional veto power over State laws, defeated (6-5).

Agreed to revised Article VII, Section 1 (debts).

"The Legislature shall fulfill the engagements and discharge the debts of the United States, and shall have the power to law and collect taxes, duties, imposts, and excises."

Resumed discussion of Senate power to make treaties, appoint Ambassadors and Judges, and referred proposal to the Committee of Five.

Friday, August 24

Heard a report from the Committee of 11 on Slave Trade Article VII, Sections 4, 5, and 6 (no interference with slave trade, capitation taxes in proportion to census, no navigation acts without 2/3 vote in each House).

Committee recommended prohibiting interference with slave trade until 1800, keeping Section 5, striking section 6 and permitting a tax to be imposed on migration.

Agreed to reconsider debt provisions and interstate commerce clause (Article VII, Section 1).

Took up Article IX, Sections 2 and 3 (controversies among states, controversies arising from conflicting land grants).

Agreed (8-2) to strike both sections.

Took up Article X, Section 1 (Executive).

Agreed on one Executive but defeated four different methods of electing the President including by the people (9-2) and by electors (6-5).

Took up Article X, Section 2 (Executive powers and duties).

Ordered adjournment at 3:00pm for the future.

Saturday, August 25

Approved (10-1) debt provision.

Defeated (10-1) motion to include common defense and general welfare clause in Article VII, Section 1, Clause 1.

Took up Article VII, Section 4 (slave trade) (see also July 23, August 8, 21, 22, 26, and 29).

Agreed (7-4) to change from 1800 to 1808 the prohibition on Congress (New Jersey, Pennsylvania, Delaware, and Virginia voting against).

Approved (7-4) "The migration or importation of such persons as the several states now existing should think proper to admit, shall not be prohibited by the Legislature prior to the year 1808."

Madison stated, "twenty years will produce all the mischief that can be apprehended from the liberty to import slaves." He also "thought it wrong to admit into the Constitution the idea that there could be property in men."

Approved import tax not to exceed $10.00 per person.

Approved Article VII, Section 5 as reported.

Postponed Article VII, Section 6.

Continued on Executive powers in Article X.

Defeated (6-3-1) motion allowing appointment to Federal offices by State Executives in Article X, Section 2.

Monday, August 27

Continued on Executive powers in Article X.

Agreed (6-2) that President would be "commander chief... of the militia when called into the actual service of the United States" (Massachusetts, New Jersey, and North Carolina absent).

Began discussion of Article XI (Judicial powers).

Took up Section 1: "The Judicial Power of the United States..."

Agreed (6-2) to Johnson's motion to add "both in law and equity" after the words "United States." Three states absent.

Approved Section 1 (6-2).

Took up Section 2.

Defeated (7-1) removal of justices by Executive on request of Legislature.

Approved Section 2 (6-2).

Took up Section 3.

Postponed clause considering the impeachment of judges.

Discussed distinction between original and appellate jurisdiction.

Agreed to add, "to which the United States is a Party" to "controversies."

Approved (8-2) several other perfecting amendments. Johnson moved to insert the words "this Constitution and the" before the word "laws" in "The jurisdiction of the Supreme Court shall extend to all cases arising under the laws passed by the Legislature of the United States."

This passed nem con on the understanding that the jurisdiction was "limited to cases of a Judiciary nature."

Massachusetts, New Jersey, and North Carolina experienced difficulties meeting quorum requirements.

Tuesday, August 28

Heard a report from August 25th committee (regulation of commerce).

Continued discussion of Article XI.

Took up Section 3 (appellate jurisdiction).

Approved Section 3 (9-1).

Took up Section 4 (local trial by jury and Writ of Habeas Corpus).

Amended to provide for crimes committed outside any state.

Agreed (7-3) to add that the privilege of the writ of Habeas Corpus shall not be suspended, unless where in cases of Rebellion or invasion the public safety may require it.

Agreed to Section 4.

Agreed to Section 5 (limit punishment under impeachment).

Took up Article XII (limits on State powers).

Agreed (8-1-1) to add prohibition on emitting bills of credit, or making anything but gold or silver legal tender.

Agreed (7-3) that no State could pass bills of attainder or ex post facto laws.

Defeated (8-3) prohibiting laying of embargoes.

Agreed to Article XII as amended.

Took up Article XIII (additional prohibition on States).

Agreed (6-5) to prohibit States from taxing exports as well as imports without consent of Congress.

Agreed (9-2) that net receipts of State taxation of imports and exports go into Federal Treasury.

Agreed to Article XIII.

Took up Article XIV (mutual privileges and immunities).

Approved it (9-1-1).

Took up Article XV (extradition): "Any person charged with treason, felony, or high misdemeanor in any State, who shall flee from justice, and shall be found in any other State, shall, on demand of the Executive power of the State from which he fled, be delivered up and removed to the State having jurisdiction of the offence."

"High misdemeanors" replaced by "other crimes."

Butler and Pinckney suggest that the extradition clause be extended to include run away slaves. They argue that "fugitive slaves (should) be delivered up like criminals."

Agreed to Article XV, nem con.

Adjourned

Wednesday, August 29

Took up Article XVI (full faith and credit).

Heard motion to establish uniform bankruptcy laws.

Committed both Article XVI and motion to Committee on State Commitments with 5 members, chaired by John Rutledge.

Took up recommendation by the Livingston Committee on Slave Trade to strike out Article VII, Section 6 (2/3 vote needed to approve Congressional regulation of international and interstate commerce).

Committee report approved (7-4).

Returned to Article XV and passed a fugitive slave clause (11-0) to be added at the end of the Article: "If any person bound to service or labor in any of the United States shall escape into another State, he or she shall not be discharged from such service or labor in consequence of any regulations susbsisting in the State to which they escape; but shall be delivered up to the person justly claiming their service or labor."

Took up Article XVII (admission of new states) and passed (6-5).

Thursday, August 30

Continued discussion on Article XVII (admission of new states).

Agreed (8-3) to permit the admission of new States on equal terms, prohibit dividing or combining states without consent of State Legislatures, and grant Congress authority to govern public lands, territory or other property of the United States.

Took up Article XVIII (guarantee of republican form of government): "The United States shall guaranty to each State a Republican form of Government; and shall protect each State against foreign invasion, and, on the application of its Legislature, against domestic violence."

Dropped "foreign" and retained "domestic violence" over "insurrection" (6-5).

Amended and agreed (9-2).

Took up Article XIX (amending process) and agreed.

Took up Article XX (oath for officers of the government).

Added "or Affirmation."

Added, "no religious test shall ever be required," which passed nem con.

Agreed to Article XX (8-1-2).

Discussed Article XXI (mode of ratification of the Constitution): "The ratifications of the Conventions of ___ States shall be sufficient for organizing this Constitution."

Friday, August 31

Continued discussing Article XXI (mode of ratification of the Constitution).

Shall the blank be filled with the number 7, 8, 9, 10, 11, or 13?

Agreed (9-1), to add "between the said states," to limit effect of ratification to states actually ratifying.

Rejected (6-4) attempt to overturn provision requiring ratification by specially elected conventions rather than ratification by State Legislatures.

Debated number of states required to secure ratification of the Constitution.

Defeated (9-1) motion requiring all 13 states to ratify.

Defeated (7-4) motion requiring 10 states to ratify

Agreed (8-3) to motion requiring 9 states to ratify.

Agreed (10-1) to Article XXI as amended.

Took up Article XXII (Authorization of the Constitution by Confederation Congress).

Agreed (8-3) to strike provision requiring Confederation Congress approval of the Constitution.

Defeated (7-4) proposal in effect permitting Confederation Congress to rewrite the Constitution.

Defeated (8-3) motion to postpone discussion on Article XXII.

Agreed (10-1) to Article XXII as amended.

Discussed Article XXIII (transition from Confederation Government to Constitutional Government).

Agreed with amendments.

Took up Committee of 11 Report of Article VII, Section 4 (Export taxes and duties).

Agreed to provision not to give preference to one state over another.

Agreed (8-2) to proposal to prohibit requiring ships bound for one state to enter, clear, or pay duties in another.

Agreed on uniformity clause.

Conclusion of discussion on Committee of Detail Report.

Referred all leftover proposals to a Committee of one delegate from each state:

Gilman, King, Sherman, Brearly, G. Morris, Dickinson, Carroll, Madison, Williamson, Butler, and Baldwin

This is known as the Brearly Committee.

Saturday, Sept. 1

Heard initial report from Brearly Committee.

Recommended alteration in Article VI, Section 9: Ineligibility of Federal Legislators to other Federal office.

Received the report of the August 29th Committee, the Rutledge Committee.

Recommended alteration in Article XVI, concerning bankruptcies.

Appearance of "Full Faith and Credit clause."

Approved (7-1-1) motion to adjourn.

New Jersey and Pennsylvania did not meet quorum requirement.

Monday, Sept. 3

Took up Article XVI (Full Faith and Credit clause).

Agreed (6-3) to the clause (New Hampshire not voting).

Agreed (9-1) to Article XVI as amended.

Took up Article XVI, uniform bankruptcy laws and agreed (9-1).

Defeated (6-4) motion to adjourn.

Took up Article VI, Section 9 (ineligibility of Federal Legislators to other Federal office).

Agreed (5-3-1) (New Jersey not voting).

Delaware did not meet quorum requirement.

Tuesday, Sept. 4

Discussed 4 out of 9 proposals submitted by Brearly Committee.

Approved Brearly Committee proposal #1 giving Federal Legislature authority to lay and collect taxes, duties and imposts and provide for "the common defense and general welfare."

Agreed to proposal #2 to amend Article VII, Section 1, interstate commerce clause, to include Congressional regulation of commerce "with the Indian tribes."

Postponed proposal #3 to amend Article IX, Section 1. The proposal reads:

"The Senate of the United States shall have the power to try all impeachments; but no person shall be convicted without the concurrence of two thirds of the members present."

Took up proposal #4 to amend Article X, Section 1 (Election of Executive).

A.) And with the Vice President, "He shall hold his office during the term of 4 years."

B.) "Each state shall appoint in such a manner as its Legislature shall direct, a number of electors equal to the whole number of Senators and members of the House of Representatives, to which the State may be entitled in the Legislature."

C.) "The person having the greatest number of (Electoral College) votes shall be the President."

D.) "If no person have a majority, then from the 5 highest on the list the Senate shall choose by ballot the President."

E.) "And in every case after the choice of the President, the person having the greatest number of votes shall be vice-president: but if there should remain two or more who have equal votes, the Senate shall choose from them the vice-president."

F.) "The Legislature may determine the time of choosing and assembling the Electors, and the manner of certifying and transmitting their votes."

Received #5: Qualifications for President including "natural born citizen" clause.

Received #6: The Vice-President.

Received #7: Advice and consent of the Senate.

Received #8: Opinion in writing.

Received #9: Removal from office.

Agreed (7-3) to postpone consideration of #4-#9.

Wednesday, Sept. 5

Received 5 additional proposals from the Brearly Committee, which were considered immediately.

Considered proposals #10, 11, 13 & 14, to amend Article VII, Section 1.

#10-Added "and grant letters of marquee and reprisal" to the war powers clause, nem con.

#11-Limited military appropriations to two years, nem con.

#13-Granted exclusive jurisdiction over Federal land to Congress, nem con.

#14-Provided limited patents to promote science and arts, nem con.

Agreed (9-2) to postpone proposal #12 concerning Article IV: A reconsideration of the Connecticut Compromise, namely, to now permit the Senate to amend money bills that originate in the House.

Gerry gave notice that he wanted to reconsider Articles XIX (amending), XX (oath), XXI (ratification), and XXII (blessing of Confedration Congress).

Returned to consideration of the 6 proposals left over from the September 4th submission of 9 proposals by the Brearly Committee (#4, 5, 6, 7, 8, 9).

Extensive discussion of proposal #4 to amend Article X, Section 1 (Election of Executive).

Defeated several motions concerning the election of the Executive.

Defeated (7-3-1) motion to overcome non-majoritarian outcomes in the Electoral College in the whole Congress instead of just the Senate.

Randolph "We have in some revolutions of this plan made a bold stroke for monarchy. We are now doing the same for an aristocracy." Mason agreed.

Defeated (9-2) motion to limit choice in the Senate to the top 3 candidates instead of the top 5 candidates.

Wilson: "This subject…is in truth the most difficult of all of which we have had to decide."

Agreed to request Congress to pay Convention expenses.

Thursday, Sept. 6

Continued discussion of proposal #4 to amend Article X, Section 1 (election of Executive).

Agreed (10-1) that the President and Vice-President to be elected to a term of 4 years.

Agreed (10-1) after discussion and amending to authorize the Senate to choose the Executive from top 4 candidates.

Agreed (10-1) to a motion by Williamson to substitute the House, with voting by states, for the Senate, or the whole Legislature, in electing the Executive from the top 4 candidates in the event of a break down of the Electoral College.

Mason liked this because it reduced "the aristocratic influence of the Senate."

Agreed Senate shall choose the Vice-President in the event of a tie for the Vice-Presidency.

Friday, Sept. 7

Continued discussion on proposal #4 to amend Article X, Section 1 (election of Executive).

Agreed (8-3) on Electoral College with majority of electoral votes needed for the election of the Executive.

Decided (10-1) that the House, rather than the Senate, shall decide in such circumstances but each State shall have one vote.

Approved (6-4-1) motion to let Legislature determine who shall act in cases of disability of President and Vice-President.

Took up Proposal #5: Qualifications of the President

Agreed (nem con) that the President should be a natural-born citizen, resident for 14 years and be 35 years of age.

Took up Proposal #6: Vice-President as President of Senate.

Agreed (8-2) that the Vice-President would serve as President of the Senate (North Carolina not voting).

Took up Proposal #7: Powers of the Executive.

Defeated (10-1) motion to include House in treaty-making.

Agreed to Presidential nomination and Senate concurrence of ambassadors, ministers, consuls, and other officers.

Approved treaty-making with "the advice and consent" of 2/3 of Senate present.

Defeated (8-3) motion for Council of Advisors to President.

Saturday, Sept. 8

Resumed discussion on Proposal #7: Powers of the Executive.

Reconsidered treaty power and engaged in lengthy discussion of role of the Senate especially the 2/3 approved rule.

Defeated (6-5) Sherman's motion that "no treaty be made without a Majority of the whole number of the Senate."

Agreed (8-3) to Brearly Committee Proposal #8 (President can request opinions of government officials in writing).

Took up Proposal #9: Impeachment of the President.

Mason wanted to add "maladministration" to "treason and bribery."

Agreed (8-3) to replace "maladministration" with "other high crimes and misdemeanors against the State."

Defeated (9-2) motion to strike Senate as body to judge on impeachment.

Agreed (11-0) to addition of Vice-President and other Civil Officers as subject to impeachment.

Returned to Proposal #12: Consideration of Money Bills.

Agreed (9-2) to Proposal #12: Origination of money bills in the House, subject to Senate amendment (This vote removes that feature of the Connecticut Compromise deemed vital by Mason, Gerry and Randolph).

Balloted for a Committee of Style (Johnson, Hamilton, G. Morris, Madison, and King) to revise the style and arrange the articles which had been agreed to."

Defeated (6-5) motion supported by Madison and Hamilton to increase the size of House membership.

Monday, Sept. 10

Reconsidered (9-1-1) Article XIX of the Committee of Detail report: Process to amend the Constitution (2/3 of State Legislatures requesting an amendment, the Congress shall call a Convention).

Madison wondered: "How was a Convention to be formed? By what rule decide? What is the force of its acts?"

Agreed (11-0) that an amendment proposal becomes part of the Constitution upon ratification of 3/4 of the State Legislatures or State Conventions.

Rutledge: Exclude changes to 1808 agreement on slave trade.

Agreed (9-1-1) to permit 2/3 House and 2/3 Senate to request an amendment.

Agreed (7-3-1) to reconsider Article XXII of the Committee of Detail Report.

Approved (11-0) Article XXI.

This Constitution becomes effective on the approbation of 9 state ratifying conventions and "binding and conclusive" on those states "assenting thereto."

Took up Article XXII.

Randolph and Gerry explain their reservations about signing the Constitution if "approbation by Congress" is not required. "Mr. Randolph took this opportunity to state his objection to the system."

Rejected nem con a motion to require the approval of the Constitution by the Confederation Congress.

Committee of Detail Report, as revised, and Brearly Committee report, as revised, sent to the Committee of Style.

Tuesday, Sept. 11

Convention met and adjourned because the Committee of Style was not ready with their report.

Wednesday, Sept. 12

Committee of Style reported a 7 Article document and "read by paragraph."

This document is preceded by a preamble, which begins, "We the People of the United States, in order to form a more perfect union..." rather than "We the people of the states of New Hampshire, etc..."

Took up Article I, Section 7.

Agreed (6-4-1) to amend section to include 2/3 instead of 3/4 for Congress to override an Executive veto.

Mason and Gerry call for a Bill of Rights; motion is defeated (10-0) (Massachusetts absent).

Thursday, Sept. 13

Resumed consideration of Report of Committee of Style.

Took up Article I and focused on Sections 2 & 7.

Agreed unanimously to substitute "service" for "servitude."

Agreed (7-3) to allow State duties to defray costs of storage and inspection.

Mason bemoans the absence of "a power to make sumptuary regulations."

Named Mason, Franklin, Dickinson, Johnson, and Livingston to a committee to suggest measures for encouraging economy, frugality, and American manufactures (this committee never made a report).

Johnson from the Committee of Style reported a substitute for Articles XXIII of the Committee of Detail Report.

Friday, Sept. 14

Took up Article I, Sections 3, 4, 5, & 6.

Agreed to sections with minimal debate.

Took up Article I, Section 8 (Powers of Congress).

Agreed (8-3) to strike election of Treasurer by Legislature.

Agreed (11-0) to add uniformity requirement to taxing power.

Madison, Randolph, Wilson, G. Morris, Mason debate meaning of "necessary and proper clause."

Defeated (6-4-1) motion to give Congress power to establish a university.

Pinckney, Gerry, and Sherman debate whether Congress has the power to interfere with freedom of the press.

Defeated (6-5) motion to insert "The Liberty of the Press shall be inviolably preserved."

Took up Article I, Section 9 (Restraints on Congressional powers).

Defeated Mason's motion "that an account of the public expenditures should be annually published."

Adopted Madison's suggestion nem con to change "annual" publications to "from time to time."

Agreed to the Section with minimal debate.

Took up Article I, Section 10 (Restraints on the powers of the States).

Gerry's motion to extend to the Federal Government "the restraint put on the states from impairing the obligations of contracts" failed to obtain a second.

Saturday, Sept. 15

The Convention resumed discussion on the report from the Committee of Style.

Decided (6-4) an address from the Convention to the people was "unnecessary and improper" (South Carolina absent).

Defeated (6-5) an attempt to add another member for Rhode Island in the House.

King threatened to withhold his signature to the Constitution if this proposition passed

Passed (10-1) an attempt to add another member for North Carolina in the House.

Took up Article I, Section 10 (Restraints on the powers of the States).

McHenry, Carroll, Langdon, Mason, G. Morris, Madison, and Sherman debate the meaning of the Interstate Commerce clause.

Does the regulatory power of Congress restrain state commerce authority?

Agreed (6-4-1) that "no state shall lay any duty on tonnage with out the consent of Congress."

Took up Article II, Section 1 (General structure of Executive Office).

Agreed (7-4) that the President shall not receive "any other emolument from the United States or any of them" during his term of office.

Took up Article II, Section 2 (Powers of the President).

Defeated (8-2-1) motion to extend the power "to grant reprieves and pardons for offenses against the United States, except in cases of impeachment" to include "cases of treason."

Agreed (after debate, nem con) to G. Morris's "Inferior Officer's" clause (Allows Congress to bypass the "advice and consent of the Senate" and vest/delegate the appointment of "inferior officers" to the President alone, the Courts of Law alone or the Heads of Departments alone). This motion was initially defeated (5-5-1).

Took up Article III, Section 2 (Trial by jury).

Defeated (nem con) an attempt to extend the "trial by jury" clause covering criminal cases to include civil cases.

Took up Article IV, Section 2 (Fugitive Slave clause).

Struck out "no person legally held to service or labor in one state escaping into another" and replaced it with "no person held to service or labor in one state, under the laws thereof, escaping into another" (emphasis added).

Addition of "under the laws thereof" removes the idea "that slavery was legal in a moral view."

Agreed to Article IV, Section 3 (Admittance of new states).

Agreed to Article IV, Section 4 (Republican guarantee).

Took up Article V (Amending the Constitution).

Agreed (nem con) that Congress shall call a convention on the application for amendments by 2/3 of the State Legislatures.

Agreed (8-3) that a state cannot be deprived of its equal suffrage in the Senate without its own consent.

Unanimously rejected a call by Randolph, Mason, and Gerry "that amendments to the plan might be offered by the States Conventions, which should be submitted to and finally decided on by another general convention."

Approved (10-0) the document as amended (North Carolina did not meet quorum call).

Monday, Sept. 17

The Constitution was presented and read aloud; several delegates expressed concerns yet restrained their reservations in order to achieve a sense of unanimity.

Randolph's prediction: "Nine states will fail to ratify the plan and confusion must ensue."

Changed the base of representation in the House of Representatives from 1:40,000 to 1:30,000 with the support of Washington.

Voted (10-1) to deposit the Journals (Secretary Jackson's notes) with the President, subject to the orders of Congress.

Heard Franklin's "Rising Sun" speech.

Signed the Constitution and adjourned, Mason, Randolph and Gerry refused to sign; Read signed Dickinson's name in his absence.

"The business being thus closed, the Members adjourned to the City Tavern, dined together and took a cordial leave of each other."

4

Major Themes at the Constitutional Convention

THE RULE OF SECRECY

On May 25, the Constitutional Convention began its work by creating a Committee to propose "rules for conducting business." On May 28, the Committee reported sixteen rules and on May 29 they reported six further rules. One of these was the rule of secrecy. According to Madison's *Notes*, the exact language of the secrecy rule was: "That nothing spoken in the house be printed, or otherwise published or communicated without leave."

The delegates adopted these rules without debate. And for the most part they adhered to the rule of secrecy. The issue of what would happen after the Convention adjourned was not addressed. Certainly Madison informed Thomas Jefferson about the main features of the deliberations. There was at least one Founder in each of the state ratifying conventions, and these conventions were open to the public with the deliberations reported widely in the press. Madison seems to have taken the vow of secrecy to the limit; his copious *Notes* weren't available until after his death despite numerous requests that he make them available to help in constitutional interpretation.

Why secrecy? There seems to be an instinctive case against secrecy since democracy and openness are often deemed to be synonymous. There is the further suspicion that secret gatherings are designed by the wicked few to shaft the innocent many. This is in large part the conclusion of twentieth century Progressive Historiography that makes a point of equating meeting in secret with smoked filled rooms and elitist betrayal of virtuous majorities.

They point to the secrecy rule, and the thick drapes over closed windows in Independence Hall during the hot Philadelphia summer, as evidence of an undemocratic founding. But anyone who has seen politicians in front of the camera knows that openness and posturing also go together and that being pressured by outside forces is not always conducive to wise deliberation and choice. Thus even contemporary society sees the need for executive sessions and private discourse.

I think the model the Founders had in mind was "the trial by jury model" where the jurors deliberated in secret in order to be candid with each other and to be free to change their mind for the right reason, namely, because they were persuaded to do so. There is also something to be said to being part of an uninterrupted conversation. It isn't so much that politics seeks darkness rather than light; rather it is from darkness that light emerges.

THE CENTRAL FEATURES OF THE VIRGINIA PLAN

Text of the Virginia Plan

On May 29, Edmund Randolph introduced the Virginia Plan containing 15 Resolutions.

Echoing, Madison's Vices of April 1787, he itemized five reasons why the Articles of Confederation must be radically altered.

1. "It does not provide against foreign attacks."
2. "It does not secure Harmony to the States."
3. "It is incapable of producing certain blessings to the States."
4. "It cannot defend itself against encroachments."
5. "It is not superior to State constitutions."

The single most important reason why the delegates were gathered was because of what Madison referred to as the multiplicity, mutability, and injustice of legislation at the state level. To correct these deficiencies, the Virginia Plan removed the state legislatures both structurally, and in terms of powers, from any place in the new continental arrangement. Most importantly,

1. The National Legislature should consist of two branches.
2. The people of each State should elect the First Branch of the National Legislature. The Second Branch of the National Legislature should be elected by the first.
3. The National Legislature shall have power "to legislate in all cases to which the separate States are incompetent," and "to negative all laws passed by the States, contravening in the opinion of the National Legislature the articles of Union."
4. The National Legislature shall elect a National Executive.
5. The Executive and a number of National Judiciary will form a Council of Revision. This Council will review laws passed by the National Legislature and have the power to reject the laws, unless the National Legislature can pass the act again.
6. The National Legislature will create the National Judiciary. The structure will consist of one or more supreme tribunals and inferior tribunals. Judges will be appointed for life, during good behavior.
7. State Legislatures, Executives, and Judges are to be bound by oath to support the Articles.
8. The new plan for government should be ratified by the people, through assemblies of representatives chosen by the people.

The "oracle" Montesquieu had argued that for a people to remain free, they must reside in small, homogeneous communities. Public virtue was needed to secure a republic and this sentiment was endangered in large, heterogeneous communities. It is the unique contribution of Madison to challenge this traditional theory of self-government head on. In fact, he stands it on its head! His first verbal articulation of this position occurs on June 6 where he argues that majority faction is the mortal disease of popular government and traditional solutions to factious politics will no longer work. He thus directly challenges the traditional claim that people are happier in small republics. Just the opposite; unless we spread people out over an extended orbit and filter their opinions, passions, and interests through a scheme of representation, then popular government will come to a violent end. This speech is the precursor to the famous *Federalist* 10 essay and is part of the political theory underlying the Virginia Plan.

There is a division of opinion in the scholarly literature concerning the motivation behind the introduction of the Virginia Plan. Some scholars credit Madison for his strategic brilliance in shifting the attention away from revising the Articles of Confederation to this new and bold plan. Other interpreters point out that it was introduced by Virginia, the largest state, that would benefit in terms of representation at the expense of the smaller states who received equal representation under the Articles of Confederation. A number of political theorists portray the Virginia Plan as making the novel case for "the large republic" theory over against the traditional "small republic" theory articulated by Roger Sherman on June 6. What is clear from both Randolph's arguments on May 29 and Madison's position on June 6 is that the Virginians saw state legislatures, in both large and small states, as dangerous to liberty and justice. What is also clear is that Madison sees no principled reason for the equal representation of states *qua* states.

WHY WAS THE NEW JERSEY PLAN INTRODUCED?

On June 11, Roger Sherman proposed a compromise: rather than have proportional representation of the people in both the House and the Senate, why not agree to proportional representation in the House and equal representation for each state in the Senate? The rejection of this compromise, led the New Jersey, Connecticut, New York, and Delaware delegations, and Mr. Martin from Maryland, to propose the New Jersey Plan.

Madison's *Notes* for June 15th records the following: "Mr. Dickinson said to Mr. Madison you see the consequence of pushing things too far." The 11 Resolutions of the New Jersey Plan restored the single chamber structure of the Articles, where each state was represented equally regardless of the size of its population. As far as powers were concerned, the power to tax and the power to regulate interstate commerce were added to the powers that the union had under the Articles.

It is tempting to see the introduction of the New Jersey Plan as an attempt by the small states to fight off the impending victory of the large state supported Virginia Plan. But this is to simplify too much. There were some "large minded" men from small states—Dickenson for example—who were willing to meet the Madisonians half way, but to no avail.

What are the principles, if any, that undergird this Plan? On June 16, for example, Pinckney observed, rather cynically, that no principles were involved: "the whole comes down to this, as he conceived. Give N. Jersey an equal vote, and she will dismiss her scruple, and concur in the Natil. system." But Pinckney, to the contrary notwithstanding, there are two "scruples" involved.

The first scruple concerns the rule of law. On February 28, 1787, the Confederation Congress endorsed the meeting of a Grand Convention, "for the sole purpose of revising the articles of confederation and reporting to Congress and the several state legislatures such alterations and provisions therein as shall, when agreed to in Congress and confirmed by the States, render the federal constitution adequate to the exigencies of government and the preservation of the Union." The defenders of the New Jersey Plan pointed to this mandate and suggested that the Virginia Plan was illegal. The second principled position was the question of prudence, namely, the improbability that the Virginia Plan will be adopted. The defenders of the New Jersey Plan argued that it would be more likely to be adopted by the electorate than the never before imagined Virginia Plan. On June 16, Lansing, in support of Patterson, stated: "The Scheme is itself totally novel. There is no parallel to it to be found."

The New Jersey Plan supporters had to cont.nd with the question, why are states *qua* states entitled to equal representation? There are two answers. 1) The colonies became the States and the States have been equally represented in every continental scheme from the start, so why the move to alter tradition? 2) The Declaration of Independence declared the independence, equality, and sovereignty of each state. And the Treaty of Paris recognized the independence of the states as part of the principles of the peace.

WHAT'S THE POINT TO THE HAMILTON PLAN?

June 13 is Hamilton day at the convention. He argued that the New Jersey Plan simply duplicated the defects of the Articles and thus failed to address the source of the problem, namely, state sovereignty. And, he argued further, that the Virginia Plan didn't go far enough. It didn't adequately subdue the state governments—Hamilton wanted the governors of the states to be selected by the national government along the lines of the previous colonial administration—and it was insufficiently high-toned.

Hamilton stated that there are five "great & essential principles necessary for the support of government." 1. " An active & constant interest in supporting it," 2. "The love of power. Men love power," 3. " An habitual attachment of the people," 4. "Force by which may be understood a coercion of laws or coercion of arms," and 5. "Influence." According to Hamilton neither plan meets these five objectives.

To Hamilton, the task was "to go as far as in order to attain stability and permanency as republican principles will admit. Let one branch of the Legislature hold their places for life or at least during good behaviour. Let the Executive also be for life." Put differently, only the British Government came close to securing good government. The feature he admired in the British system was the duration in office for the office holders. He suggested that the duration in office proposed by the delegates supporting both plans were inadequate; as long as the chief executive and Senators were elected, for example, and subject to impeachment, then we could trust them to have life terms! This was a major departure from what was accepted as a republican form of government.

It is tempting to speculate why Hamilton spent so much time on his eleven point plan and what impact he had. One bit of American mythology has Hamilton deliberately introducing such an outrageous Plan in order to make the Virginia rather than the New Jersey plan look moderate. This lovely story concludes by demonstrating that the very next day the amended Virginia Plan is adopted and subsequently Hamilton leaves the convention for New York. But there is no evidence that Hamilton's speech swayed anyone to change their vote from the New Jersey plan to the Virginia Plan.

The importance of Hamilton's speech is that it pushed the delegates, but much later on, to consider the true from the false definition of monarchy and aristocracy. The false definition, says Hamilton, is longevity in office; the true characteristic is how you get into office. And by the latter stages of the convention, the delegates were willing to entertain a much more "elevated" form of government that Hamilton so brashly presented a couple of months earlier. Hamilton's point is that the key to monarchy and aristocracy is that the office holders: inherit their position and are not elected by the people. This distinction is critical because it challenges the traditional republican doctrine that "where annual elections end, tyranny begins," and that intrinsic to republicanism are short terms in office with provisions for recall and rotation.

THE CONNECTICUT COMPROMISE

The Virginia Plan, introduced on May 29, was "wholly national." Of particular importance is the absence of any structural representation for the states. According to Resolutions 3, 4, and 5, the general government shall have a bicameral legislative structure with neither branch elected by the states and with neither representing the states.

On June 11, the delegates overwhelmingly agreed that the lower house should be based on population and elected by the people. By a 6-5 vote, the delegates rejected a proposal by Roger Sherman that supported popular representation in the lower house and equal representation for the states in the upper branch. Thus on June 15, William Paterson submitted the New Jersey Plan, one that scrapped all the popular representation provisions of the Virginia Plan.

On 19 June, the New Jersey Plan was defeated 7-3-1. For the remainder of June, however, the delegates returned repeatedly to the compromise proposal of June 11. And on June 29, Ellsworth reintroduced the motion of June 11: equal representation for the states in the upper house with proportional representation in the lower house.

For the first time, the case for the representation of the states was elevated from one of convenience to one of principle. Ellsworth declared, "We were partly national; partly federal. He trusted that on this middle ground a compromise would take place." On June 30, the youngest delegate, Jonathan Dayton of New Jersey—until then a pretty staunch nationalist—spoke for the first time: "We were partly federal, partly national in our Union," he declared. "And he did not see why the Govt. might (not) in some respects operate on the States, in others on the people."

On July 2, the Ellsworth proposal was defeated on a tie vote: 5-5-1. Nevertheless, a Committee of 11—one delegate from each state—was created to seek a compromise on the representation question. The composition of the committee reveals that Madison's attempt to exclude the states from the structure of the general government had been halted in its tracks. Gerry was chosen over King from Massachusetts, Yates over Hamilton from New York, Franklin over Wilson from Pennsylvania, Davie over Williamson from North Carolina, Rutledge over Pinckney from South Carolina, and Mason over Madison from Virginia.

From July 5 to July 7, the Gerry Committee defended equal representation for the states in the Senate and popular representation in the House. We need to put theoretical niceties to one side, Gerry said, and think about "accommodation." "We were… in a peculiar situation. We were neither the same Nation nor different Nations. If no compromise should take place what will be the consequence."? Mason concurred: "There must be some accommodation." Paterson, also on the committee, urged adoption of the report for "there was no other ground of accommodation."

The key to the Compromise was winning over such former wholly national supporters like Gerry and Mason. An often-overlooked component of the Compromise was the agreement that money bills would originate in the House and could not be amended in the Senate. This feature was vital in winning over Mason and Gerry, as well as Randolph who introduced the wholly national

Virginia Plan. These three delegates were willing to buy into the partly national (popular representation in the House), partly federal (equal representation for the states in the Senate) arrangement if the principle of no taxation without popular representation was adhered to.

On July 16, the delegates agreed (5-4-1) to the Gerry Committee Report, also known as the Connecticut Compromise. The losing delegates, Madison, Wilson, G. Morris, Pinckney, and King, decided not to challenge the outcome.

THE NECESSARY AND PROPER CLAUSE

Article One, Section 8 of the Constitution enumerates the powers of Congress. The eighteenth and final entry says: "To make all Laws which shall be necessary and proper for carrying into Execution the foregoing Powers vested by this Constitution in the Government of the United States, or in any Department or Officer thereof." When and how did this phrase make its appearance in the convention deliberations?

The necessary and proper clause is a constitutional compromise, one somewhere between the Federalist disposition not to enumerate any Congressional powers at all—a vital part of a wholly national arrangement—and the Antifederalist concern to limit the reach of Congress to those items expressly itemized

The Virginia Plan was wholly national in terms of powers. Of particular importance, here, is the absence of 1) an enumeration of Congressional powers whatsoever—Congress was empowered to legislate in all areas where the states were "incompetent"—and 2) a Bill of Rights on behalf of either the states or the people.

On July 17, the delegates agreed (6-4) to adhere to the "incompetent" powers provision of the Virginia Plan. This vote, however, should not be interpreted as a Madisonian victory; rather it is a prelude to his fourth serious defeat on the federal-national issue. Prior to July 17, the "incompetent" clause sailed through without more than a murmur of opposition. Now it was on its last gasp. On August 6, the Committee of Detail presented the first draft of the Constitution and, the next day, the delegates began their deliberations of the 23 Articles. What is really significant about the report is that the powers of Congress are enumerated for the first time.

On August 20, the delegates turned to the final enumerated power which had never before been part of the constitutional conversation: "And to make all laws that shall be necessary and proper for carrying into execution the foregoing powers and all other powers vested, by this Constitution, in the government of the United States, or in any department or officer thereof."

According to Madison's Notes, on August 20, the clause was read and then: "Mr. Madison and Mr. Pinckney moved to insert between "laws" and "necessary" "and establish all offices," it appearing to them liable to cavil that the latter was not included in the former."

It is unclear, however, what future "cavil" Madison and Pinckney hoped to avoid, but what is clear is that they thought that the clause, as at it stood, had the "potentiality" to undermine the ability of the nation to take care of itself. Apparently three members of the Committee of Detail thought it unnecessary to adopt the Madison-Pinckney amendment.

From September 12 to September 17, the delegates debated The Committee of Style Report; the necessary and proper clause received the most attention. One gets the impression, especially during the September 14 discussion, that the Framers were engaged in an initial "liquidation" of the meaning of the necessary and proper clause. An exchange on September 14 leaves us pondering what is included from what is excluded.

Mr. Madison and Mr. Pinckney then moved to insert in the list of powers vested in Congress a power—"to establish an University, in which no preferences or distinctions should be allowed on account of religion."

Mr. Wilson supported the motion.

Mr. Govr Morris. It was not necessary. The exclusive power at the Seat of Government will reach the object.

On the question, it was defeated Ayes 4, Noes 6, divided 1.

THE SLAVE TRADE

No issue is more in need of careful consideration than the slavery question, because no issue is more likely to impeach the entire Founding enterprise than the slavery issue. Unfortunately, historians have a way of reading history backwards rather than forwards and when we read the slavery issue backwards it looks like in the most critical area—Article I, Section 9 on the Slave Trade—the delegates are unequivocally and perpetually endorsing the institution of slavery. It is as if Judge Roger Taney, in the Dred Scott Case—the Constitution embraces the perpetual enslavement of African Americans—has the story correct and Abraham Lincoln, in his debates with Douglas—the Framers intended to put slavery in the course of ultimate extinction—has it all wrong. There is no evidence that either Taney or Lincoln read Madison's *Notes*. When we turn to the evidence in Madison's *Notes*, which position makes more sense?

We need to ask a prior question: how did Article I, Section 9 get to be the way it is? Was there unanimity among the delegates, was there even a discussion, and if, so, was there anybody who put up the slightest resistance to the continuation of slavery?

On August 6, the Committee of Detail Report was presented to the delegates. Article VII, Section 1 itemized the powers of Congress and sections two through seven placed limitations on the powers of Congress. Section 4 stated that:

No tax or duty shall be laid by the Legislature... on the migration or importation of such persons as the several States shall think proper to admit; nor shall such migration or importation be prohibited.

This is clearly a slaveholder's document: Congress is forbidden forever from prohibiting the salve trade and any incentive through taxation is also prohibited. This section is the result of a demand from the North Carolina, South Carolina and Georgia delegations to think practically rather than in terms of humanity and religion.

On September 17, the delegates signed the Constitution, Article I, Section 9 of which states the following:

The Migration or Importation of such persons as any of the States now existing shall think proper to admit, shall not be prohibited by the Congress prior to the year one thousand eight hundred and eight, but a Tax or duty may be imposed on such importation.

Note that the final version permits Congress to eliminate the slave trade in 1808—which it did effective January 1, 1808—and permits Congress in the meantime to discourage the trade by taxation. Also the final version limits the Congressional prohibition to the existing States thus inviting the future restriction of slavery in the territories. In this regard, it is important to note that the Confederation Congress restricted slavery in the Northwest Territories in exchange for the return of fugitive slaves. The delegates adopt this Ordinance solution as part of Article IV.

What took place between August 6 and September 17? Rutledge of South Carolina argued on August 21, "Interest alone is the governing principle with Nations. The true question at present is whether the Southern States shall or not be parties of the Union." Sherman and Ellsworth, moreover, recommended not making the slave trade a divisive issue: "Slavery in time will not be a speck in our Country." Luther Martin disagreed: slavery "was inconsistent with the principles of the revolution." On August 22, Mason supported Martin's position: "Every master of slaves is born a petty tyrant. They bring the judgment of heaven on a Country." Dickinson, from Delaware, considered slavery "as inadmissible on every principle of honor & safety." And Randolph stated, "he could never agree to the clause as it stands."

On August 25, the delegates received a Committee compromise recommendation to permit Congress to prohibit the slave trade in 1800. Pinckney moved to alter this to 1808. Madison's response was prophetic: "twenty years will produce all the mischief that can be apprehended from the liberty to import slaves." The first time the slavery issue was raised in the convention is by Madison on June 6. There in his itemization of the causes of faction, or the unjust use of power, he says "that we have seen the mere distinction of colour made in the most enlightened period of time, a ground of the most oppressive dominion ever exercised by man over man."

G. Morris from Pennsylvania, on August 25, was rather blunt: why not say that this part of the Constitution was a compliance with... North Carolina, South Carolina & Georgia."

The delegates agreed to the 1808 prohibition by a vote of Ayes 7, Noes 4. The 4 noes were New Jersey, Pennsylvania, Delaware, and Virginia and they voted "no" because they thought that 1808 was too compromising. Lincoln, and not Taney, has the weight of the Founders on his side of the argument.

ESTABLISHING THE ELECTORAL COLLEGE AND THE PRESIDENCY

The Virginia Plan, introduced by Edmund Randolph on May 29, called for the creation of a National Executive elected by the Congress. On the initial consideration of the proposal, the delegates on June 1, June 2, and June 4 agreed on a single executive who would serve a seven year term and be ineligible for re-election. Some delegates wanted to settle the issue of 1) re-eligibility first, others wanted to 2) fix the length of term before proceeding further, still other delegates wanted to discuss how 3) the executive would be elected before considering anything else, and still other delegates thought 4) that the powers of the President should be the primary question to be settled.

On the first reading, and every time thereafter, the convention agreed to provide the chief executive with a veto subject to Congressional override. (See Judicial Review Theme.) The biggest issue was how to elect the President. On June 9, the delegates defeated a motion to have the President elected by state executives. On June 18, Hamilton surprised the delegates with a proposal for a President for life.

The delegates revisited the four main issues—without settling any one once and for all—involved in the construction of the executive on July 17, 18, 19, 20, 24, and 26. On July 17, the delegates agreed to a single executive elected by the legislature, and to be re-elected rather than serve during good behaviour. On July 18 and 19, the delegates revisited the issue of whether the President should be re-eligible and embraced the idea that perhaps the president should be chosen by electors chosen by state legislatures. On July 20, a proposal permitting the impeachment of the president was approved. On July 24, the delegates returned to the earlier position: the President should be elected by the national legislature. Finally, on July 26, the delegates approved a seven-year term for the President. But he would be ineligible for re-election!

The Committee of Detail Report of August 6, summarized where the delegates stood. On August 24, the delegates turned to the Presidential article and defeated four different modes of electing the President. In the end, the Convention selected members of the Brearly Committee whose objective was to settle outstanding issues. The chief of these was the Presidential clause. On September 4, the Brearly Committee recommended that the Convention support the Electoral College method of choosing a president. On September 6 and 7, the delegates agreed to a four-year renewable term for the President and that he be a natural born citizen. On September 8, the delegates settled the treaty making power and agreed on the impeachment of the President for "high crimes and misdemeanours." Finally, on September 15, the delegates added "the inferior officers clause."

To summarize, the Brearly Committee, composed of Gilman, King, Sherman, Brearly, G. Morris, Dickinson, Carroll, Madison, Williamson, Butler, and Baldwin—a veritable cross-section of the delegates—proposed the adoption of an Electoral College in which both the people and the States are represented in the election of the President. This resolution of the difficult matter of Presidential election clearly meant that the partly national-partly federal model had become the deliberate sense of the convention. This structural compromise—Congress is partly federal and partly national—became the deliberate sense of the community by the end of the Convention. It is the model to which the delegates returned for the resolution of the most durable of issues, namely, the election of the President.

JUDICIAL REVIEW AND JUDICIAL POWERS

The Virginia Plan, introduced on May 29, called for the creation of a National Judiciary with judges holding office during good behavior. Another feature of the Virginia Plan proposed that before a bill becomes a law it must be reviewed by the Executive branch and "a convenient number of the National Judiciary." This "Council of Revision" would "have the authority to examine every act of the of the national Legislature before it shall operate, & every act of a particular Legislature before a negative thereon shall be final; and that the dissent of the said Council shall amount to a rejection, unless the Act of the National legislature be again passed, or that of a particular Legislature be again negatived by___________of the members of each branch."

In his Vices, Madison had indicated that two of the vices of the American system were the ability of state legislatures to pass multiple and mutable laws. The Council is his answer to these vices at both the state and national level. It is important to note that the Council gives the Executive and Judiciary joint prior review before a bill becomes a law.

On three separate occasions— June 4, July 21, and August 15— the delegates considered this novel Council of Revision proposal. Although the idea was abandoned, the reasons for doing so are vital for understanding the Framers's position on the role of the Judiciary. At the heart of the objection to the Council was that the Executive alone should have the power to review legislation before it became law. And in doing so, the Framers excluded the Judiciary from having the power of policy review or what we might call prior review. That was a political function to be performed by the Executive alone. But the Framers simultaneously bestowed on the judiciary the power of subsequent review or to exercise a judicial review after policy has been jointly made by the Legislature and the Executive.

On June 4, Gerry opposed giving the judges the power of prior review because they have the power of "exposition of the laws, which involved a power of deciding on their constitutionality. In some of the States the Judges had (actually) set aside laws as being agst. The Constitution. This was done too with general approbation." King concurred: "the Judges ought to be able to expound the law as it should come before them, free of the bias of having participated in its formation." On July 21, Gerry repeated his objection to the Council: " It was making the Expositors of the Laws, the Legislators which ought never to be done. " Strong agreed that the distinction between making laws ought to be distinguished "from that of expounding the laws." Gorham thought, "the judges ought to carry into the exposition of the laws no prepossessions with regard to them." Mr. G. Morris argued similarly: "Expositors of laws ought to have no hand in making them." And Luther Martin stated that the judges ought not to "have a double negative." And finally, Rutledge thought "the Judges ought never to give their opinion on a law until it comes before them." On August 15, Pinckney reiterated the same theme: he "opposed the interference of the judges in the legislative business; it will involve them in parties, and give a previous tincture to their opposition." Sherman "disapproved of judges meddling in politics and parties, "and Williamson objected to "admitting the judges into the business of legislation."

It is often remarked by judicial scholars that Article III of the Constitution makes no mention of judicial review. This is true. So, the presumption is that the Framers didn't intend to establish judicial review otherwise they would have put it in the Constitution. Thus the question, where and when did judicial review make its appearance in our constitutional heritage? The conventional answer is that John Marshall, in *Marbury v Madison*, 1803, established judicial review. But if we need to find the exact words "judicial review," to establish judicial review, then the *Marbury* case isn't good enough because the phrase doesn't occur there either. The phrase "judicial review" does not make its appearance until the 1880s and then in a law review article by Edwin Corwin.

The evidence suggests that the Framers recognized what we now call judicial review, but were serious about the distinction between policy and constitutional review.

On August 27, Johnson moved to "insert the words 'this Constitution and the' before the word 'laws.'"

Mr. Madison doubted whether it was not going too far to extend the jurisdiction of the Court generally to cases arising Under the Constitution, & whether it ought not to be limited to cases of a Judiciary Nature. The right of expounding the cases not of this nature ought not to be given to that Department.

The motion of Docr. Johnson was agreed to nem:con: it being generally supposed that the jurisdiction given was constructively limited to cases of a Judiciary nature.

WHY THREE DELEGATES DIDN'T SIGN

Mason and Gerry were members of the Gerry Committee that proposed the Connecticut Compromise. A generally overlooked component of the Compromise was the agreement that money bills would originate in the House and could not be amended in the Senate. This feature was vital in winning over Mason and Gerry, as well as Randolph who introduced the wholly national Virginia Plan. These three delegates were willing to buy into the partly national, partly federal arrangement if the principle of no taxation without popular representation was followed.

On August 6, the Committee of Detail Report was presented and Article IV, Section 5 honored this agreement. On August 8, however, the delegates agreed to drop this provision. On August 13, Dickinson attempted to reassure Randolph et al that as far as money bills are be concerned," Experience should be our only guide. Reason may mislead us." The defeat of the money bills provision marks the critical moment for the three dissenters. By early September, all three delegates had become concerned that Constitution had given far too much authority to the Senate and that the executive contained the seeds of monarchy.

By September 10, Randolph was convinced that Congress now possessed sufficient powers to turn the Philadelphia Constitution into a wholly national document. He decided to withhold his signature because he thought the Constitution contained the potentiality to shift rapidly from the republican foundation insisted upon in the Virginia Plan that Randolph introduced.

Randolph listed 12 objections among which were: "on the necessity of 3/4 instead of 2/3 of each house to overrule the negative of the President (&) on the smallness of the number of the representative branch." The delegates reached out to Randolph during the last week and responded to each of these objections, but to no avail. He was particularly concerned about "the general clause concerning necessary and proper laws," as a major source of future tyranny.

On September 15, Gerry concurred: "the rights of the citizens were… rendered insecure" by 1. The general power of the Legislature to make what laws they may please to call necessary and proper. 2. To raise armies and money without limit. 3. To establish a tribunal without juries, which will be a Star-Chamber as to Civil Cases. "He could… get over" his eight other objections if these three were overcome.

On September 15, Mason listed sixteen objections among which were the absence of a declaration of rights, the 1808 compromise on the slave trade, and the general power of the Senate in the system, the "shadow of representation" in the House, and the powers of the President. He too criticized the presence of the necessary and proper clause in the Constitution:

Under their own construction of the general clause, at the end of the enumerated powers, the Congress may grant monopolies in trade and commerce, constitute new crimes, inflict unusual and severe punishments, and extend their powers as far as they think proper; so that the State legislatures have no security for the powers not presumed to remain to them, or the people for their rights.

Interestingly, Mason, Gerry, and Randolph were more concerned that the Constitution departed from the traditional principles of republicanism than that the Constitution departed too far from the traditional principles of federalism.

GEORGE WASHINGTON AND THE VIRGINIA DELEGATION

1) Virginia was the first state to select delegates to the Grand Convention and took the lead in encouraging other states to do the same. The Virginia Legislature selected 7 delegates: Washington, Blair, Madison, Mason, McClurg, Randolph, and Wythe. They arrived in Philadelphia on time, but had to wait a couple of weeks until a quorum of seven states

was achieved. The delegates were also united in their approach and this consensus was displayed right away with the presentation of the Virginia Plan.

2) Mr. Wythe left in early June, but there were no cracks then in the Virginia delegation. With the passage of the Connecticut Compromise on July 16, and the creation of the Committee of Detail at the end of July, Dr. McClurg returned to his medical practice in Virginia. All seemed to be pretty smooth sailing. But there were strains. Virginia voted no on the Connecticut Compromise that was adopted by the Convention. The alliance of Madison, Blair, and McClurg carried the no vote. Mason voted yes; he was part of the Compromise Committee, and certainly by the next day, Randolph came to agree with Mason that it was best to forge ahead.
3) The Connecticut Compromise has three parts a) equal representation for people in the House, b) equal representation for the states in the Senate and c) money bills can only be introduced in the House and can't be amended by the Senate. This third component was critical in persuading Mason and Randolph to deviate from the Virginia Plan.
4) But things started to unravel in August. The once united and leading state was now divided and McClurg had returned to Virginia. And they divide on August 8 and 9 when Madison attempted to remove the third feature of the Compromise. Mason said that to "strike out this section was to unhinge the compromise of which it made a part." Randolph said that the removal would lead to "endangering the success of the plan." The delegations voted 7 yes, 4, no to strike out the third feature. Virginia voted to strike, so the internal Virginia vote must have been 3-2 and that could only have happened if Washington sided with Madison and Blair over against Mason and Randolph.
5) Randolph refused to accept defeat. On August 11, he persuaded the Convention to reconsider the August 8 vote to strike and the issue was debated thoroughly on August

13. Mason and Randolph saw principle to be at sake, Madison said nothing of principle was at stake in the Connecticut Compromise, and Dickinson observed that "experience must be our only guide. Reason may mislead us." A vote was taken as to the "exclusive originating of money bills in the H. of Reps."

6) Madison gives details of the August 13 vote that reinstated exclusive origination accompanied by a footnote explanation:

   N. H. ay. Mas. ay. Ct. no. N. J. no. P. no. Md. No. Virga. ay. Mr Blair & Mr M. no" Mr. R. Col. Mason and General Washington* ay. N. C. ay. S. C. no. Geo. No [Ayes"4; noes"7.]

   *He disapproved & till now voted agst., the exclusive privilege *(see 4 above)*, he gave up his judgment he said, because it was not of very material weight with him & was made an essential point with others, who if disappointed, might be less cordial in other points of real weight.

   Now I interpret this vote switch by Washington to be the action of a prudent leader, not only of a national convention, but of a Virginia delegation that was in serious disagreement. He realized that it was important to keep Randolph and Mason on board if possible so long as no fundamental principle had been violated. But Randolph and Mason held out for more.

7) On August 31, September 5, 8, and 10, the delegates, especially the Virginia delegates, divided over ratification procedures. Should ratification be by state legislatures or state conventions, and if by conventions, how many should say "yes" for ratification? What is the role of these conventions? Can they propose amendments? What about the role of the existing Congress? Can they make alterations? Should there be a Second Grand Convention where all these things are pulled together?

8) Randolph and Mason wanted maximum flexibility otherwise they would refuse to sign. On September 10, Randolph gave 12 reasons why he couldn't sign"including the "smallness of the number of the Representative branch""that could only

be overcome by following a long ratification route through the Congress, the states, and back to a SECOND CONVENTION. Mason urged the delegates to see what they could do to accommodate Randolph, but on September 12 he issued 16 reasons why he too couldn't sign the Constitution.

9) Mason and Randolph repeated their objections on September 15. Randolph, seconded by Mason, moved that if the delegates agreed "with the expedient of another Convention as proposed, he could sign." Madison reports: "On the question on the proposition of Mr. Randolph. All the States answered-no." Virginia could only have voted no if Washington sided with Madison and Blair over against Mason and Randolph.

10) The last three lines of Madison's *Notes* on the 15th are worth citation: "on the question to agree to the Constitution as amended. All the States ay. The Constitution was then ordered to be engrossed. And the House adjourned."

If Washington had not acted, Virginia would have been divided between the two camps and could not have voted "ay." Even on the last day, September 17, Washington reached out to Randolph and spoke for the first time urging the delegates to increase the size of the representative branch. The delegates agreed, but it was not enough to get Randolph and Mason to sign.

5

Committee Assignments Chart and Commentary

TWELVE ACTION COMMITTEES

There are important moments in the life of a political gathering, such as an assembly of delegates, when recourse to a smaller number of the membership is necessary. The Constitutional Convention of 1787 found the need to resort to this on twelve different occasions during their four months. Each one of these twelve committees of the Convention is an "Action Committee," in the sense that each one helps the Convention move to the next stage of the deliberative and decision-making process.

We suggest that it is useful to distinguish between two different kinds of action committees. The first is on behalf of the deliberative process and is an effort to set down the rules or secure a breakthrough so that deliberation can continue in a productive fashion. The second is on behalf of the decision-making process itself. In other words, the action involved is not primarily focused on keeping the deliberative process alive and well, but bringing the gathering toward making some decisions from which there is little possibility of reversal.

During the months of May, June, and July, the Convention sat as a Committee of the Whole. That meant that the entire membership was involved in the give and take together on essential questions—sitting as a Committee of the Whole makes it far easier to explore, alter, and prod—rather than the emphasis being on the delegates having to decide, once and for all as it were, on specific articles, sections, and clauses. The decision-making stage occurs during the months of August and September where the task of filling in the details and hammering out specific compromises are delegated to members of committees selected by the entire Convention. This is where the votes of the delegates become crucial to the outcome.

ACT ONE AND ACT TWO

Acts One and Two of the Four Act Drama capture the deliberative stage of the Convention. Accordingly, it is not surprising that out of the twelve committees listed, only four occur during this earlier phase of the Convention: the Rules Committee and the three Committees of Representation, which can be collapsed into the "Gerry Committee." So we actually have only two important committees to examine in this stage of the conversation.

The three member Rules Committee, under the leadership of the Virginia legal scholar, George Wythe, laid down rules for what they considered to be a civilized conversation. Hamilton and Pinckney—later accused of being a monarchist and aristocrat respectively—joined Wythe in proposing rules aimed to foster open deliberation among the delegates. One of the more controversial recommendations was the rule of secrecy. Madison, both at the time of the Convention and later, vigorously defended this rule; he thought it encouraged the free exchange of ideas among the members so vital for the success of the deliberative process. The secrecy rule has been criticized by influential Progressive Historians of the twentieth century who portray it as evidence of an upper class and reactionary disposition at the Convention to undermine the democratic spirit of the Revolution of 1776.

The membership of the Gerry Committee provides a crucial insight into the mood of the Convention at the end of June and the beginning of July. At the end of Act One, the wholly national Virginia Plan, albeit slightly amended, was on the table for further consideration. But the opposition, led by Sherman and Ellsworth of Connecticut, insisted on a compromise between the wholly national Virginia Plan and the wholly federal New Jersey Plan introduced by Paterson of New Jersey. Or if no compromise were possible, then they favored the adoption of the federal New Jersey Plan. The last two weeks of June marks the low point of the Convention. Conversation and deliberation had given way to threats of secession, lines were drawn in the sand, and frustration ran high. At the end of June, Ellsworth tried one more time to break the deadlock with his partly national-partly federal proposal. This time it worked, and the more pragmatic delegates decided to create a committee to move the deliberative process forward. The Convention, still sitting as a committee of the Whole, on July 2 elected 11 members—one from each State present—to seek a partly national-partly federal compromise.

But the Gerry Committee could not have made that recommendation, and made it stick, unless the members of the committee, and thus the Convention itself, were so inclined. Davie from North Carolina announced his support for the partly national and partly federal compromise in late June, as did Franklin, Luther Martin, Paterson, Sherman-Ellsworth, and Yates. The Convention could have chosen Madison rather than Mason from Virginia, Wilson rather than Franklin from Pennsylvania, and King rather than Gerry from Massachusetts, but the delegates did not. The 11 members chosen by the entire body of delegates were selected because of their inclination to seek a compromise; the members of the Gerry Committee were those representatives from each state that could be relied upon to propose and secure the passage of the Connecticut Compromise on July 16.

ACT THREE AND ACT FOUR

8 of the 12 committees met during Act Three and Act Four, and four of these committees were crucial in the framing of the Constitution: The Committee of Detail, the Committee of Slave Trade, the Brearly Committee, and the Committee of Style. Of the other four, the Committee of Trade was actually a companion to the Slave Trade Committee and worked out the final North South compromise on navigation issues. Two other committees dealt with existing state debts and state commitments under the new Constitution. The eighth committee on "economy, frugality, and

manufactures" was created during the last week of the Convention and never filed a report.

The 5 members of the Committee of Detail—Rutledge (chair), Ellsworth, Gorham, Randolph, and Wilson—were chosen by the entire Convention to turn the various proposals and recommendations made in Act One and Act Two into the first draft of the Constitution. They met for nearly two weeks and produced the Committee of Detail Report that became the focus of conversation of the entire Convention during August. It is beyond the scope of this commentary to speculate on the twists and turns that must have taken place among the delegates over that period. Or even why these five were chosen. Suffice it to note, that Rutledge managed to secure a strong pro-slave trade provision, Randolph, by his subsequent actions, must have been insistent upon the money bills provision of the Connecticut Compromise, Ellsworth was there to secure the structural importance and reserved powers of the states, and Wilson and King probably urged the inclusion of as much high-toned government as possible in the elevation of the Senate to a central player. Interestingly, the Committee agreed that the powers of Congress be enumerated—this is where the interstate and international commerce clause and the necessary and proper clause make their appearance—but the structure and powers of the Executive branch are still in an inconclusive situation.

I suggest that once the Convention shifted from an emphasis on committees of deliberation to an emphasis on committees of decision-making, then the work of the committees takes on a privileged position. Accordingly, the delegates reviewing and debating the work of the committees are probably likely to challenge the recommendations of the committee only when something big is at stake. Thus, we should pay close attention to important concerns generated by the Committee of Detail Report.

There were two major concerns that attracted the attention of the delegates. The provision in the Report that banned Congress from ever regulating (international commerce just granted in) the slave trade generated considerable division near the end of August. The Slave Trade Committee, also known as the Livingston Committee, was created to find a "middle ground" between the Committee of Detail Report that guaranteed the permanent existence of the international slave trade and those delegates who wished to limit the slave trade in the foreseeable future. This committee recommended that Congress be released from this restriction in 1800. Anti-slave trade delegates Madison, L. Martin, King, and Dickinson were members of the Committee of the 11 elected by the entire Convention. The final decision of the Convention was to release the Congressional prohibition in 1808.

The delegates were also concerned about "left overs," especially the Presidency. The Brearly Committee that included Madison, King, G. Morris, Dickinson and Sherman settled on the Electoral College as the compromise mode of electing the President. And in the process they elevated the Executive to a position of importance in the separation of powers system.

The Convention, in mid-September, also elected five members to the Committee of Style: Hamilton, Johnson (Chairman), King, Madison, and G. Morris. With the possible exception of Johnson, the members were very warm supporters of the original Virginia Plan that proposed a wholly national remedy for the ills of republicanism and defended time and again any possible move for a higher toned government.

The mood of the Convention had shifted once again, but this time, in September, it had shifted back toward the supporters of the original Virginia Plan. This is revealed by the election of Madison, King, and G. Morris to the Brearly Committee and the Committee of Style. It's almost like the delegates at the Convention let the initial promoters of the national movement have the last say after the Sherman opposition had their say in July and August.

A — Rules Committee (created May 25, delivered report on May 28) – 3 members

B — First Committee of Representation (created July 2, also known as "the Gerry Committee") – 11 members

C — Second Committee of Representation (created July 6, also known as "the Committee of Five") – 5 members

D — Third Committee of Representation (created July 9) – 11 members

E — Committee of Detail (created July 24, report delivered on August 6 and discussed throughout August) – 5 members

F — Committee of Assumption of State Debts (created August 18) – 11 members

G — Committee of Slave Trade (created Aug. 22, also known as "the Livingston Committee," delivered report on Aug. 24) – 11 members

H — Committee of Trade (created August 25) – 11 members

I — Committee of State Commitments (created August 29) – 11 members

J — Committee of Leftovers (created August 31, also known as "the Brearly Committee") – 11 members

K — Committee of Style (created Sept. 10, report delivered on Sept. 12 and discussed during the remainder of the Convention) 5 members

L — Committee of Economy, Frugality and Manufactures (created September 13) – 5 members

6

Selected Correspondence from Summer 1787

INTRODUCTION TO THE SELECTED CORRESPONDENCE

The delegates to the Constitutional Convention in Philadelphia adopted a rule of secrecy right at the start of their deliberations. Writing from Paris to John Adams in London, Jefferson says: "I am sorry they began their deliberations by so abominable a precedent as that of tying up the tongues of their members. Nothing can justify this example but the innocence of their intentions, and ignorance of the value of public discussions. I have no doubt that all their other measures will be good and wise." This comes after he has declared the delegates to be "an assembly of demigods." The adoption of the secrecy rule also means, to the extent that it was observed—and it was pretty scrupulously observed—that subsequent generations of scholars have limited access to the private thoughts of the delegates during the time the deliberations were taking place. There are numerous post convention observations and reflections by the delegates, but these are not quite the same as an unfolding authentic observation.

What follows, then, is a list of essential correspondence. My criterion for essential is that they were written by people who played an essential part in the drama of the American Founding and that the letters reveal some of the twists and turns along with the initial hopes, the frustration during the middle months, the homesickness of the delegates, and the relief that it was all over. I have selected those letters that give a personal flavor to my coverage of the Constitutional Convention as a Four Act Drama. To be sure, there are other letters that could have been included, but they repeat the same twists and turns and the missing of the "felicity" of family life etc that have already been essentially included.

The fact that some of the delegates left Philadelphia—especially the New Jersey and Delaware delegates—for certain periods of time and exchanged comments with those still in Philadelphia provides some valuable information. They talked as openly and as frankly with each other in the mail as they would have done on the floor of the convention. The exchange in early July between Hamilton and Washington is particularly noteworthy in this regard. Also of interest is the correspondence that delegates received from concerned and influential folks back home who shared what they heard being "whispered" about the proceedings. Nor were people like John Jay and Nathan Dane reluctant to provide their own opinions to the selected delegates. And despite his protestations about how the secrecy rule demonstrated "an ignorance of the value of public discussions," Jefferson was kept informed by Madison of the general flow of the debates and, in turn, he openly exchanged ideas with Madison about the separation of powers and the construction of the executive branch.

DELEGATE CORRESPONDENCE AND THE FOUR ACT DRAMA

Act One

May 20. George Mason to George Mason Jr. How the Virginia delegates occupied themselves in Philadelphia waiting for a quorum of states to take place.

May 20. George Washington to Arthur Lee. The general is livid at the absence of a quorum: "the delays our the temper of the punctual members."

May 21. George Read to John Dickinson. Housing is at a premium and the Virginians have a plan.

May 27. James Madison to Edmund Pendleton. Finally, we have a quorum.

June 1. George Mason to George Mason Jr. What we do here will "impact millions unborn."

June 1. Robert Yates to Abraham Yates. He doesn't like the secrecy rule, but will obey it and keep "an exact journal."

June 3. Nathaniel Gorham to Nathan Dane. He is not supposed to tell what the delegates are doing, "but to you in confidence I can say" what has been agreed to.

June 3. Jeremiah Wadsworth to Rufus King. On Connecticut delegate Roger Sherman: "he is as cunning as the devil."

June 6. Edmund Randolph to Beverley Randolph. The former decides to send for his wife because the delegates will be in Philadelphia for a long time.

June 6. James Madison to Thomas Jefferson. He is restrained by rules of confidentiality, but what we do here "will in some way or other have a powerful effect on our destiny."

June 6. James Madison to William Short. "The convention contains in several instances the most respectable characters" and "the eyes and hopes of all are turned towards this new assembly."

June 10. James Madison to James Monroe. The secrecy rule "will effectively secure the requisite freedom of discussion."

June 15. John Dickinson to Polly Dickinson. The "convention is very busy," and "of an excellent temper."

June 18. Nathaniel Gorham to Theophilus Parsons. He is not supposed to say anything, but here is what we are doing. "I beg you not to have heard anything on the subject from me, except to your brother."

Act Two

June 19. Nathan Dane to Rufus King. Delegate Pierce Butler from Philadelphia is in New York visiting his wife and attending Congress; he doesn't "fully understand the true meaning, full and just extent of the order not to communicate."

June 26. Oliver Ellsworth to Abigail Ellsworth. He longs for the sincerity of the "little domestic circle."

June 26. John Lansing to Philip Schuyler. "The business of the Convention is going along very slowly."

June 27. William Pierce to George Tucker. "We are enjoined in secrecy. I dare not say any thing."

June 30. George Mason to Beverley Randolph. Silence forbids giving information, but the next two or three days are decisive.

July 1. George Washington to David Stuart. "Everybody expects something from the convention." He anticipates opposition from local politicians unwilling to lose their current powers in state government.

July 2. William Paterson to Euphemia Paterson. "Much remains to be done, and the work is full of labour and difficulty."

July 3. Alexander Hamilton to George Washington. The people are ready for a "strong well mounted government."

July 7. William Jackson to William Rawle. He thanks Rawle for extending the library privileges of the Library of Philadelphia to the delegates.

July 10. George Washington to Alexander Hamilton. He despairs of "seeing a favourable issue to the proceedings of the Convention, and do therefore repent having had any agency in the business."

July 18. James Madison to Thomas Jefferson. The Antifederalists are already mounting their out of doors pamphlet opposition to the new plan. Essays by A Mechanic and Columbiadis have appeared.

July 25. William Pierce to William Short: The "first principles" have been settled.

July 25. Edmund Randolph to David Shepherd. "A committee was appointed to prepare a constitution conformable to those (general) principles" that have been agreed on.

July 25. John Jay to George Washington. Only a natural born citizen should be President.

Intermission

July 27. David Brearly to Jonathan Dayton. "Westerday we completed the great principles."

July 28. James Madison to James Madison Sr. A committee is at work during the adjournment.

August 5. James McClurg to James Madison. Patrick Henry is stirring up opposition in Virginia.

Act Three

August 12. Richard Dobbs Spaight to James Iredell. The Committee of Detail Report is under consideration. He anticipates opposition by local politicians during ratification.

August 14. Thomas Jefferson to George Washington. Americans are "in the happiest political situation which exists."

August 16. Thomas McKean to William Atlee. The convention is still sitting; "some say, they will continue together about two more weeks, others say two months."

August 19. George Washington to Henry Knox. "I am fully persuaded it is the best that can be obtained at the present moment under such diversity of ideas as prevail."

August 21. Elbridge Gerry to Ann Gerry. "We meet now at ten and sit till after four, but entre-nous, I do not expect to give my voice to the measures."

August 23. William Paterson to Oliver Ellsworth. "It is said that you are afraid of the very windows, and have a man planted under them to prevent the secrets and doings from flying out."

August 26. Elbridge Gerry to Ann Gerry. "I am exceedingly distressed at the proceedings of the Convention."

August 28. Alexander Hamilton to Rufus King. He will return to sign. It is "whispered here" that the Constitution has recently taken on a "higher tone."

August 30. Thomas Jefferson to John Adams. "It is really an assembly of demigods." However they were wrong to adopt a rule of secrecy.

Act Four

September 1. William Johnson to Ann Johnson. He expects to be home in a fortnight.

September 4. James Madison to James Madison Sr. We won't be here much longer.

September 6. James Madison to Thomas Jefferson, "If the present moment be lost, it is hard to say what may be our fate."

September 7. Jonas Phillips to George Washington. Urges departure from state practices that require an oath to the New Testament as a qualification for holding office.

September 9. Elbridge Gerry to Ann Gerry. "I have every prospect at present of my giving my negative."

September 9. George Washington to George Augustine Washington. "I am homesick."

September 11. Joseph Jones to James Madison. "it is whispered here that the Virginia delegation is less than unanimous" on the mode of ratification.

September 15. John Dickinson to George Read. Due to a severe headache, "I am now setting off for Wilmington." (Read signed Dickenson's name to the Constitution.)

September 16. James McHenry to Peggy McHenry. "The plan of government passed by an unanimous vote." I am coming home.

Between 1774 and 1789, 13 colonies became a nation-the United States of America. In 1774, Great Britain's North American colonies first came together to defend themselves against wrongs committed by their "mother country." By 1789, these colonies had become independent states, joined by a new federal constitution into a single nation.

Assembling representatives from every colony, the Continental Congress (1774-1789) began as a coordinated effort to resist the British. With the outbreak of the Revolutionary War, the Congress became the central institution for managing the struggle for American independence.

Independence raised new issues. How could thirteen separate self-governed states unite? What form would that union take? The Articles of Confederation (1781-1789) were America's first attempt to govern itself as an independent nation. They united the states as a confederation-a loose league of states represented in a Congress.

In 1783, with the war formally drawing to a close, the Congress faced a wider range of issues: the disbanding of the Continental Army, the large debts owed by each state, foreign debts owed by the Confederation, the governing of territories won from the British, and the establishment of formal relationships with foreign countries.

Despite the Congress's continued efforts to improve its effectiveness, many Americans saw the need for a more powerful central authority; the Congress as defined by the Articles of Confederation was too weak to make the states obey congressional mandates. Anxious for change, in 1786, leading statesmen called for a special convention to revise the Articles — the Constitutional Convention.

The Constitutional Convention of 1787 proposed a new constitution establishing a much stronger national government. Although this controversial new Constitution provoked a great deal of resistance, it was eventually ratified by the necessary number of states, replacing the Articles of Confederation as the framework of the United States government.

Debate and compromise, controversy and tedious detail, foreign affairs and domestic problems, are all included in the 267 documents of the Continental Congress and Constitutional Convention Broadside Collections. Including public announcements of congressional actions, drafts of legislation, committee reports, and final versions of legislation or treaties, these broadsides illustrate the evolution of a government, from a legislative body called together in the crisis of war, to an intricate system of checks and balances. These documents show the birth of the American nation.

Organizing a War

The huge task of organizing thirteen separate governments and militia into a united, effective fighting force was a main concern of the Continental Congress. The hastily assembled Continental Army was an army without a precedent; Congress had to create rules for organization and conduct, and invent an effective system of raising money to fund the war effort.

Congress Makes Rules for Plundering Enemy Ships

In December 1775, Great Britain passed the Prohibitory Act, removing the colonies from the protection of the crown, banning trade with them, and allowing seizure of American ships at sea. The Continental Congress responded by issuing "letters of marque and reprisal", permitting Americans to arm private ships for attacking and seizing British vessels and cargoes at sea. Intended to supplement the infant Continental Navy, recently established under the command of Esek Hopkins, privateering was a frequent practice throughout the war, with the Continental Congress commissioning more than a thousand private vessels.

The displayed document, printed in 1781 by Benjamin Franklin, American Minister to France, reproduces congressional instructions to captains of privateers issued in May 1780.

CONGRESS PROVIDES FOR PRISONERS OF WAR

The colonies' first measures of resistance to British rule were enacted before they had officially declared themselves independent, and without a formal declaration of war. As combat between British troops and American militia increased, Congress quickly saw the need for formal rules and procedures in handling prisoners. A resolution, passed on May 21, 1776 and published by order of Congress, included specific instructions for feeding, housing, and imprisoning British prisoners of war. Although most prisoners were eventually exchanged, British Major John André suffered a different fate.

Congress Reorganizes the Army

Throughout the Revolutionary War, the Continental Army suffered problems of low recruitment, supply shortages, and sinking morale. In January 1778, at General George Washington's urging,

Congress sent a committee to military headquarters at Valley Forge, to confer with Washington on necessary improvements. Although the committee made proposals for reorganizing supply procedures and revising recruitment regulations, Congress's response was slow and piecemeal; other issues, such as the controversy surrounding a prisoner exchange, kept Congress distracted. Congress did not approve the plan for rearrangement of the army until May 1778, and it was November before implementation was completed.

Fanning the Flames of Patriotism

As the only institution encompassing all thirteen states, the Continental Congress served as a symbol of national unity, laboring to inspire patriotic spirit in support of the war, and communicating news of victories, defeats, and major political decisions.

Congress Declares Independence

On June 7, 1776, Virginia delegate Richard Henry Lee offered a formal resolution that the united colonies "are, and of right ought to be, free and independent States." After some debate, a committee was appointed to write a formal declaration of independence; Thomas Jefferson of Virginia drafted the document. On July 2, 1776, Congress officially resolved that the united colonies should be free and independent states, and on July 4, the Declaration of Independence was formally approved by Congress. The displayed copy of the Declaration — the first official printing with the names of the signers attached — was printed by Baltimore printer Mary Katherine Goddard.

The new nation celebrated with prayer, speeches, fireworks, and formal readings of the Declaration. Delegate John Adams later stated that the vote for American independence was "the greatest question...which ever was debated in America, and a greater, perhaps, never was nor will be decided among men."

Congress Warns: "The British Are Coming"

On December 10, 1776, Congress warned citizens of Pennsylvania that British troops were fast approaching. It encouraged them to unite and offer strong resistance, and assured them that

General Charles Lee was on his way with reinforcements. Despite its strong pleas to resist the British until Lee could arrive, Congress packed its bags and departed Philadelphia two days later, reassembling in Baltimore.

Congress Boosts Public Morale

In an effort to rally the nation in the midst of war, and attract popular support for itself, Congress addressed the inhabitants of the United States, reminding them of the cruelties they had suffered at the hands of the British, and warning them that more such treatment would result from a reunion with Britain. Because people regularly gathered at places of worship, Congress distributed the address to "churches and chapels and other places of religious worship" with the request that ministers read it aloud to their congregation immediately after divine service. Written by Congressman Gouverneur Morris, the address was sent throughout the states, and 50 copies were given to General Washington, to disperse throughout the army.

Congress Publicly Threatens the British

News of the French alliance with America in 1778 panicked the British, prompting them to send commissioners to America, with offers of peace. Congress replied that it would happily discuss peace, if Britain would accept American independence and recall its troops. The British commissioners, however, had no intention of granting American independence. They continued to press Congress to accept their proposals, even offering bribes to individual Congressmen, such as Joseph Reed, in exchange for help in re-uniting England and its colonies. Frustrated in their efforts, in October 1778, the British issued a manifesto questioning Congress's authority to make a treaty with France, and threatening dire consequences if their offer of conciliation was rejected. On October 30, 1778, Congress responded with a manifesto — intended as a morale-boosting national statement of strength and confidence — declaring that the American cause was just, success was assured, and if Britain carried through with its threats, "we will take such exemplary vengeance, as shall deter others from a like conduct."

Incorporating the Western Territories

Under the Treaty of Paris (1783) which ended the Revolutionary War, Britain relinquished to the United States a large tract of land west of the Appalachian mountains, doubling the size of the new nation. How would this territory be incorporated into the United States? Congressional debates about the division and government of the new territories resulted in precedents which were followed throughout the settlement of the west.

Congress Discusses Slavery in the Western Territories

In 1783, Congress formed a committee to "prepare a plan for the temporary government of the western territory." Thomas Jefferson, chairman of the committee, delivered a report in March 1784 proposing the division of the land into ten territories, and their eventual admission to the Union on an equal footing with the original thirteen states. In addition, Jefferson proposed the prohibition of slavery in any of the new states. Congress rejected Jefferson's ban on slavery, but in 1785 Rufus King attempted to restore it, offering the displayed resolution. Congress, once again, rejected the proposal by a slight margin. Slavery was officially barred from the new western states in 1787.

Congress Decides How to Divide the Western Territories

Congressman David Howell of Rhode Island complained that America's new western territories were "the most complicated and embarrassing Subject before Congress since peace has taken place." Deliberation over what to do with the territory continued for several years, but on May 18, 1785, a burst of activity resulted in a proposal for the orderly settlement of the western public lands. Rufus King of Massachusetts, a key figure in the debate, made many of the notations that appear in the document's margins. Congress adopted the final version of the Land Ordinance of 1785 on May 20.

Congress Determines How New States Can Enter the Union

In 1787, Congress was approached by agents of the Ohio Company, a group of New England Revolutionary War veterans seeking to purchase vast tracts of western land. The prospect of earning real revenue for the western territories inspired Congress to resolve the long debate over the west; the Northwest Ordinance, passed on July 13, 1787, provided for a government in the western territories, created a procedure for the formation of states, established a formal method for the new states to enter the union as equals, guaranteed the inhabitants civil and religious liberties, and prohibited slavery. The president of Congress, Arthur St. Clair, was named first governor of the territory. The document above shows some of the final changes made in the ordinance before its passage.

Relations With Native Americans

Before permanently settling the western territories, the United States had to consider the presence of Native Americans already living on these lands. Great Britain may have agreed to give the United States the land, but no one had consulted with the Indian people concerning this change. Reacting to the pressure of American settlers anxious for new land, Congress sought treaties with Native Americans to insure the safety of the settlers, and to obtain clear title for the land.

Congress Tries to Appease Southern Indian Peoples

Although treaties with the Indian people were usually negotiated in good faith, the Congress found itself politically unwilling and actually unable to halt illegal settlement of Indian lands by a growing number of American settlers. These treaties are attempts by Congress to establish friendship between Congress and the Shawnee and Cherokee nations; the Southern states, as typified by North Carolinian delegate William Blount, objected so violently to the treaties's moderate land claims that the agreed-upon boundaries became impossible to enforce.

Congress Increases the Army in the Northwest

By the early spring of 1786, Congressional commissioners had signed several treaties with a number of Indian nations. However, the Indian people were far from satisfied with America's increasing expansion into the west; many Indian tribes of the Northwest, such as the Mohawk nation, represented by Mohawk Joseph Brant, were not willing to concede that all of their land was destined to be occupied and settled by Americans. By the summer of 1786, skirmishes between Native Americans and settlers were on the rise, and war was a clear possibility. Unwilling to halt the expansion, on October 20, 1786, Congress responded to the crisis by calling for additional troops and increased fortifications in the west.

A Cash-Poor Congress Decides to Strive for Peace

Although confident that America would continue its western expansion, Congress altered its policy due to the threat of warfare with the Indian people, combined with an empty treasury. In response to a report from Secretary of War Henry Knox, Congress retreated from its more aggressive attitude towards Native American lands, and on February 20, 1787, admitted that "certain encroachments are made on the lands of the Creek and Cherokee nations." Congress promised to strive for "peace with the Indians, provided it can be obtained and preserved consistently with the justice and dignity of the nation."

Identifying Defects in the Confederation

With the passage of time, weaknesses in the Articles of Confederation became apparent; Congress commanded little respect and no support from state governments anxious to maintain their power. Congress could not raise funds, regulate trade, or conduct foreign policy without the voluntary agreement of the states. Recognizing the need to improve the government, Congress tried to strengthen the Articles, but problems persisted.

Congress Can Not Improve Poor Attendance by Delegates

In November 1783, American diplomats sent Congress the final version of the Treaty of Paris, which formally ended America's war with Great Britain. A quorum of nine states had to be present for Congress to ratify the treaty, yet throughout December, scarcely that number was present. Weeks passed, the treaty sat, and Congress remained unable to act upon it. Some desperate congressmen went so far as to contemplate holding Congress in the sickroom of an ailing delegate, to add him to their numbers. After years of experiencing frustrating delays due to lackadaisical attendance, delegate James Wilson of Pennsylvania expected this predicament. In anticipation of the crisis, he voiced the need to "devise means for procuring a full representation in Congress." The displayed report, produced by a committee appointed to address the problem, does little more than agree with Wilson; Congress lacked the authority to do much more. Although some statesmen, like Secretary Charles Thomson, took their congressional responsibilities seriously, the weakness of Congress under the Articles of Confederation encouraged many delegates to pay far more attention to politics in their home states and to their personal affairs than to the nation's legislative body.

Congress Pleads with the States to Contribute Money to the National Treasury

By the end of the war, the new nation had a large debt. Although Congress proposed a number of ways for the states to raise revenue towards the national debt, the states almost never complied with Congress's suggestions. By June of 1786, the situation was desperate. The Board of Treasury submitted a report, warning that unless the states immediately adopted the measures recommended by Congress in 1783, "...nothing...can rescue us from Bankruptcy, or preserve the Union of the several States from Dissolution." Congress agreed with the board's findings, and prepared to address the states on the subject. William Samuel Johnson of Connecticut, whose copy of the document is included in the collection, chaired the committee in charge of drafting the address; friends warned him, however, that "Your Address to the States will (I fear) prove like Water spilled upon the Ground and have no Influence to awake us from our Stupor." Eventually, after much revision and argument, Congress decided not to send any address at all.

Congress is Unable to Control Commerce Between America and Foreign Nations

Under the Articles of Confederation, Congress lacked the authority to regulate commerce, making it unable to protect or standardize trade between foreign nations and the various states. In 1784, Congress requested that the states grant it limited power over commerce for a period of fifteen years, but many of the states did not comply. In 1785, twenty-seven-year-old delegate James Monroe again stressed the need for increased congressional power over commerce. Congress appointed a committee, chaired by Monroe, to investigate the problem. On February 16, 1785, the committee recommended amending the Articles of Confederation so that Congress would have power over commerce. Although Congress sent the proposed amendment to the state legislatures, along with a letter urging immediate action, few states responded. Monroe later concluded that the issue was so crucial, and potentially granted so much power to Congress, that the states were afraid to act.

Creating a Constitution

The Constitutional Convention of 1787 was called to revise the ailing Articles of Confederation. However, the Convention soon abandoned the Articles, drafting a new Constitution with a much stronger national government. Nine states had to approve the Constitution before it could go into effect. After a long and often bitter debate, eleven states ratified the Constitution, which instituted a new form of government for the United States.

Congress Tries to Revise the Articles of Confederation

In May 1786, Charles Pinckney of South Carolina proposed that Congress revise the Articles of Confederation. Congress responded by appointing a committee to draft amendments to the Articles. On August 7, 1786, the committee produced these amendments, written chiefly by committee chairman Pinckney.

Among many changes, the amendments would have granted Congress exclusive power over commerce, and outlined punishments for poor attendance by members of Congress. Although the most ambitious effort to revise the Articles of Confederation, the amendments were never acted upon; a new convention meeting in Annapolis, Maryland, seemed likely to devise a plan for granting Congress power over trade.

The Constitutional Convention Drafts a New Constitution

On July 26, 1787, after two months of fierce debate over the structure and powers of a new federal government, the Constitutional Convention was ready to commit its resolutions to writing. Appointing a "committee of detail" to draft a written constitution, the Convention adjourned until August 6.

To prepare themselves, the committee first studied the Convention's resolutions, state constitutions, the Articles of Confederation, and other applicable reports and documents. Then, Edmund Randolph of Virginia wrote out a rough draft of a constitution, which the committee then discussed. James Wilson revised Randolph's draft, the committee reviewed it, and a clean copy was sent to prominent Philadelphia printers John Dunlap and David Claypoole. The Convention told them to print just enough copies for use by the delegates; the draft was to be kept secret to avoid controversy.

The Constitutional Convention Completes a New Constitution

After five weeks of debate over the committee of detail's draft Constitution, the Constitutional Convention appointed a committee of style to prepare a final version; Gouverneur Morris, later known as the "penman of the Constitution," did most of the work. On September 17, 1787, after several days of further revision, the Constitutional Convention voted in favor of the Constitution. The states were left to accept or reject this new plan of government. Delegate James Madison, one of the Constitution's most fervent advocates, felt that the success or failure of the American Constitution "would decide forever the fate of republican government."

The Continental Congress Institutes a New Government

As the states considered the proposed Constitution, Congress assembled, but with a new government in the making, the old government had little to do. As one delegate wrote: "To your demand to know what we are doing in Congress? I answer — Nothing. To your enquiry what we have done? I answer — almost nothing... The

States have been in such a flutter about the New, that they have hardly paid attention to the old Government." On July 2, 1788, Congress received the momentous news that New Hampshire had just become the ninth state to ratify the new Constitution, making it the law of the land.

Congress responded by appointing a committee to schedule the first federal elections and fix the date when the new government would begin operation in New York City. This was the last major act of the Continental Congress.

General Introduction
For the Independent Journal.
HAMILTON

To the People of the State of New York:

AFTER an unequivocal experience of the inefficiency of the subsisting federal government, you are called upon to deliberate on a new Constitution for the United States of America. The subject speaks its own importance; comprehending in its consequences nothing less than the existence of the UNION, the safety and welfare of the parts of which it is composed, the fate of an empire in many respects the most interesting in the world. It has been frequently remarked that it seems to have been reserved to the people of this country, by their conduct and example, to decide the important question, whether societies of men are really capable or not of establishing good government from reflection and choice, or whether they are forever destined to depend for their political constitutions on accident and force. If there be any truth in the remark, the crisis at which we are arrived may with propriety be regarded as the era in which that decision is to be made; and a wrong election of the part we shall act may, in this view, deserve to be considered as the general misfortune of mankind. This idea will add the inducements of philanthropy to those of patriotism, to heighten the solicitude which all considerate and good men must feel for the event. Happy will it be if our choice should be directed by a judicious estimate of our true interests, unperplexed and unbiased by considerations not connected with the public good. But this is a thing more ardently to be wished than seriously to be expected. The plan offered to our deliberations affects too many particular interests, innovates upon too many local institutions, not to involve in its discussion a variety of objects foreign to its merits, and of views, passions and prejudices little favorable to the discovery of truth.

Among the most formidable of the obstacles which the new Constitution will have to encounter may readily be distinguished the obvious interest of a certain class of men in every State to resist all changes which may hazard a diminution of the power, emolument, and consequence of the offices they hold under the State establishments; and the perverted ambition of another class of men, who will either hope to aggrandize themselves by the confusions of their country, or will flatter themselves with fairer prospects of elevation from the subdivision of the empire into several partial confederacies than from its union under one government.

It is not, however, my design to dwell upon observations of this nature. I am well aware that it would be disingenuous to resolve indiscriminately the opposition of any set of men (merely because their situations might subject them to suspicion) into interested or ambitious views. Candor will oblige us to admit that even such men may be actuated by upright intentions; and it cannot be doubted that much of the opposition which has made its appearance, or may hereafter make its appearance, will spring from sources, blameless at least, if not respectable—the honest errors of minds led astray by preconceived jealousies and fears. So numerous indeed and so powerful are the causes which serve to give a false bias to the judgment, that we, upon many occasions, see wise and good men on the wrong as well as on the right side of questions of the first magnitude to society. This circumstance, if duly attended to, would furnish a lesson of moderation to those who are ever so much persuaded of their being in the right in any controversy. And a further reason for caution, in this respect, might be drawn from the reflection that we are not always sure that those who advocate the truth are influenced by purer principles than their antagonists. Ambition, avarice, personal animosity, party opposition, and many other motives not more laudable than these, are apt to operate as well upon those who support as those who oppose the right side of a question. Were there not even these inducements to moderation, nothing could be more ill-judged than that intolerant spirit which has, at all times, characterized political parties. For in politics, as in religion, it is equally absurd to aim at making proselytes by fire and sword. Heresies in either can rarely be cured by persecution.

And yet, however just these sentiments will be allowed to be, we have already sufficient indications that it will happen in this as in all former cases of great national discussion. A torrent of angry and malignant passions will be let loose. To judge from the conduct of the opposite parties, we shall be led to conclude that they will mutually hope to evince the justness of their opinions, and to increase the number of their converts by the loudness of their declamations and the bitterness of their invectives. An enlightened zeal for the energy and efficiency of government will be stigmatized as the offspring of a temper fond of despotic power and hostile to the principles of liberty. An over-scrupulous jealousy of danger to the rights of the people, which is more commonly the fault of the head than of the heart, will be represented as mere pretense and artifice, the stale bait for popularity at the expense of the public good.

It will be forgotten, on the one hand, that jealousy is the usual concomitant of love, and that the noble enthusiasm of liberty is apt to be infected with a spirit of narrow and illiberal distrust. On the other hand, it will be equally forgotten that the vigor of government is essential to the security of liberty; that, in the contemplation of a sound and well-informed judgment, their interest can never be separated; and that a dangerous ambition more often lurks behind the specious mask of zeal for the rights of the people than under the forbidden appearance of zeal for the firmness and efficiency of government. History will teach us that the former has been found a much more certain road to the introduction of despotism than the latter, and that of those men who have overturned the liberties of republics, the greatest number have begun their career by paying an obsequious court to the people; commencing demagogues, and ending tyrants.

In the course of the preceding observations, I have had an eye, my fellow-citizens, to putting you upon your guard against all attempts, from whatever quarter, to influence your decision in a matter of the utmost moment to your welfare, by any impressions other than those which may result from the evidence of truth. You will, no doubt, at the same time, have collected from the general scope of them, that they proceed from a source not unfriendly to the new Constitution.

Yes, my countrymen, I own to you that, after having given it an attentive consideration, I am clearly of opinion it is your interest to adopt it. I am convinced that this is the safest course for your liberty, your dignity, and your happiness. I affect not reserves which I do not feel. I will not amuse you with an appearance of deliberation when I have decided. I frankly acknowledge to you my convictions, and I will freely lay before you the reasons on which they are founded. The consciousness of good intentions disdains ambiguity. I shall not, however, multiply professions on this head. My motives must remain in the depository of my own breast. My arguments will be open to all, and may be judged of by all. They shall at least be offered in a spirit which will not disgrace the cause of truth.

I propose, in a series of papers, to discuss the following interesting particulars:

THE UTILITY OF THE UNION TO YOUR POLITICAL PROSPERITY THE INSUFFICIENCY OF THE PRESENT CONFEDERATION TO PRESERVE THAT UNION THE NECESSITY OF A GOVERNMENT AT LEAST EQUALLY ENERGETIC WITH THE ONE PROPOSED, TO THE ATTAINMENT OF THIS OBJECT THE CONFORMITY OF THE PROPOSED CONSTITUTION TO THE TRUE PRINCIPLES OF REPUBLICAN GOVERNMENT ITS ANALOGY TO YOUR OWN STATE CONSTITUTION and lastly, THE ADDITIONAL SECURITY WHICH ITS ADOPTION WILL AFFORD TO THE PRESERVATION OF THAT SPECIES OF GOVERNMENT, TO LIBERTY, AND TO PROPERTY.

In the progress of this discussion I shall endeavor to give a satisfactory answer to all the objections which shall have made their appearance, that may seem to have any claim to your attention. It may perhaps be thought superfluous to offer arguments to prove the utility of the UNION, a point, no doubt, deeply engraved on the hearts of the great body of the people in every State, and one, which it may be imagined, has no adversaries. But the fact is, that we already hear it whispered in the private circles of those who oppose the new Constitution, that the thirteen States are of too great extent for any general system, and that we must of necessity resort to separate confederacies of distinct portions of the whole.1 This doctrine will, in all probability, be gradually propagated, till it has votaries enough to countenance an open avowal of it. For nothing can be more evident, to those who are able to take an enlarged view of the subject, than the alternative of an adoption of the new Constitution or a dismemberment of the Union. It will therefore be of use to begin by examining the advantages of that Union, the certain evils, and the probable dangers, to which every State will be exposed from its dissolution. This shall accordingly constitute the subject of my next address.

Concerning Dangers from Foreign Force and Influence For the Independent Journal.

JAY

To the People of the State of New York:

WHEN the people of America reflect that they are now called upon to decide a question, which, in its consequences, must prove one of the most important that ever engaged their attention, the propriety of their taking a very comprehensive, as well as a very serious, view of it, will be evident.

Nothing is more certain than the indispensable necessity of government, and it is equally undeniable, that whenever and however it is instituted, the people must cede to it some of their natural rights in order to vest it with requisite powers. It is well worthy of consideration therefore, whether it would conduce more to the interest of the people of America that they should, to all general purposes, be one nation, under one federal government, or that they should divide themselves into separate confederacies, and give to the head of each the same kind of powers which they are advised to place in one national government.

It has until lately been a received and uncontradicted opinion that the prosperity of the people of America depended on their continuing firmly united, and the wishes, prayers, and efforts of our best and wisest citizens have been constantly directed to that object. But politicians now appear, who insist that this opinion is erroneous, and that instead of looking for safety and happiness in union, we ought to seek it in a division of the States into distinct confederacies or sovereignties. However extraordinary this new doctrine may appear, it nevertheless has its advocates; and certain characters who were much opposed to it formerly, are at present of the number. Whatever may be the arguments or inducements which have wrought this change in the sentiments and declarations of these gentlemen, it certainly would not be wise in the people at large to adopt these new political tenets without being fully convinced that they are founded in truth and sound policy.

It has often given me pleasure to observe that independent America was not composed of detached and distant territories, but that one connected, fertile, widespreading country was the portion of our western sons of liberty. Providence has in a particular manner blessed it with a variety of soils and productions, and watered it with innumerable streams, for the delight and accommodation of its inhabitants. A succession of navigable waters forms a kind of chain round its borders, as if to bind it together; while the most noble rivers in the world, running at convenient distances, present them with highways for the easy communication of friendly aids, and the mutual transportation and exchange of their various commodities.

With equal pleasure I have as often taken notice that Providence has been pleased to give this one connected country to one united people—a people descended from the same ancestors, speaking the same language, professing the same religion, attached to the same principles of government, very similar in their manners and customs, and who, by their joint counsels, arms, and efforts, fighting side by side throughout a long and bloody war, have nobly established general liberty and independence.

This country and this people seem to have been made for each other, and it appears as if it was the design of Providence, that an inheritance so proper and convenient for a band of brethren, united to each other by the strongest ties, should never be split into a number of unsocial, jealous, and alien sovereignties.

Similar sentiments have hitherto prevailed among all orders and denominations of men among us. To all general purposes we have uniformly been one people each individual citizen everywhere enjoying the same national rights, privileges, and protection. As a nation we have made peace and war; as a nation we have vanquished our common enemies; as a nation we have formed alliances, and made treaties, and entered into various compacts and conventions with foreign states.

A strong sense of the value and blessings of union induced the people, at a very early period, to institute a federal government to preserve and perpetuate it. They formed it almost as soon as they had a political existence; nay, at a time when their habitations were in flames, when many of their citizens were bleeding, and when the progress of hostility and desolation left little room for those calm and mature inquiries and reflections which must ever precede the formation of a wise and wellbalanced government for a free people. It is not to be wondered at, that a government instituted in times so inauspicious, should on experiment be found greatly deficient and inadequate to the purpose it was intended to answer.

This intelligent people perceived and regretted these defects. Still continuing no less attached to union than enamored of liberty, they observed the danger which immediately threatened the former and more remotely the latter; and being pursuaded that ample security for both could only be found in a national government more wisely framed, they as with one voice, convened the late convention at Philadelphia, to take that important subject under consideration.

This convention composed of men who possessed the confidence of the people, and many of whom had become highly distinguished by their patriotism, virtue and wisdom, in times which tried the minds and hearts of men, undertook the arduous task. In the mild season of peace, with minds unoccupied by other subjects, they passed many months in cool, uninterrupted, and daily consultation; and finally, without having been awed by power, or influenced by any passions except love for their country, they presented and recommended to the people the plan produced by their joint and very unanimous councils.

Admit, for so is the fact, that this plan is only **RECOMMENDED**, not imposed, yet let it be remembered that it is neither recommended to **BLIND** approbation, nor to **BLIND** reprobation; but to that sedate and candid consideration which the magnitude and importance of the subject demand, and which it certainly ought to receive. But this (as was remarked in the foregoing number of this paper) is more to be wished than expected, that it may be so considered and examined. Experience on a former occasion teaches us not to be too sanguine in such hopes. It is not yet forgotten that well-grounded apprehensions of imminent danger induced the people of America to form the memorable Congress of 1774. That body recommended certain measures to their constituents, and the event proved their wisdom; yet it is fresh in our memories how soon the press began to teem with pamphlets and weekly papers against those very measures. Not only many of the officers of government, who obeyed the dictates of personal interest, but others, from a mistaken estimate of consequences, or the undue influence of former attachments, or whose ambition aimed at objects which did not correspond with the public good, were indefatigable in their efforts to pursuade the people to reject the advice of that patriotic Congress. Many, indeed, were deceived and deluded, but the great majority of the people reasoned and decided judiciously; and happy they are in reflecting that they did so.

They considered that the Congress was composed of many wise and experienced men. That, being convened from different parts of the country, they brought with them and communicated to each other a variety of useful information. That, in the course of the time they passed together in inquiring into and discussing the true interests of their country, they must have acquired very accurate knowledge on that head. That they were individually interested in the public liberty and prosperity, and therefore that it was not less their inclination than their duty to recommend only such measures as, after the most mature deliberation, they really thought prudent and advisable.

These and similar considerations then induced the people to rely greatly on the judgment and integrity of the Congress; and they took their advice, notwithstanding the various arts and endeavors used to deter them from it. But if the people at large had reason to confide in the men of that Congress, few of whom had been fully tried or generally known, still greater reason have they now to respect the judgment and advice of the convention, for it is well known that some of the most distinguished members of that Congress, who have been since tried and justly approved for patriotism and abilities, and who have grown old in acquiring political information, were also members of this convention, and carried into it their accumulated knowledge and experience.

It is worthy of remark that not only the first, but every succeeding Congress, as well as the late convention, have invariably joined with the people in thinking that the prosperity of America depended on its Union. To preserve and perpetuate it was the great object of the people in forming that convention, and it is also the great object of the plan which the convention has advised them to adopt. With what propriety, therefore, or for what good purposes, are attempts at this particular period made by some men to depreciate the importance of the Union? Or why is it suggested that three or four confederacies would be better than one? I am persuaded in my own mind that the people have always thought right on this subject, and that their universal and uniform attachment to the cause of the Union rests on great and weighty reasons, which I shall endeavor to develop and explain in some ensuing papers. They who promote the idea of substituting a number of distinct confederacies in the room of the plan of the convention, seem clearly to foresee that the rejection of it would put the continuance of the Union in the utmost jeopardy. That certainly would be the case, and I sincerely wish that it may be as clearly foreseen by every good citizen, that whenever the dissolution of the Union arrives, America will have reason to exclaim, in the words of the poet: "FAREWELL! A LONG FAREWELL TO ALL MY GREATNESS."

The Same Subject Continued: Concerning Dangers From Foreign Force and Influence For the Independent Journal.

JAY

To the People of the State of New York:

IT IS not a new observation that the people of any country (if, like the Americans, intelligent and wellinformed) seldom adopt and steadily persevere for many years in an erroneous opinion respecting their interests. That consideration naturally tends to create great respect for the high opinion which the people of America have so long and uniformly entertained of the importance of their continuing firmly united under one federal government, vested with sufficient powers for all general and national purposes.

The more attentively I consider and investigate the reasons which appear to have given birth to this opinion, the more I become convinced that they are cogent and conclusive.

Among the many objects to which a wise and free people find it necessary to direct their attention, that of providing for their **SAFETY** seems to be the first. The **SAFETY** of the people doubtless has relation to a great variety of circumstances and considerations, and consequently affords great latitude to those who wish to define it precisely and comprehensively.

At present I mean only to consider it as it respects security for the preservation of peace and tranquillity, as well as against dangers from **FOREIGN ARMS AND INFLUENCE**, as from dangers of the **LIKE KIND** arising from domestic causes. As the former of these comes first in order, it is proper it should be the first discussed. Let us therefore proceed to examine whether the people are not right in their opinion that a cordial Union, undc : an efficient national government, affords them the best security that can be devised against **HOSTILITIES** from abroad.

The number of wars which have happened or will happen in the world will always be found to be in proportion to the number and weight of the causes, whether **REAL** or **PRETENDED**, which **PROVOKE** or **INVITE** them. If this remark be just, it becomes useful to inquire whether so many JUST causes of war are likely to be given by **UNITED AMERICA** as by **DISUNITED** America; for if it should turn out that United America will probably give the fewest, then it will follow that in this respect the Union tends most to preserve the people in a state of peace with other nations.

The **JUST** causes of war, for the most part, arise either from violation of treaties or from direct violence. America has already formed treaties with no less than six foreign nations (*), and all of them, except Prussia, are maritime, and therefore able to annoy and injure us. She has also extensive commerce with Portugal, Spain, and Britain, and, with respect to the two latter, has, in addition, the circumstance of neighborhood to attend to.

It is of high importance to the peace of America that she observe the laws of nations towards all these powers, and to me it appears evident that this will be more perfectly and punctually done by one national government than it could be either by thirteen separate States or by three or four distinct confederacies.

Because when once an efficient national government is established, the best men in the country will not only consent to serve, but also will generally be appointed to manage it; for, although town or country, or other contracted influence, may place men in State assemblies, or senates, or courts of justice, or executive departments, yet more general and extensive reputation for talents and other qualifications will be necessary to recommend men to offices under the national government,—especially as it will have the widest field for choice, and never experience that want of proper persons which is not uncommon in some of the States.

Hence, it will result that the administration, the political counsels, and the judicial decisions of the national government will be more wise, systematical, and judicious than those of individual States, and consequently more satisfactory with respect to other nations, as well as more **SAFE** with respect to us.

Because, under the national government, treaties and articles of treaties, as well as the laws of nations, will always be expounded in one sense and executed in the same manner,—whereas, adjudications on the same points and questions, in thirteen States, or in three or four confederacies, will not always accord or be consistent; and that, as well from the variety of independent courts and judges appointed by different and independent governments, as from the different local laws and interests which may affect and influence them. The wisdom of the convention, in committing such questions to the jurisdiction and judgment of courts appointed by and responsible only to one national government, cannot be too much commended.

Because the prospect of present loss or advantage may often tempt the governing party in one or two States to swerve from good faith and justice; but those temptations, not reaching the other States, and consequently having little or no influence on the national government, the temptation will be fruitless, and good faith and justice be preserved. The case of the treaty of peace with Britain adds great weight to this reasoning.

Because, even if the governing party in a State should be disposed to resist such temptations, yet as such temptations may, and commonly do, result from circumstances peculiar to the State, and may affect a great number of the inhabitants, the governing party may not always be able, if willing, to prevent the injustice meditated, or to punish the aggressors. But the national government, not being affected by those local circumstances, will neither be induced to commit the wrong themselves, nor want power or inclination to prevent or punish its commission by others.

So far, therefore, as either designed or accidental violations of treaties and the laws of nations afford **JUST** causes of war, they are less to be apprehended under one general government than under several lesser ones, and in that respect the former most favors the SAFETY of the people.

As to those just causes of war which proceed from direct and unlawful violence, it appears equally clear to me that one good national government affords vastly more security against dangers of that sort than can be derived from any other quarter. Because such violences are more frequently caused by the passions and interests of a part than of the whole; of one or two States than of the Union. Not a single Indian war has yet been occasioned by aggressions of the present federal government, feeble as it is; but there are several instances of Indian hostilities having been provoked by the improper conduct of individual States, who, either unable or unwilling to restrain or punish offenses, have given occasion to the slaughter of many innocent inhabitants.

The neighborhood of Spanish and British territories, bordering on some States and not on others, naturally confines the causes of quarrel more immediately to the borderers. The bordering States, if any, will be those who, under the impulse of sudden irritation, and a quick sense of apparent interest or injury, will be most likely, by direct violence, to excite war with these nations; and nothing can so effectually obviate that danger as a national government, whose wisdom and prudence will not be diminished by the passions which actuate the parties immediately interested.

But not only fewer just causes of war will be given by the national government, but it will also be more in their power to accommodate and settle them amicably. They will be more temperate and cool, and in that respect, as well as in others, will be more in capacity to act advisedly than the offending State. The pride of states, as well as of men, naturally disposes them to justify all their actions, and opposes their acknowledging, correcting, or repairing their errors and offenses. The national government, in such cases, will not be affected by this pride, but will proceed with moderation and candor to consider and decide on the means most proper to extricate them from the difficulties which threaten them.

Besides, it is well known that acknowledgments, explanations, and compensations are often accepted as satisfactory from a strong united nation, which would be rejected as unsatisfactory if offered by a State or confederacy of little consideration or power.

In the year 1685, the state of Genoa having offended Louis XIV., endeavored to appease him. He demanded that they should send their Doge, or chief magistrate, accompanied by four of their senators, to FRANCE, to ask his pardon and receive his terms. They were obliged to submit to it for the sake of peace. Would he on any occasion either have demanded or have received the like humiliation from Spain, or Britain, or any other POWERFUL nation?

The Same Subject Continued: Concerning Dangers From Foreign Force and Influence For the Independent Journal.

JAY

To the People of the State of New York:

MY LAST paper assigned several reasons why the safety of the people would be best secured by union against the danger it may be exposed to by **JUST** causes of war given to other nations; and those reasons show that such causes would not only be more rarely given, but would also be more easily accommodated, by a national government than either by the State governments or the proposed little confederacies.

But the safety of the people of America against dangers from **FOREIGN** force depends not only on their forbearing to give **JUST** causes of war to other nations, but also on their placing and continuing themselves in such a situation as not to **INVITE** hostility or insult; for it need not be observed that there are **PRETENDED** as well as just causes of war.

It is too true, however disgraceful it may be to human nature, that nations in general will make war whenever they have a prospect of getting anything by it; nay, absolute monarchs will often make war when their nations are to get nothing by it, but for the purposes and objects merely personal, such as thirst for military glory, revenge for personal affronts, ambition, or private compacts to aggrandize or support their particular families or partisans. These and a variety of other motives, which affect only the mind of the sovereign, often lead him to engage in wars not sanctified by justice or the voice and interests of his people. But, independent of these inducements to war, which are more prevalent in absolute monarchies, but which well deserve our attention, there are others which affect nations as often as kings; and some of them will on examination be found to grow out of our relative situation and circumstances. With France and with Britain we are rivals in the fisheries, and can supply their markets cheaper than they can themselves, notwithstanding any efforts to prevent it by bounties on their own or duties on foreign fish.

With them and with most other European nations we are rivals in navigation and the carrying trade; and we shall deceive ourselves if we suppose that any of them will rejoice to see it flourish; for, as our carrying trade cannot increase without in some degree diminishing theirs, it is more their interest, and will be more their policy, to restrain than to promote it.

In the trade to China and India, we interfere with more than one nation, inasmuch as it enables us to partake in advantages which they had in a manner monopolized, and as we thereby supply ourselves with commodities which we used to purchase from them.

The extension of our own commerce in our own vessels cannot give pleasure to any nations who possess territories on or near this continent, because the cheapness and excellence of our productions, added to the circumstance of vicinity, and the enterprise and address of our merchants and navigators, will give us a greater share in the advantages which those territories afford, than consists with the wishes or policy of their respective sovereigns.

Spain thinks it convenient to shut the Mississippi against us on the one side, and Britain excludes us from the Saint Lawrence on the other; nor will either of them permit the other waters which are between them and us to become the means of mutual intercourse and traffic. From these and such like considerations, which might, if consistent with prudence, be more amplified and detailed, it is easy to see that jealousies and uneasinesses may gradually slide into the minds and cabinets of other nations, and that we are not to expect that they should regard our advancement in union, in power and consequence by land and by sea, with an eye of indifference and composure.

The people of America are aware that inducements to war may arise out of these circumstances, as well as from others not so obvious at present, and that whenever such inducements may find fit time and opportunity for operation, pretenses to color and justify them will not be wanting. Wisely, therefore, do they consider union and a good national government as necessary to put and keep them in **SUCH A SITUATION** as, instead of **INVITING** war, will tend to repress and discourage it. That situation consists in the best possible state of defense, and necessarily depends on the government, the arms, and the resources of the country.

As the safety of the whole is the interest of the whole, and cannot be provided for without government, either one or more or many, let us inquire whether one good government is not, relative to the object in question, more competent than any other given number whatever.

One government can collect and avail itself of the talents and experience of the ablest men, in whatever part of the Union they may be found. It can move on uniform principles of policy. It can harmonize, assimilate, and protect the several parts and members, and extend the benefit of its foresight and precautions to each. In the formation of treaties, it will regard the interest of the whole, and the particular interests of the parts as connected with that of the whole.

It can apply the resources and power of the whole to the defense of any particular part, and that more easily and expeditiously than State governments or separate confederacies can possibly do, for want of concert and unity of system. It can place the militia under one plan of discipline, and, by putting their officers in a proper line of subordination to the Chief Magistrate, will, as it were, consolidate them into one corps, and thereby render them more efficient than if divided into thirteen or into three or four distinct independent companies.

What would the militia of Britain be if the English militia obeyed the government of England, if the Scotch militia obeyed the government of Scotland, and if the Welsh militia obeyed the government of Wales? Suppose an invasion; would those three governments (if they agreed at all) be able, with all their respective forces, to operate against the enemy so effectually as the single government of Great Britain would?

We have heard much of the fleets of Britain, and the time may come, if we are wise, when the fleets of America may engage attention. But if one national government, had not so regulated the navigation of Britain as to make it a nursery for seamen—if one national government had not called forth all the national means and materials for forming fleets, their prowess and their thunder would never have been celebrated. Let England have its navigation and fleet—let Scotland have its navigation and fleet—let Wales have its navigation and fleet—let Ireland have its navigation and fleet—let those four of the constituent parts of the British empire be be under four independent governments, and it is easy to perceive how soon they would each dwindle into comparative insignificance.

Apply these facts to our own case. Leave America divided into thirteen or, if you please, into three or four independent governments—what armies could they raise and pay—what fleets could they ever hope to have? If one was attacked, would the others fly to its succor, and spend their blood and money in its defense? Would there be no danger of their being flattered into neutrality by its specious promises, or seduced by a too great fondness for peace to decline hazarding their tranquillity and present safety for the sake of neighbors, of whom perhaps they have been jealous, and whose importance they are content to see diminished? Although such conduct would not be wise, it would, nevertheless, be natural. The history of the states of Greece, and of other countries, abounds with such instances, and it is not improbable that what has so often happened would, under similar circumstances, happen again.

But admit that they might be willing to help the invaded State or confederacy. How, and when, and in what proportion shall aids of men and money be afforded? Who shall command the allied armies, and from which of them shall he receive his orders? Who shall settle the terms of peace, and in case of disputes what umpire shall decide between them and compel acquiescence? Various difficulties and inconveniences would be inseparable from such a situation; whereas one government, watching over the general and common interests, and combining and directing the powers and resources of the whole, would be free from all these embarrassments, and conduce far more to the safety of the people. But whatever may be our situation, whether firmly united under one national government, or split into a number of confederacies, certain it is, that foreign nations will know and view it exactly as it is; and they will act toward us accordingly. If they see that our national government is efficient and well administered, our trade prudently regulated, our militia properly organized and disciplined, our resources and finances discreetly managed, our credit re-established, our people free, contented, and united, they will be much more disposed to cultivate our friendship than provoke our resentment. If, on the other hand, they find us either destitute of an effectual government (each State doing right or wrong, as to its rulers may seem convenient), or split into three or four independent and probably discordant republics or confederacies, one inclining to Britain, another to France, and a third to Spain, and perhaps played off against each other by the three, what a poor, pitiful figure will America make in their eyes! How liable would she become not only to their contempt but to their outrage, and how soon would dear-bought experience proclaim that when a people or family so divide, it never fails to be against themselves.

The Same Subject Continued: Concerning Dangers From Foreign Force and Influence For the Independent Journal.

JAY

To the People of the State of New York: **QUEEN ANNE**, in her letter of the 1st July, 1706, to the Scotch Parliament, makes some observations on the importance of the **UNION** then forming between England and Scotland, which merit our attention. I shall present the public with one or two extracts from it: "An entire and perfect union will be the solid foundation of lasting peace: It will secure your religion, liberty, and property; remove the animosities amongst yourselves, and the jealousies and differences betwixt our two kingdoms. It must increase your strength, riches, and trade; and by this union the whole island, being joined in affection and free from all apprehensions of different interest, will be **ENABLED TO RESIST ALL ITS ENEMIES**." "We most earnestly recommend to you calmness and unanimity in this great and weighty affair, that the union may be brought to a happy conclusion, being the only EFFECTUAL way to secure our present and future happiness, and disappoint the designs of our and your enemies, who will doubtless, on this occasion, **USE THEIR UTMOST ENDEAVORS TO PREVENT OR DELAY THIS UNION.**"

It was remarked in the preceding paper, that weakness and divisions at home would invite dangers from abroad; and that nothing would tend more to secure us from them than union, strength, and good government within ourselves. This subject is copious and cannot easily be exhausted.

The history of Great Britain is the one with which we are in general the best acquainted, and it gives us many useful lessons. We may profit by their experience without paying the price which it cost them. Although it seems obvious to common sense that the people of such an island should be but one nation, yet we find that they were for ages divided into three, and that those three were almost constantly embroiled in quarrels and wars with one another. Notwithstanding their true interest with respect to the continental nations was really the same, yet by the arts and policy and practices of those nations, their mutual jealousies were perpetually kept inflamed, and for a long series of years they were far more inconvenient and troublesome than they were useful and assisting to each other.

Should the people of America divide themselves into three or four nations, would not the same thing happen? Would not similar jealousies arise, and be in like manner cherished? Instead of their being "joined in affection" and free from all apprehension of different "interests," envy and jealousy would soon extinguish confidence and affection, and the partial interests of each confederacy, instead of the general interests of all America, would be the only objects of their policy and pursuits. Hence, like most other **BORDERING** nations, they would always be either involved in disputes and war, or live in the constant apprehension of them.

The most sanguine advocates for three or four confederacies cannot reasonably suppose that they would long remain exactly on an equal footing in point of strength, even if it was possible to form them so at first; but, admitting that to be practicable, yet what human contrivance can secure the continuance of such equality? Independent of those local circumstances which tend to beget and increase power in one part and to impede its progress in another, we must advert to the effects of that superior policy and good management which would probably distinguish the government of one above the rest, and by which their relative equality in strength and consideration would be destroyed. For it cannot be presumed that the same degree of sound policy, prudence, and foresight would uniformly be observed by each of these confederacies for a long succession of years.

Whenever, and from whatever causes, it might happen, and happen it would, that any one of these nations or confederacies should rise on the scale of political importance much above the degree of her neighbors, that moment would those neighbors behold her with envy and with fear.

Both those passions would lead them to countenance, if not to promote, whatever might promise to diminish her importance; and would also restrain them from measures calculated to advance or even to secure her prosperity. Much time would not be necessary to enable her to discern these unfriendly dispositions. She would soon begin, not only to lose confidence in her neighbors, but also to feel a disposition equally unfavorable to them. Distrust naturally creates distrust, and by nothing is good-will and kind conduct more speedily changed than by invidious jealousies and uncandid imputations, whether expressed or implied.

The North is generally the region of strength, and many local circumstances render it probable that the most Northern of the proposed confederacies would, at a period not very distant, be unquestionably more formidable than any of the others. No sooner would this become evident than the **NORTHERN HIVE** would excite the same ideas and sensations in the more southern parts of America which it formerly did in the southern parts of Europe. Nor does it appear to be a rash conjecture that its young swarms might often be tempted to gather honey in the more blooming fields and milder air of their luxurious and more delicate neighbors.

They who well consider the history of similar divisions and confederacies will find abundant reason to apprehend that those in contemplation would in no other sense be neighbors than as they would be borderers; that they would neither love nor trust one another, but on the contrary would be a prey to discord, jealousy, and mutual injuries; in short, that they would place us exactly in the situations in which some nations doubtless wish to see us, viz., **FORMIDABLE ONLY TO EACH OTHER**.

From these considerations it appears that those gentlemen are greatly mistaken who suppose that alliances offensive and defensive might be formed between these confederacies, and would produce that combination and union of wills of arms and of resources, which would be necessary to put and keep them in a formidable state of defense against foreign enemies.

When did the independent states, into which Britain and Spain were formerly divided, combine in such alliance, or unite their forces against a foreign enemy? The proposed confederacies will be **DISTINCT NATIONS**. Each of them would have its commerce with foreigners to regulate by distinct treaties; and as their productions and commodities are different and proper for different markets, so would those treaties be essentially different. Different commercial concerns must create different interests, and of course different degrees of political attachment to and connection with different foreign nations. Hence it might and probably would happen that the foreign nation with whom the **SOUTHERN** confederacy might be at war would be the one with whom the **NORTHERN** confederacy would be the most desirous of preserving peace and friendship. An alliance so contrary to their immediate interest would not therefore be easy to form, nor, if formed, would it be observed and fulfilled with perfect good faith.

Nay, it is far more probable that in America, as in Europe, neighboring nations, acting under the impulse of opposite interests and unfriendly passions, would frequently be found taking different sides. Considering our distance from Europe, it would be more natural for these confederacies to apprehend danger from one another than from distant nations, and therefore that each of them should be more desirous to guard against the others by the aid of foreign alliances, than to guard against foreign dangers by alliances between themselves. And here let us not forget how much more easy it is to receive foreign fleets into our ports, and foreign armies into our country, than it is to persuade or compel them to depart. How many conquests did the Romans and others make in the characters of allies, and what innovations did they under the same character introduce into the governments of those whom they pretended to protect.

Let candid men judge, then, whether the division of America into any given number of independent sovereignties would tend to secure us against the hostilities and improper interference of foreign nations.

Concerning Dangers from Dissensions Between the States
For the Independent Journal.
HAMILTON

To the People of the State of New York:

THE three last numbers of this paper have been dedicated to an enumeration of the dangers to which we should be exposed, in a state of disunion, from the arms and arts of foreign nations. I shall now proceed to delineate dangers of a different and, perhaps, still more alarming kind—those which will in all probability flow from dissensions between the States themselves, and from domestic factions and convulsions. These have been already in some instances slightly anticipated; but they deserve a more particular and more full investigation.

A man must be far gone in Utopian speculations who can seriously doubt that, if these States should either be wholly disunited, or only united in partial confederacies, the subdivisions into which they might be thrown would have frequent and violent contests with each other. To presume a want of motives for such contests as an argument against their existence, would be to forget that men are ambitious, vindictive, and rapacious. To look for a continuation of harmony between a number of independent, unconnected sovereignties in the same neighborhood, would be to disregard the uniform course of human events, and to set at defiance the accumulated experience of ages.

The causes of hostility among nations are innumerable. There are some which have a general and almost constant operation upon the collective bodies of society. Of this description are the love of power or the desire of pre-eminence and dominion—the jealousy of power, or the desire of equality and safety. There are others which have a more circumscribed though an equally operative influence within their spheres. Such are the rivalships and competitions of commerce between commercial nations. And there are others, not less numerous than either of the former, which take their origin entirely in private passions; in the attachments, enmities, interests, hopes, and fears of leading individuals in the communities of which they are members. Men of this class, whether the favorites of a king or of a people, have in too many instances abused the confidence they possessed; and assuming the pretext of some public motive, have not scrupled to sacrifice the national tranquillity to personal advantage or personal gratification.

The celebrated Pericles, in compliance with the resentment of a prostitute,1 at the expense of much of the blood and treasure of his countrymen, attacked, vanquished, and destroyed the city of the **SAMNIANS**. The same man, stimulated by private pique against the MEGARENSIANS,2 another nation of Greece, or to avoid a prosecution with which he was threatened as an accomplice of a supposed theft of the statuary Phidias,3 or to get rid of the accusations prepared to be brought against him for dissipating the funds of the state in the purchase of popularity,4 or from a combination of all these causes, was the primitive author of that famous and fatal war, distinguished in the Grecian annals by the name of the **PELOPONNESIAN** war; which, after various vicissitudes, intermissions, and renewals, terminated in the ruin of the Athenian commonwealth.

The ambitious cardinal, who was prime minister to Henry VIII., permitting his vanity to aspire to the triple crown,5 entertained hopes of succeeding in the acquisition of that splendid prize by the influence of the Emperor Charles V. To secure the favor and interest of this enterprising and powerful monarch, he precipitated England into a war with France, contrary to the plainest dictates of policy, and at the hazard of the safety and independence, as well of the kingdom over which he presided by his counsels, as of Europe in general. For if there ever was a sovereign who bid fair to realize the project of universal monarchy, it was the Emperor Charles V., of whose intrigues Wolsey was at once the instrument and the dupe.

The influence which the bigotry of one female,6 the petulance of another,7 and the cabals of a third,8 had in the contemporary policy, ferments, and pacifications, of a considerable part of Europe, are topics that have been too often descanted upon not to be generally known.

To multiply examples of the agency of personal considerations in the production of great national events, either foreign or domestic, according to their direction, would be an unnecessary waste of time. Those who have but a superficial acquaintance with the sources from which they are to be drawn, will themselves recollect a variety of instances; and those who have a tolerable knowledge of human nature will not stand in need of such lights to form their opinion either of the reality or extent of that agency. Perhaps, however, a reference, tending to illustrate the general principle, may with propriety be made to a case which has lately happened among ourselves. If Shays had not been a **DESPERATE DEBTOR**, it is much to be doubted whether Massachusetts would have been plunged into a civil war.

But notwithstanding the concurring testimony of experience, in this particular, there are still to be found visionary or designing men, who stand ready to advocate the paradox of perpetual peace between the States, though dismembered and alienated from each other. The genius of republics (say they) is pacific; the spirit of commerce has a tendency to soften the manners of men, and to extinguish those inflammable humors which have so often kindled into wars. Commercial republics, like ours, will never be disposed to waste themselves in ruinous contentions with each other. They will be governed by mutual interest, and will cultivate a spirit of mutual amity and concord.

Is it not (we may ask these projectors in politics) the true interest of all nations to cultivate the same benevolent and philosophic spirit? If this be their true interest, have they in fact pursued it? Has it not, on the contrary, invariably been found that momentary passions, and immediate interest, have a more active and imperious control over human conduct than general or remote considerations of policy, utility or justice? Have republics in practice been less addicted to war than monarchies? Are not the former administered by **MEN** as well as the latter? Are there not aversions, predilections, rivalships, and desires of unjust acquisitions, that affect nations as well as kings? Are not popular assemblies frequently subject to the impulses of rage, resentment, jealousy, avarice, and of other irregular and violent propensities? Is it not well known that their determinations are often governed by a few individuals in whom they place confidence, and are, of course, liable to be tinctured by the passions and views of those individuals? Has commerce hitherto done anything more than change the objects of war? Is not the love of wealth as domineering and enterprising a passion as that of power or glory? Have there not been as many wars founded upon commercial motives since that has become the prevailing system of nations, as were before occasioned by the cupidity of territory or dominion? Has not the spirit of commerce, in many instances, administered new incentives to the appetite, both for the one and for the other? Let experience, the least fallible guide of human opinions, be appealed to for an answer to these inquiries.

Sparta, Athens, Rome, and Carthage were all republics; two of them, Athens and Carthage, of the commercial kind. Yet were they as often engaged in wars, offensive and defensive, as the neighboring monarchies of the same times. Sparta was little better than a wellregulated camp; and Rome was never sated of carnage and conquest.

Carthage, though a commercial republic, was the aggressor in the very war that ended in her destruction. Hannibal had carried her arms into the heart of Italy and to the gates of Rome, before Scipio, in turn, gave him an overthrow in the territories of Carthage, and made a conquest of the commonwealth.

Venice, in later times, figured more than once in wars of ambition, till, becoming an object to the other Italian states, Pope Julius II. found means to accomplish that formidable league,9 which gave a deadly blow to the power and pride of this haughty republic.

The provinces of Holland, till they were overwhelmed in debts and taxes, took a leading and conspicuous part in the wars of Europe. They had furious contests with England for the dominion of the sea, and were among the most persevering and most implacable of the opponents of Louis XIV.

In the government of Britain the representatives of the people compose one branch of the national legislature. Commerce has been for ages the predominant pursuit of that country. Few nations, nevertheless, have been more frequently engaged in war; and the wars in which that kingdom has been engaged have, in numerous instances, proceeded from the people.

There have been, if I may so express it, almost as many popular as royal wars. The cries of the nation and the importunities of their representatives have, upon various occasions, dragged their monarchs into war, or continued them in it, contrary to their inclinations, and sometimes contrary to the real interests of the State. In that memorable struggle for superiority between the rival houses of **AUSTRIA** and **BOURBON**, which so long kept Europe in a flame, it is well known that the antipathies of the English against the French, seconding the ambition, or rather the avarice, of a favorite leader,10 protracted the war beyond the limits marked out by sound policy, and for a considerable time in opposition to the views of the court.

The wars of these two last-mentioned nations have in a great measure grown out of commercial considerations,—the desire of supplanting and the fear of being supplanted, either in particular branches of traffic or in the general advantages of trade and navigation.

From this summary of what has taken place in other countries, whose situations have borne the nearest resemblance to our own, what reason can we have to confide in those reveries which would seduce us into an expectation of peace and cordiality between the members of the present confederacy, in a state of separation? Have we not already seen enough of the fallacy and extravagance of those idle theories which have amused us with promises of an exemption from the imperfections, weaknesses and evils incident to society in every shape? Is it not time to awake from the deceitful dream of a golden age, and to adopt as a practical maxim for the direction of our political conduct that we, as well as the other inhabitants of the globe, are yet remote from the happy empire of perfect wisdom and perfect virtue? Let the point of extreme depression to which our national dignity and credit have sunk, let the inconveniences felt everywhere from a lax and ill administration of government, let the revolt of a part of the State of North Carolina, the late menacing disturbances in Pennsylvania, and the actual insurrections and rebellions in Massachusetts, declare—!

So far is the general sense of mankind from corresponding with the tenets of those who endeavor to lull asleep our apprehensions of discord and hostility between the States, in the event of disunion, that it has from long observation of the progress of society become a sort of axiom in politics, that vicinity or nearness of situation, constitutes nations natural enemies. An intelligent writer expresses himself on this subject to this effect: "**NEIGHBORING NATIONS** (says he) are naturally enemies of each other unless their common weakness forces them to league in a **CONFEDERATE REPUBLIC**, and their constitution prevents the differences that neighborhood occasions, extinguishing that secret jealousy which disposes all states to aggrandize themselves at the expense of their neighbors." This passage, at the same time, points out the **EVIL** and suggests the **REMEDY**.

The Same Subject Continued:
Concerning Dangers from Dissensions Between the States
For the Independent Journal.
HAMILTON

To the People of the State of New York:

IT IS sometimes asked, with an air of seeming triumph, what inducements could the States have, if disunited, to make war upon each other? It would be a full answer to this question to say—precisely the same inducements which have, at different times, deluged in blood all the nations in the world. But, unfortunately for us, the question admits of a more particular answer. There are causes of differences within our immediate contemplation, of the tendency of which, even under the restraints of a federal constitution, we have had sufficient experience to enable us to form a judgment of what might be expected if those restraints were removed.

Territorial disputes have at all times been found one of the most fertile sources of hostility among nations. Perhaps the greatest proportion of wars that have desolated the earth have sprung from this origin. This cause would exist among us in full force. We have a vast tract of unsettled territory within the boundaries of the United States. There still are discordant and undecided claims between several of them, and the dissolution of the Union would lay a foundation for similar claims between them all. It is well known that they have heretofore had serious and animated discussion concerning the rights to the lands which were ungranted at the time of the Revolution, and which usually went under the name of crown lands. The States within the limits of whose colonial governments they were comprised have claimed them as their property, the others have contended that the rights of the crown in this article devolved upon the Union; especially as to all that part of the Western territory which, either by actual possession, or through the submission of the Indian proprietors, was subjected to the jurisdiction of the king of Great Britain, till it was relinquished in the treaty of peace. This, it has been said, was at all events an acquisition to the Confederacy by compact with a foreign power. It has been the prudent policy of Congress to appease this controversy, by prevailing upon the States to make cessions to the United States for the benefit of the whole. This has been so far accomplished as, under a continuation of the Union, to afford a decided prospect of an amicable termination of the dispute. A dismemberment of the Confederacy, however, would revive this dispute, and would create others on the same subject. At present, a large part of the vacant Western territory is, by cession at least, if not by any anterior right, the common property of the Union. If that were at an end, the States which made the cession, on a principle of federal compromise, would be apt when the motive of the grant had ceased, to reclaim the lands as a reversion. The other States would no doubt insist on a proportion, by right of representation. Their argument would be, that a grant, once made, could not be revoked; and that the justice of participating in territory acquired or secured by the joint efforts of the Confederacy, remained undiminished. If, contrary to probability, it should be admitted by all the States, that each had a right to a share of this common stock, there would still be a difficulty to be surmounted, as to a proper rule of apportionment. Different principles would be set up by different States for this purpose; and as they would affect the opposite interests of the parties, they might not easily be susceptible of a pacific adjustment.

In the wide field of Western territory, therefore, we perceive an ample theatre for hostile pretensions, without any umpire or common judge to interpose between the contending parties. To reason from the past to the future, we shall have good ground to apprehend, that the sword would sometimes be appealed to as the arbiter of their differences. The circumstances of the dispute between Connecticut and Pennsylvania, respecting the land at Wyoming, admonish us not to be sanguine in expecting an easy accommodation of such differences. The articles of confederation obliged the parties to submit the matter to the decision of a federal court. The submission was made, and the court decided in favor of Pennsylvania. But Connecticut gave strong indications of dissatisfaction with that determination; nor did she appear to be entirely resigned to it, till, by negotiation and management, something like an equivalent was found for the loss she supposed herself to have sustained. Nothing here said is intended to convey the slightest censure on the conduct of that State. She no doubt sincerely believed herself to have been injured by the decision; and States, like individuals, acquiesce with great reluctance in determinations to their disadvantage.

Those who had an opportunity of seeing the inside of the transactions which attended the progress of the controversy between this State and the district of Vermont, can vouch the opposition we experienced, as well from States not interested as from those which were interested in the claim; and can attest the danger to which the peace of the Confederacy might have been exposed, had this State attempted to assert its rights by force. Two motives preponderated in that opposition: one, a jealousy entertained of our future power; and the other, the interest of certain individuals of influence in the neighboring States, who had obtained grants of lands under the actual government of that district. Even the States which brought forward claims, in contradiction to ours, seemed more solicitous to dismember this State, than to establish their own pretensions. These were New Hampshire, Massachusetts, and Connecticut. New Jersey and Rhode Island, upon all occasions, discovered a warm zeal for the independence of Vermont; and Maryland, till alarmed by the appearance of a connection between Canada and that State, entered deeply into the same views. These being small States, saw with an unfriendly eye the perspective of our growing greatness. In a review of these transactions we may trace some of the causes which would be likely to embroil the States with each other, if it should be their unpropitious destiny to become disunited.

The competitions of commerce would be another fruitful source of contention. The States less favorably circumstanced would be desirous of escaping from the disadvantages of local situation, and of sharing in the advantages of their more fortunate neighbors. Each State, or separate confederacy, would pursue a system of commercial policy peculiar to itself. This would occasion distinctions, preferences, and exclusions, which would beget discontent. The habits of intercourse, on the basis of equal privileges, to which we have been accustomed since the earliest settlement of the country, would give a keener edge to those causes of discontent than they would naturally have independent of this circumstance. **WE SHOULD BE READY TO DENOMINATE INJURIES THOSE THINGS WHICH WERE IN REALITY THE JUSTIFIABLE ACTS OF INDEPENDENT SOVEREIGNTIES CONSULTING A DISTINCT INTEREST**. The spirit of enterprise, which characterizes the commercial part of America, has left no occasion of displaying itself unimproved. It is not at all probable that this unbridled spirit would pay much respect to those regulations of trade by which particular States might endeavor to secure exclusive benefits to their own citizens. The infractions of these regulations, on one side, the efforts to prevent and repel them, on the other, would naturally lead to outrages, and these to reprisals and wars.

The opportunities which some States would have of rendering others tributary to them by commercial regulations would be impatiently submitted to by the tributary States. The relative situation of New York, Connecticut, and New Jersey would afford an example of this kind. New York, from the necessities of revenue, must lay duties on her importations. A great part of these duties must be paid by the inhabitants of the two other States in the capacity of consumers of what we import. New York would neither be willing nor able to forego this advantage. Her citizens would not consent that a duty paid by them should be remitted in favor of the citizens of her neighbors; nor would it be practicable, if there were not this impediment in the way, to distinguish the customers in our own markets. Would Connecticut and New Jersey long submit to be taxed by New York for her exclusive benefit? Should we be long permitted to remain in the quiet and undisturbed enjoyment of a metropolis, from the possession of which we derived an advantage so odious to our neighbors, and, in their opinion, so oppressive? Should we be able to preserve it against the incumbent weight of Connecticut on the one side, and the co-operating pressure of New Jersey on the other? These are questions that temerity alone will answer in the affirmative.

The public debt of the Union would be a further cause of collision between the separate States or confederacies. The apportionment, in the first instance, and the progressive extinguishment afterward, would be alike productive of ill-humor and animosity. How would it be possible to agree upon a rule of apportionment satisfactory to all? There is scarcely any that can be proposed which is entirely free from real objections. These, as usual, would be exaggerated by the adverse interest of the parties. There are even dissimilar views among the States as to the general principle of discharging the public debt. Some of them, either less impressed with the importance of national credit, or because their citizens have little, if any, immediate interest in the question, feel an indifference, if not a repugnance, to the payment of the domestic debt at any rate. These would be inclined to magnify the difficulties of a distribution. Others of them, a numerous body of whose citizens are creditors to the public beyond proportion of the State in the total amount of the national debt, would be strenuous for some equitable and effective provision. The procrastinations of the former would excite the resentments of the latter. The settlement of a rule would, in the meantime, be postponed by real differences of opinion and affected delays. The citizens of the States interested would clamour; foreign powers would urge for the satisfaction of their just demands, and the peace of the States would be hazarded to the double contingency of external invasion and internal contention.

Suppose the difficulties of agreeing upon a rule surmounted, and the apportionment made. Still there is great room to suppose that the rule agreed upon would, upon experiment, be found to bear harder upon some States than upon others. Those which were sufferers by it would naturally seek for a mitigation of the burden. The others would as naturally be disinclined to a revision, which was likely to end in an increase of their own incumbrances. Their refusal would be too plausible a pretext to the complaining States to withhold their contributions, not to be embraced with avidity; and the non-compliance of these States with their engagements would be a ground of bitter discussion and altercation. If even the rule adopted should in practice justify the equality of its principle, still delinquencies in payments on the part of some of the States would result from a diversity of other causes—the real deficiency of resources; the mismanagement of their finances; accidental disorders in the management of the government; and, in addition to the rest, the reluctance with which men commonly part with money for purposes that have outlived the exigencies which produced them, and interfere with the supply of immediate wants. Delinquencies, from whatever causes, would be productive of complaints, recriminations, and quarrels. There is, perhaps, nothing more likely to disturb the tranquillity of nations than their being bound to mutual contributions for any common object that does not yield an equal and coincident benefit. For it is an observation, as true as it is trite, that there is nothing men differ so readily about as the payment of money.

Laws in violation of private contracts, as they amount to aggressions on the rights of those States whose citizens are injured by them, may be considered as another probable source of hostility. We are not authorized to expect that a more liberal or more equitable spirit would preside over the legislations of the individual States hereafter, if unrestrained by any additional checks, than we have heretofore seen in too many instances disgracing their several codes. We have observed the disposition to retaliation excited in Connecticut in consequence of the enormities perpetrated by the Legislature of Rhode Island; and we reasonably infer that, in similar cases, under other circumstances, a war, not of **PARCHMENT**, but of the sword, would chastise such atrocious breaches of moral obligation and social justice.

The probability of incompatible alliances between the different States or confederacies and different foreign nations, and the effects of this situation upon the peace of the whole, have been sufficiently unfolded in some preceding papers. From the view they have exhibited of this part of the subject, this conclusion is to be drawn, that America, if not connected at all, or only by the feeble tie of a simple league, offensive and defensive, would, by the operation of such jarring alliances, be gradually entangled in all the pernicious labyrinths of European politics and wars; and by the destructive contentions of the parts into which she was divided, would be likely to become a prey to the artifices and machinations of powers equally the enemies of them all. Divide et impera1 must be the motto of every nation that either hates or fears us.

The Consequences of Hostilities Between the States
From the New York Packet. Tuesday, November 20, 1787.
HAMILTON

To the People of the State of New York:

ASSUMING it therefore as an established truth that the several States, in case of disunion, or such combinations of them as might happen to be formed out of the wreck of the general Confederacy, would be subject to those vicissitudes of peace and war, of friendship and enmity, with each other, which have fallen to the lot of all neighboring nations not united under one government, let us enter into a concise detail of some of the consequences that would attend such a situation.

War between the States, in the first period of their separate existence, would be accompanied with much greater distresses than it commonly is in those countries where regular military establishments have long obtained. The disciplined armies always kept on foot on the continent of Europe, though they bear a malignant aspect to liberty and economy, have, notwithstanding, been productive of the signal advantage of rendering sudden conquests impracticable, and of preventing that rapid desolation which used to mark the progress of war prior to their introduction. The art of fortification has contributed to the same ends. The nations of Europe are encircled with chains of fortified places, which mutually obstruct invasion. Campaigns are wasted in reducing two or three frontier garrisons, to gain admittance into an enemy's country. Similar impediments occur at every step, to exhaust the strength and delay the progress of an invader. Formerly, an invading army would penetrate into the heart of a neighboring country almost as soon as intelligence of its approach could be received; but now a comparatively small force of disciplined troops, acting on the defensive, with the aid of posts, is able to impede, and finally to frustrate, the enterprises of one much more considerable. The history of war, in that quarter of the globe, is no longer a history of nations subdued and empires overturned, but of towns taken and retaken; of battles that decide nothing; of retreats more beneficial than victories; of much effort and little acquisition.

In this country the scene would be altogether reversed. The jealousy of military establishments would postpone them as long as possible. The want of fortifications, leaving the frontiers of one state open to another, would facilitate inroads. The populous States would, with little difficulty, overrun their less populous neighbors. Conquests would be as easy to be made as difficult to be retained. War, therefore, would be desultory and predatory. **PLUNDER** and devastation ever march in the train of irregulars. The calamities of individuals would make the principal figure in the events which would characterize our military exploits.

This picture is not too highly wrought; though, I confess, it would not long remain a just one. Safety from external danger is the most powerful director of national conduct. Even the ardent love of liberty will, after a time, give way to its dictates. The violent destruction of life and property incident to war, the continual effort and alarm attendant on a state of continual danger, will compel nations the most attached to liberty to resort for repose and security to institutions which have a tendency to destroy their civil and political rights. To be more safe, they at length become willing to run the risk of being less free.

The institutions chiefly alluded to are **STANDING ARMIES** and the correspondent appendages of military establishments. Standing armies, it is said, are not provided against in the new Constitution; and it is therefore inferred that they may exist under it.1 Their existence, however, from the very terms of the proposition, is, at most, problematical and uncertain. But standing armies, it may be replied, must inevitably result from a dissolution of the Confederacy. Frequent war and constant apprehension, which require a state of as constant preparation, will infallibly produce them. The weaker States or confederacies would first have recourse to them, to put themselves upon an equality with their more potent neighbors. They would endeavor to supply the inferiority of population and resources by a more regular and effective system of defense, by disciplined troops, and by fortifications. They would, at the same time, be necessitated to strengthen the executive arm of government, in doing which their constitutions would acquire a progressive direction toward monarchy. It is of the nature of war to increase the executive at the expense of the legislative authority.

The expedients which have been mentioned would soon give the States or confederacies that made use of them a superiority over their neighbors. Small states, or states of less natural strength, under vigorous governments, and with the assistance of disciplined armies, have often triumphed over large states, or states of greater natural strength, which have been destitute of these advantages. Neither the pride nor the safety of the more important States or confederacies would permit them long to submit to this mortifying and adventitious superiority. They would quickly resort to means similar to those by which it had been effected, to reinstate themselves in their lost pre-eminence. Thus, we should, in a little time, see established in every part of this country the same engines of despotism which have been the scourge of the Old World. This, at least, would be the natural course of things; and our reasonings will be the more likely to be just, in proportion as they are accommodated to this standard.

These are not vague inferences drawn from supposed or speculative defects in a Constitution, the whole power of which is lodged in the hands of a people, or their representatives and delegates, but they are solid conclusions, drawn from the natural and necessary progress of human affairs.

It may, perhaps, be asked, by way of objection to this, why did not standing armies spring up out of the contentions which so often distracted the ancient republics of Greece? Different answers, equally satisfactory, may be given to this question. The industrious habits of the people of the present day, absorbed in the pursuits of gain, and devoted to the improvements of agriculture and commerce, are incompatible with the condition of a nation of soldiers, which was the true condition of the people of those republics. The means of revenue, which have been so greatly multiplied by the increase of gold and silver and of the arts of industry, and the science of finance, which is the offspring of modern times, concurring with the habits of nations, have produced an entire revolution in the system of war, and have rendered disciplined armies, distinct from the body of the citizens, the inseparable companions of frequent hostility.

There is a wide difference, also, between military establishments in a country seldom exposed by its situation to internal invasions, and in one which is often subject to them, and always apprehensive of them. The rulers of the former can have a good pretext, if they are even so inclined, to keep on foot armies so numerous as must of necessity be maintained in the latter. These armies being, in the first case, rarely, if at all, called into activity for interior defense, the people are in no danger of being broken to military subordination. The laws are not accustomed to relaxations, in favor of military exigencies; the civil state remains in full vigor, neither corrupted, nor confounded with the principles or propensities of the other state. The smallness of the army renders the natural strength of the community an over-match for it; and the citizens, not habituated to look up to the military power for protection, or to submit to its oppressions, neither love nor fear the soldiery; they view them with a spirit of jealous acquiescence in a necessary evil, and stand ready to resist a power which they suppose may be exerted to the prejudice of their rights. The army under such circumstances may usefully aid the magistrate to suppress a small faction, or an occasional mob, or insurrection; but it will be unable to enforce encroachments against the united efforts of the great body of the people.

In a country in the predicament last described, the contrary of all this happens. The perpetual menacings of danger oblige the government to be always prepared to repel it; its armies must be numerous enough for instant defense. The continual necessity for their services enhances the importance of the soldier, and proportionably degrades the condition of the citizen. The military state becomes elevated above the civil. The inhabitants of territories, often the theatre of war, are unavoidably subjected to frequent infringements on their rights, which serve to weaken their sense of those rights; and by degrees the people are brought to consider the soldiery not only as their protectors, but as their superiors. The transition from this disposition to that of considering them masters, is neither remote nor difficult; but it is very difficult to prevail upon a people under such impressions, to make a bold or effectual resistance to usurpations supported by the military power.

The kingdom of Great Britain falls within the first description. An insular situation, and a powerful marine, guarding it in a great measure against the possibility of foreign invasion, supersede the necessity of a numerous army within the kingdom. A sufficient force to make head against a sudden descent, till the militia could have time to rally and embody, is all that has been deemed requisite. No motive of national policy has demanded, nor would public opinion have tolerated, a larger number of troops upon its domestic establishment. There has been, for a long time past, little room for the operation of the other causes, which have been enumerated as the consequences of internal war. This peculiar felicity of situation has, in a great degree, contributed to preserve the liberty which that country to this day enjoys, in spite of the prevalent venality and corruption. If, on the contrary, Britain had been situated on the continent, and had been compelled, as she would have been, by that situation, to make her military establishments at home coextensive with those of the other great powers of Europe, she, like them, would in all probability be, at this day, a victim to the absolute power of a single man. 'T is possible, though not easy, that the people of that island may be enslaved from other causes; but it cannot be by the prowess of an army so inconsiderable as that which has been usually kept up within the kingdom.

If we are wise enough to preserve the Union we may for ages enjoy an advantage similar to that of an insulated situation. Europe is at a great distance from us. Her colonies in our vicinity will be likely to continue too much disproportioned in strength to be able to give us any dangerous annoyance. Extensive military establishments cannot, in this position, be necessary to our security. But if we should be disunited, and the integral parts should either remain separated, or, which is most probable, should be thrown together into two or three confederacies, we should be, in a short course of time, in the predicament of the continental powers of Europe — our liberties would be a prey to the means of defending ourselves against the ambition and jealousy of each other.

This is an idea not superficial or futile, but solid and weighty. It deserves the most serious and mature consideration of every prudent and honest man of whatever party. If such men will make a firm and solemn pause, and meditate dispassionately on the importance of this interesting idea; if they will contemplate it in all its attitudes, and trace it to all its consequences, they will not hesitate to part with trivial objections to a Constitution, the rejection of which would in all probability put a final period to the Union. The airy phantoms that flit before the distempered imaginations of some of its adversaries would quickly give place to the more substantial forms of dangers, real, certain, and formidable.

The Union as a Safeguard Against Domestic Faction and Insurrection

For the Independent Journal.

HAMILTON

To the People of the State of New York:

A FIRM Union will be of the utmost moment to the peace and liberty of the States, as a barrier against domestic faction and insurrection. It is impossible to read the history of the petty republics of Greece and Italy without feeling sensations of horror and disgust at the distractions with which they were continually agitated, and at the rapid succession of revolutions by which they were kept in a state of perpetual vibration between the extremes of tyranny and anarchy. If they exhibit occasional calms, these only serve as short-lived contrast to the furious storms that are to succeed. If now and then intervals of felicity open to view, we behold them with a mixture of regret, arising from the reflection that the pleasing scenes before us are soon to be overwhelmed by the tempestuous waves of sedition and party rage. If momentary rays of glory break forth from the gloom, while they dazzle us with a transient and fleeting brilliancy, they at the same time admonish us to lament that the vices of government should pervert the direction and tarnish the lustre of those bright talents and exalted endowments for which the favored soils that produced them have been so justly celebrated.

From the disorders that disfigure the annals of those republics the advocates of despotism have drawn arguments, not only against the forms of republican government, but against the very principles of civil liberty. They have decried all free government as inconsistent with the order of society, and have indulged themselves in malicious exultation over its friends and partisans. Happily for mankind, stupendous fabrics reared on the basis of liberty, which have flourished for ages, have, in a few glorious instances, refuted their gloomy sophisms. And, I trust, America will be the broad and solid foundation of other edifices, not less magnificent, which will be equally permanent monuments of their errors.

But it is not to be denied that the portraits they have sketched of republican government were too just copies of the originals from which they were taken. If it had been found impracticable to have devised models of a more perfect structure, the enlightened friends to liberty would have been obliged to abandon the cause of that species of government as indefensible. The science of politics, however, like most other sciences, has received great improvement. The efficacy of various principles is now well understood, which were either not known at all, or imperfectly known to the ancients. The regular distribution of power into distinct departments; the introduction of legislative balances and checks; the institution of courts composed of judges holding their offices during good behavior; the representation of the people in the legislature by deputies of their own election: these are wholly new discoveries, or have made their principal progress towards perfection in modern times. They are means, and powerful means, by which the excellences of republican government may be retained and its imperfections lessened or avoided. To this catalogue of circumstances that tend to the amelioration of popular systems of civil government, I shall venture, however novel it may appear to some, to add one more, on a principle which has been made the foundation of an objection to the new Constitution; I mean the **ENLARGEMENT** of the **ORBIT** within which such systems are to revolve, either in respect to the dimensions of a single State or to the consolidation of several smaller States into one great Confederacy. The latter is that which immediately concerns the object under consideration. It will, however, be of use to examine the principle in its application to a single State, which shall be attended to in another place.

The utility of a Confederacy, as well to suppress faction and to guard the internal tranquillity of States, as to increase their external force and security, is in reality not a new idea. It has been practiced upon in different countries and ages, and has received the sanction of the most approved writers on the subject of politics. The opponents of the plan proposed have, with great assiduity, cited and circulated the observations of Montesquieu on the necessity of a contracted territory for a republican government. But they seem not to have been apprised of the sentiments of that great man expressed in another part of his work, nor to have adverted to the consequences of the principle to which they subscribe with such ready acquiescence.

When Montesquieu recommends a small extent for republics, the standards he had in view were of dimensions far short of the limits of almost every one of these States. Neither Virginia, Massachusetts, Pennsylvania, New York, North Carolina, nor Georgia can by any means be compared with the models from which he reasoned and to which the terms of his description apply. If we therefore take his ideas on this point as the criterion of truth, we shall be driven to the alternative either of taking refuge at once in the arms of monarchy, or of splitting ourselves into an infinity of little, jealous, clashing, tumultuous commonwealths, the wretched nurseries of unceasing discord, and the miserable objects of universal pity or contempt. Some of the writers who have come forward on the other side of the question seem to have been aware of the dilemma; and have even been bold enough to hint at the division of the larger States as a desirable thing. Such an infatuated policy, such a desperate expedient, might, by the multiplication of petty offices, answer the views of men who possess not qualifications to extend their influence beyond the narrow circles of personal intrigue, but it could never promote the greatness or happiness of the people of America.

Referring the examination of the principle itself to another place, as has been already mentioned, it will be sufficient to remark here that, in the sense of the author who has been most emphatically quoted upon the occasion, it would only dictate a reduction of the **SIZE** of the more considerable **MEMBERS** of the Union, but would not militate against their being all comprehended in one confederate government. And this is the true question, in the discussion of which we are at present interested.

So far are the suggestions of Montesquieu from standing in opposition to a general Union of the States, that he explicitly treats of a **CONFEDERATE REPUBLIC** as the expedient for extending the sphere of popular government, and reconciling the advantages of monarchy with those of republicanism.

"It is very probable," (says he1) "that mankind would have been obliged at length to live constantly under the government of a single person, had they not contrived a kind of constitution that has all the internal advantages of a republican, together with the external force of a monarchical government. I mean a **CONFEDERATE REPUBLIC**.

"This form of government is a convention by which several smaller **STATES** agree to become members of a larger **ONE**, which they intend to form. It is a kind of assemblage of societies that constitute a new one, capable of increasing, by means of new associations, till they arrive to such a degree of power as to be able to provide for the security of the united body.

"A republic of this kind, able to withstand an external force, may support itself without any internal corruptions. The form of this society prevents all manner of inconveniences.

"If a single member should attempt to usurp the supreme authority, he could not be supposed to have an equal authority and credit in all the confederate states. Were he to have too great influence over one, this would alarm the rest. Were he to subdue a part, that which would still remain free might oppose him with forces independent of those which he had usurped and overpower him before he could be settled in his usurpation.

"Should a popular insurrection happen in one of the confederate states the others are able to quell it. Should abuses creep into one part, they are reformed by those that remain sound. The state may be destroyed on one side, and not on the other; the confederacy may be dissolved, and the confederates preserve their sovereignty.

"As this government is composed of small republics, it enjoys the internal happiness of each; and with respect to its external situation, it is possessed, by means of the association, of all the advantages of large monarchies." I have thought it proper to quote at length these interesting passages, because they contain a luminous abridgment of the principal arguments in favor of the Union, and must effectually remove the false impressions which a misapplication of other parts of the work was calculated to make. They have, at the same time, an intimate connection with the more immediate design of this paper; which is, to illustrate the tendency of the Union to repress domestic faction and insurrection.

A distinction, more subtle than accurate, has been raised between a **CONFEDERACY** and a **CONSOLIDATION** of the States. The essential characteristic of the first is said to be, the restriction of its authority to the members in their collective capacities, without reaching to the individuals of whom they are composed. It is contended that the national council ought to have no concern with any object of internal administration. An exact equality of suffrage between the members has also been insisted upon as a leading feature of a confederate government. These positions are, in the main, arbitrary; they are supported neither by principle nor precedent. It has indeed happened, that governments of this kind have generally operated in the manner which the distinction taken notice of, supposes to be inherent in their nature; but there have been in most of them extensive exceptions to the practice, which serve to prove, as far as example will go, that there is no absolute rule on the subject. And it will be clearly shown in the course of this investigation that as far as the principle contended for has prevailed, it has been the cause of incurable disorder and imbecility in the government.

The definition of a **CONFEDERATE REPUBLIC** seems simply to be "an assemblage of societies," or an association of two or more states into one state. The extent, modifications, and objects of the federal authority are mere matters of discretion. So long as the separate organization of the members be not abolished; so long as it exists, by a constitutional necessity, for local purposes; though it should be in perfect subordination to the general authority of the union, it would still be, in fact and in theory, an association of states, or a confederacy. The proposed Constitution, so far from implying an abolition of the State governments, makes them constituent parts of the national sovereignty, by allowing them a direct representation in the Senate, and leaves in their possession certain exclusive and very important portions of sovereign power. This fully corresponds, in every rational import of the terms, with the idea of a federal government.

In the Lycian confederacy, which consisted of twenty-three **CITIES** or republics, the largest were entitled to **THREE** votes in the **COMMON COUNCIL**, those of the middle class to **TWO**, and the smallest to **ONE**. The **COMMON COUNCIL** had the appointment of all the judges and magistrates of the respective **CITIES**. This was certainly the most, delicate species of interference in their internal administration; for if there be any thing that seems exclusively appropriated to the local jurisdictions, it is the appointment of their own officers. Yet Montesquieu, speaking of this association, says: "Were I to give a model of an excellent Confederate Republic, it would be that of Lycia." Thus we perceive that the distinctions insisted upon were not within the contemplation of this enlightened civilian; and we shall be led to conclude, that they are the novel refinements of an erroneous theory.

The Union as a Safeguard Against Domestic Faction and Insurrection

From the New York Packet. Friday, November 23, 1787.

MADISON

To the People of the State of New York:

AMONG the numerous advantages promised by a wellconstructed Union, none deserves to be more accurately developed than its tendency to break and control the violence of faction. The friend of popular governments never finds himself so much alarmed for their character and fate, as when he contemplates their propensity to this dangerous vice. He will not fail, therefore, to set a due value on any plan which, without violating the principles to which he is attached, provides a proper cure for it. The instability, injustice, and confusion introduced into the public councils, have, in truth, been the mortal diseases under which popular governments have everywhere perished; as they continue to be the favorite and fruitful topics from which the adversaries to liberty derive their most specious declamations. The valuable improvements made by the

American constitutions on the popular models, both ancient and modern, cannot certainly be too much admired; but it would be an unwarrantable partiality, to contend that they have as effectually obviated the danger on this side, as was wished and expected. Complaints are everywhere heard from our most considerate and virtuous citizens, equally the friends of public and private faith, and of public and personal liberty, that our governments are too unstable, that the public good is disregarded in the conflicts of rival parties, and that measures are too often decided, not according to the rules of justice and the rights of the minor party, but by the superior force of an interested and overbearing majority. However anxiously we may wish that these complaints had no foundation, the evidence, of known facts will not permit us to deny that they are in some degree true. It will be found, indeed, on a candid review of our situation, that some of the distresses under which we labor have been erroneously charged on the operation of our governments; but it will be found, at the same time, that other causes will not alone account for many of our heaviest misfortunes; and, particularly, for that prevailing and increasing distrust of public engagements, and alarm for private rights, which are echoed from one end of the continent to the other. These must be chiefly, if not wholly, effects of the unsteadiness and injustice with which a factious spirit has tainted our public administrations.

By a faction, I understand a number of citizens, whether amounting to a majority or a minority of the whole, who are united and actuated by some common impulse of passion, or of interest, adversed to the rights of other citizens, or to the permanent and aggregate interests of the community.

There are two methods of curing the mischiefs of faction: the one, by removing its causes; the other, by controlling its effects.

There are again two methods of removing the causes of faction: the one, by destroying the liberty which is essential to its existence; the other, by giving to every citizen the same opinions, the same passions, and the same interests.

It could never be more truly said than of the first remedy, that it was worse than the disease. Liberty is to faction what air is to fire, an aliment without which it instantly expires. But it could not be less folly to abolish liberty, which is essential to political life, because it nourishes faction, than it would be to wish the annihilation of air, which is essential to animal life, because it imparts to fire its destructive agency.

The second expedient is as impracticable as the first would be unwise. As long as the reason of man continues fallible, and he is at liberty to exercise it, different opinions will be formed. As long as the connection subsists between his reason and his self-love, his opinions and his passions will have a reciprocal influence on each other; and the former will be objects to which the latter will attach themselves. The diversity in the faculties of men, from which the rights of property originate, is not less an insuperable obstacle to a uniformity of interests. The protection of these faculties is the first object of government. From the protection of different and unequal faculties of acquiring property, the possession of different degrees and kinds of property immediately results; and from the influence of these on the sentiments and views of the respective proprietors, ensues a division of the society into different interests and parties.

The latent causes of faction are thus sown in the nature of man; and we see them everywhere brought into different degrees of activity, according to the different circumstances of civil society. A zeal for different opinions concerning religion, concerning government, and many other points, as well of speculation as of practice; an attachment to different leaders ambitiously contending for pre-eminence and power; or to persons of other descriptions whose fortunes have been interesting to the human passions, have, in turn, divided mankind into parties, inflamed them with mutual animosity, and rendered them much more disposed to vex and oppress each other than to co-operate for their common good. So strong is this propensity of mankind to fall into mutual animosities, that where no substantial occasion presents itself, the most frivolous and fanciful distinctions have been sufficient to kindle their unfriendly passions and excite their most violent conflicts. But the most common and durable source of factions has been the various and unequal distribution of property. Those who hold and those who are without property have ever formed distinct interests in society. Those who are creditors, and those who are debtors, fall under a like discrimination. A landed interest, a manufacturing interest, a mercantile interest, a moneyed interest, with many lesser interests, grow up of necessity in civilized nations, and divide them into different classes, actuated by different sentiments and views. The regulation of these various and interfering interests forms the principal task of modern legislation, and involves the spirit of party and faction in the necessary and ordinary operations of the government.

No man is allowed to be a judge in his own cause, because his interest would certainly bias his judgment, and, not improbably, corrupt his integrity. With equal, nay with greater reason, a body of men are unfit to be both judges and parties at the same time; yet what are many of the most important acts of legislation, but so many judicial determinations, not indeed concerning the rights of single persons, but concerning the rights of large bodies of citizens? And what are the different classes of legislators but advocates and parties to the causes which they determine? Is a law proposed concerning private debts? It is a question to which the creditors are parties on one side and the debtors on the other. Justice ought to hold the balance between them. Yet the parties are, and must be, themselves the judges; and the most numerous party, or, in other words, the most powerful faction must be expected to prevail. Shall domestic manufactures be encouraged, and in what degree, by restrictions on foreign manufactures? are questions which would be differently decided by the landed and the manufacturing classes, and probably by neither with a sole regard to justice and the public good. The apportionment of taxes on the various descriptions of property is an act which seems to require the most exact impartiality; yet there is, perhaps, no legislative act in which greater opportunity and temptation are given to a predominant party to trample on the rules of justice. Every shilling with which they overburden the inferior number, is a shilling saved to their own pockets.

It is in vain to say that enlightened statesmen will be able to adjust these clashing interests, and render them all subservient to the public good. Enlightened statesmen will not always be at the helm. Nor, in many cases, can such an adjustment be made at all without taking into view indirect and remote considerations, which will rarely prevail over the immediate interest which one party may find in disregarding the rights of another or the good of the whole.

The inference to which we are brought is, that the **CAUSES** of faction cannot be removed, and that relief is only to be sought in the means of controlling its **EFFECTS**.

If a faction consists of less than a majority, relief is supplied by the republican principle, which enables the majority to defeat its sinister views by regular vote. It may clog the administration, it may convulse the society; but it will be unable to execute and mask its violence under the forms of the Constitution. When a majority is included in a faction, the form of popular government, on the other hand, enables it to sacrifice to its ruling passion or interest both the public good and the rights of other citizens. To secure the public good and private rights against the danger of such a faction, and at the same time to preserve the spirit and the form of popular government, is then the great object to which our inquiries are directed. Let me add that it is the great desideratum by which this form of government can be rescued from the opprobrium under which it has so long labored, and be recommended to the esteem and adoption of mankind.

By what means is this object attainable? Evidently by one of two only. Either the existence of the same passion or interest in a majority at the same time must be prevented, or the majority, having such coexistent passion or interest, must be rendered, by their number and local situation, unable to concert and carry into effect schemes of oppression. If the impulse and the opportunity be suffered to coincide, we well know that neither moral nor religious motives can be relied on as an adequate control. They are not found to be such on the injustice and violence of individuals, and lose their efficacy in proportion to the number combined together, that is, in proportion as their efficacy becomes needful.

From this view of the subject it may be concluded that a pure democracy, by which I mean a society consisting of a small number of citizens, who assemble and administer the government in person, can admit of no cure for the mischiefs of faction. A common passion or interest will, in almost every case, be felt by a majority of the whole; a communication and concert result from the form of government itself; and there is nothing to check the inducements to sacrifice the weaker party or an obnoxious individual. Hence it is that such democracies have ever been spectacles of turbulence and contention; have ever been found incompatible with personal security or the rights of property; and have in general been as short in their lives as they have been violent in their deaths. Theoretic politicians, who have patronized this species of government, have erroneously supposed that by reducing mankind to a perfect equality in their political rights, they would, at the same time, be perfectly equalized and assimilated in their possessions, their opinions, and their passions.

A republic, by which I mean a government in which the scheme of representation takes place, opens a different prospect, and promises the cure for which we are seeking. Let us examine the points in which it varies from pure democracy, and we shall comprehend both the nature of the cure and the efficacy which it must derive from the Union.

The two great points of difference between a democracy and a republic are: first, the delegation of the government, in the latter, to a small number of citizens elected by the rest; secondly, the greater number of citizens, and greater sphere of country, over which the latter may be extended.

The effect of the first difference is, on the one hand, to refine and enlarge the public views, by passing them through the medium of a chosen body of citizens, whose wisdom may best discern the true interest of their country, and whose patriotism and love of justice will be least likely to sacrifice it to temporary or partial considerations. Under such a regulation, it may well happen that the public voice, pronounced by the representatives of the people, will be more consonant to the public good than if pronounced by the people themselves, convened for the purpose. On the other hand, the effect may be inverted. Men of factious tempers, of local prejudices, or of sinister designs, may, by intrigue, by corruption, or by other means, first obtain the suffrages, and then betray the interests, of the people. The question resulting is, whether small or extensive republics are more favorable to the election of proper guardians of the public weal; and it is clearly decided in favor of the latter by two obvious considerations:

In the first place, it is to be remarked that, however small the republic may be, the representatives must be raised to a certain number, in order to guard against the cabals of a few; and that, however large it may be, they must be limited to a certain number, in order to guard against the confusion of a multitude. Hence, the number of representatives in the two cases not being in proportion to that of the two constituents, and being proportionally greater in the small republic, it follows that, if the proportion of fit characters be not less in the large than in the small republic, the former will present a greater option, and consequently a greater probability of a fit choice.

In the next place, as each representative will be chosen by a greater number of citizens in the large than in the small republic, it will be more difficult for unworthy candidates to practice with success the vicious arts by which elections are too often carried; and the suffrages of the people being more free, will be more likely to centre in men who possess the most attractive merit and the most diffusive and established characters.

It must be confessed that in this, as in most other cases, there is a mean, on both sides of which inconveniences will be found to lie. By enlarging too much the number of electors, you render the representatives too little acquainted with all their local circumstances and lesser interests; as by reducing it too much, you render him unduly attached to these, and too little fit to comprehend and pursue great and national objects. The federal Constitution forms a happy combination in this respect; the great and aggregate interests being referred to the national, the local and particular to the State legislatures.

The other point of difference is, the greater number of citizens and extent of territory which may be brought within the compass of republican than of democratic government; and it is this circumstance principally which renders factious combinations less to be dreaded in the former than in the latter. The smaller the society, the fewer probably will be the distinct parties and interests composing it; the fewer the distinct parties and interests, the more frequently will a majority be found of the same party; and the smaller the number of individuals composing a majority, and the smaller the compass within which they are placed, the more easily will they concert and execute their plans of oppression. Extend the sphere, and you take in a greater variety of parties and interests; you make it less probable that a majority of the whole will have a common motive to invade the rights of other citizens; or if such a common motive exists, it will be more difficult for all who feel it to discover their own strength, and to act in unison with each other. Besides other impediments, it may be remarked that, where there is a consciousness of unjust or dishonorable purposes, communication is always checked by distrust in proportion to the number whose concurrence is necessary.

Hence, it clearly appears, that the same advantage which a republic has over a democracy, in controlling the effects of faction, is enjoyed by a large over a small republic,—is enjoyed by the Union over the States composing it. Does the advantage consist in the substitution of representatives whose enlightened views and virtuous sentiments render them superior to local prejudices and schemes of injustice? It will not be denied that the representation of the Union will be most likely to possess these requisite endowments. Does it consist in the greater security afforded by a greater variety of parties, against the event of any one party being able to outnumber and oppress the rest? In an equal degree does the increased variety of parties comprised within the Union, increase this security. Does it, in fine, consist in the greater obstacles opposed to the concert and accomplishment of the secret wishes of an unjust and interested majority? Here, again, the extent of the Union gives it the most palpable advantage.

The influence of factious leaders may kindle a flame within their particular States, but will be unable to spread a general conflagration through the other States. A religious sect may degenerate into a political faction in a part of the Confederacy; but the variety of sects dispersed over the entire face of it must secure the national councils against any danger from that source. A rage for paper money, for an abolition of debts, for an equal division of property, or for any other improper or wicked project, will be less apt to pervade the whole body of the Union than a particular member of it; in the same proportion as such a malady is more likely to taint a particular county or district, than an entire State.

In the extent and proper structure of the Union, therefore, we behold a republican remedy for the diseases most incident to republican government. And according to the degree of pleasure and pride we feel in being republicans, ought to be our zeal in cherishing the spirit and supporting the character of Federalists.

7

The Utility of the Union in Respect to Commercial Relations and a Navy

To the People of the State of New York:

THE importance of the Union, in a commercial light, is one of those points about which there is least room to entertain a difference of opinion, and which has, in fact, commanded the most general assent of men who have any acquaintance with the subject. This applies as well to our intercourse with foreign countries as with each other.

There are appearances to authorize a supposition that the adventurous spirit, which distinguishes the commercial character of America, has already excited uneasy sensations in several of the maritime powers of Europe. They seem to be apprehensive of our too great interference in that carrying trade, which is the support of their navigation and the foundation of their naval strength. Those of them which have colonies in America look forward to what this country is capable of becoming, with painful solicitude. They foresee the dangers that may threaten their American dominions from the neighborhood of States, which have all the dispositions, and would possess all the means, requisite to the creation of a powerful marine. Impressions of this kind will naturally indicate the policy of fostering divisions among us, and of depriving us, as far as possible, of an **ACTIVE COMMERCE** in our own bottoms. This would answer the threefold purpose of preventing our interference in their navigation, of monopolizing the profits of our trade, and of clipping the wings by which we might soar to a dangerous greatness. Did not prudence forbid the detail, it would not be difficult to trace, by facts, the workings of this policy to the cabinets of ministers.

If we continue united, we may counteract a policy so unfriendly to our prosperity in a variety of ways. By prohibitory regulations, extending, at the same time, throughout the States, we may oblige foreign countries to bid against each other, for the privileges of our markets. This assertion will not appear chimerical to those who are able to appreciate the importance of the markets of three millions of people—increasing in rapid progression, for the most part exclusively addicted to agriculture, and likely from local circumstances to remain so—to any manufacturing nation; and the immense difference there would be to the trade and navigation of such a nation, between a direct communication in its own ships, and an indirect conveyance of its products and returns, to and from America, in the ships of another country. Suppose, for instance, we had a government in America, capable of excluding Great Britain (with whom we have at present no treaty of commerce) from all our ports; what would be the probable operation of this step upon her politics? Would it not enable us to negotiate, with the fairest prospect of success, for commercial privileges of the most valuable and extensive kind, in the dominions of that kingdom? When these questions have been asked, upon other occasions, they have received a plausible, but not a solid or satisfactory answer. It has been said that prohibitions on our part would produce no change in the system of Britain, because she could prosecute her trade with us through the medium of the Dutch, who would be her immediate customers and paymasters for those articles which were wanted for the supply of our markets. But would not her navigation be materially injured by the loss of the important advantage of being her own carrier in that trade? Would not the principal part of its profits be intercepted by the Dutch, as a compensation for their agency and risk? Would not the mere circumstance of freight occasion a considerable deduction? Would not so circuitous an intercourse facilitate the competitions of other nations, by enhancing the price of British commodities in our markets, and by transferring to other hands the management of this interesting branch of the British commerce?

A mature consideration of the objects suggested by these questions will justify a belief that the real disadvantages to Britain from such a state of things, conspiring with the pre-possessions of a great part of the nation in favor of the American trade, and with the importunities of the West India islands, would produce a relaxation in her present system, and would let us into the enjoyment of privileges in the markets of those islands elsewhere, from which our trade would derive the most substantial benefits. Such a point gained from the British government, and which could not be expected without an equivalent in exemptions and immunities in our markets, would be likely to have a correspondent effect on the conduct of other nations, who would not be inclined to see themselves altogether supplanted in our trade.

A further resource for influencing the conduct of European nations toward us, in this respect, would arise from the establishment of a federal navy. There can be no doubt that the continuance of the Union under an efficient government would put it in our power, at a period not very distant, to create a navy which, if it could not vie with those of the great maritime powers, would at least be of respectable weight if thrown into the scale of either of two contending parties. This would be more peculiarly the case in relation to operations in the West Indies. A few ships of the line, sent opportunely to the reinforcement of either side, would often be sufficient to decide the fate of a campaign, on the event of which interests of the greatest magnitude were suspended. Our position is, in this respect, a most commanding one. And if to this consideration we add that of the usefulness of supplies from this country, in the prosecution of military operations in the West Indies, it will readily be perceived that a situation so favorable would enable us to bargain with great advantage for commercial privileges. A price would be set not only upon our friendship, but upon our neutrality. By a steady adherence to the Union we may hope, erelong, to become the arbiter of Europe in America, and to be able to incline the balance of European competitions in this part of the world as our interest may dictate.

But in the reverse of this eligible situation, we shall discover that the rivalships of the parts would make them checks upon each other, and would frustrate all the tempting advantages which nature has kindly placed within our reach. In a state so insignificant our commerce would be a prey to the wanton intermeddlings of all nations at war with each other; who, having nothing to fear from us, would with little scruple or remorse, supply their wants by depredations on our property as often as it fell in their way. The rights of neutrality will only be respected when they are defended by an adequate power. A nation, despicable by its weakness, forfeits even the privilege of being neutral.

Under a vigorous national government, the natural strength and resources of the country, directed to a common interest, would baffle all the combinations of European jealousy to restrain our growth. This situation would even take away the motive to such combinations, by inducing an impracticability of success. An active commerce, an extensive navigation, and a flourishing marine would then be the offspring of moral and physical necessity. We might defy the little arts of the little politicians to control or vary the irresistible and unchangeable course of nature.

But in a state of disunion, these combinations might exist and might operate with success. It would be in the power of the maritime nations, availing themselves of our universal impotence, to prescribe the conditions of our political existence; and as they have a common interest in being our carriers, and still more in preventing our becoming theirs, they would in all probability combine to embarrass our navigation in such a manner as would in effect destroy it, and confine us to a **PASSIVE COMMERCE**. We should then be compelled to content ourselves with the first price of our commodities, and to see the profits of our trade snatched from us to enrich our enemies and p rsecutors. That unequaled spirit of enterprise, which signalizes the genius of the American merchants and navigators, and which is in itself an inexhaustible mine of national wealth, would be stifled and lost, and poverty and disgrace would overspread a country which, with wisdom, might make herself the admiration and envy of the world.

There are rights of great moment to the trade of America which are rights of the Union—I allude to the fisheries, to the navigation of the Western lakes, and to that of the Mississippi. The dissolution of the Confederacy would give room for delicate questions concerning the future existence of these rights; which the interest of more powerful partners would hardly fail to solve to our disadvantage. The disposition of Spain with regard to the Mississippi needs no comment. France and Britain are concerned with us in the fisheries, and view them as of the utmost moment to their navigation. They, of course, would hardly remain long indifferent to that decided mastery, of which experience has shown us to be possessed in this valuable branch of traffic, and by which we are able to undersell those nations in their own markets. What more natural than that they should be disposed to exclude from the lists such dangerous competitors?

This branch of trade ought not to be considered as a partial benefit. All the navigating States may, in different degrees, advantageously participate in it, and under circumstances of a greater extension of mercantile capital, would not be unlikely to do it. As a nursery of seamen, it now is, or when time shall have more nearly assimilated the principles of navigation in the several States, will become, a universal resource. To the establishment of a navy, it must be indispensable.

To this great national object, a **NAVY**, union will contribute in various ways. Every institution will grow and flourish in proportion to the quantity and extent of the means concentred towards its formation and support. A navy of the United States, as it would embrace the resources of all, is an object far less remote than a navy of any single State or partial confederacy, which would only embrace the resources of a single part. It happens, indeed, that different portions of confederated America possess each some peculiar advantage for this essential establishment. The more southern States furnish in greater abundance certain kinds of naval stores—tar, pitch, and turpentine. Their wood for the construction of ships is also of a more solid and lasting texture. The difference in the duration of the ships of which the navy might be composed, if chiefly constructed of Southern wood, would be of signal importance, either in the view of naval strength or of national economy. Some of the Southern and of the Middle States yield a greater plenty of iron, and of better quality. Seamen must chiefly be drawn from the Northern hive. The necessity of naval protection to external or maritime commerce does not require a particular elucidation, no more than the conduciveness of that species of commerce to the prosperity of a navy. An unrestrained intercourse between the States themselves will advance the trade of each by an interchange of their respective productions, not only for the supply of reciprocal wants at home, but for exportation to foreign markets. The veins of commerce in every part will be replenished, and will acquire additional motion and vigor from a free circulation of the commodities of every part. Commercial enterprise will have much greater scope, from the diversity in the productions of different States. When the staple of one fails from a bad harvest or unproductive crop, it can call to its aid the staple of another. The variety, not less than the value, of products for exportation contributes to the activity of foreign commerce. It can be conducted upon much better terms with a large number of materials of a given value than with a small number of materials of the same value; arising from the competitions of trade and from the fluctations of markets. Particular articles may be in great demand at certain periods, and unsalable at others; but if there be a variety of articles, it can scarcely happen that they should all be at one time in the latter predicament, and on this account the operations of the merchant would be less liable to any considerable obstruction or stagnation. The speculative trader will at once perceive the force of these observations, and will acknowledge that the aggregate balance of the commerce of the United States would bid fair to be much more favorable than that of the thirteen States without union or with partial unions.

It may perhaps be replied to this, that whether the States are united or disunited, there would still be an intimate intercourse between them which would answer the same ends; this intercourse would be fettered, interrupted, and narrowed by a multiplicity of causes, which in the course of these papers have been amply detailed.

A unity of commercial, as well as political, interests, can only result from a unity of government.

There are other points of view in which this subject might be placed, of a striking and animating kind. But they would lead us too far into the regions of futurity, and would involve topics not proper for a newspaper discussion. I shall briefly observe, that our situation invites and our interests prompt us to aim at an ascendant in the system of American affairs. The world may politically, as well as geographically, be divided into four parts, each having a distinct set of interests. Unhappily for the other three, Europe, by her arms and by her negotiations, by force and by fraud, has, in different degrees, extended her dominion over them all. Africa, Asia, and America, have successively felt her domination. The superiority she has long maintained has tempted her to plume herself as the Mistress of the World, and to consider the rest of mankind as created for her benefit. Men admired as profound philosophers have, in direct terms, attributed to her inhabitants a physical superiority, and have gravely asserted that all animals, and with them the human species, degenerate in America—that even dogs cease to bark after having breathed awhile in our atmosphere.[1] Facts have too long supported these arrogant pretensions of the Europeans. It belongs to us to vindicate the honor of the human race, and to teach that assuming brother, moderation. Union will enable us to do it. Disunion will will add another victim to his triumphs. Let Americans disdain to be the instruments of European greatness! Let the thirteen States, bound together in a strict and indissoluble Union, concur in erecting one great American system, superior to the control of all transatlantic force or influence, and able to dictate the terms of the connection between the old and the new world!

The Utility of the Union In Respect to Revenue
From the New York Packet. Tuesday, November 27, 1787.
HAMILTON

To the People of the State of New York:

THE effects of Union upon the commercial prosperity of the States have been sufficiently delineated. Its tendency to promote the interests of revenue will be the subject of our present inquiry. The prosperity of commerce is now perceived and acknowledged by all enlightened statesmen to be the most useful as well as the most productive source of national wealth, and has accordingly become a primary object of their political cares. By multipying the means of gratification, by promoting the introduction and circulation of the precious metals, those darling objects of human avarice and enterprise, it serves to vivify and invigorate the channels of industry, and to make them flow with greater activity and copiousness. The assiduous merchant, the laborious husbandman, the active mechanic, and the industrious manufacturer,—all orders of men, look forward with eager expectation and growing alacrity to this pleasing reward of their toils. The often-agitated question between agriculture and commerce has, from indubitable experience, received a decision which has silenced the rivalship that once subsisted between them, and has proved, to the satisfaction of their friends, that their interests are intimately blended and interwoven. It has been found in various countries that, in proportion as commerce has flourished, land has risen in value. And how could it have happened otherwise? Could that which procures a freer vent for the products of the earth, which furnishes new incitements to the cultivation of land, which is the most powerful instrument in increasing the quantity of money in a state—could that, in fine, which is the faithful handmaid of labor and industry, in every shape, fail to augment that article, which is the prolific parent of far the greatest part of the objects upon which they are exerted? It is astonishing that so simple a truth should ever have had an adversary; and it is one, among a multitude of proofs, how apt a spirit of ill-informed jealousy, or of too great abstraction and refinement, is to lead men astray from the plainest truths of reason and conviction.

The ability of a country to pay taxes must always be proportioned, in a great degree, to the quantity of money in circulation, and to the celerity with which it circulates. Commerce, contributing to both these objects, must of necessity render the payment of taxes easier, and facilitate the requisite supplies to the treasury. The hereditary dominions of the Emperor of Germany contain a great extent of fertile, cultivated, and populous territory, a large proportion of which is situated in mild and luxuriant climates. In some parts of this territory are to be found the best gold and silver mines in Europe. And yet, from the want of the fostering influence of commerce, that monarch can boast but slender revenues. He has several times been compelled to owe obligations to the pecuniary succors of other nations for the preservation of his essential interests, and is unable, upon the strength of his own resources, to sustain a long or continued war.

But it is not in this aspect of the subject alone that Union will be seen to conduce to the purpose of revenue. There are other points of view, in which its influence will appear more immediate and decisive. It is evident from the state of the country, from the habits of the people, from the experience we have had on the point itself, that it is impracticable to raise any very considerable sums by direct taxation. Tax laws have in vain been multiplied; new methods to enforce the collection have in vain been tried; the public expectation has been uniformly disappointed, and the treasuries of the States have remained empty. The popular system of administration inherent in the nature of popular government, coinciding with the real scarcity of money incident to a languid and mutilated state of trade, has hitherto defeated every experiment for extensive collections, and has at length taught the different legislatures the folly of attempting them.

No person acquainted with what happens in other countries will be surprised at this circumstance. In so opulent a nation as that of Britain, where direct taxes from superior wealth must be much more tolerable, and, from the vigor of the government, much more practicable, than in America, far the greatest part of the national revenue is derived from taxes of the indirect kind, from imposts, and from excises. Duties on imported articles form a large branch of this latter description.

In America, it is evident that we must a long time depend for the means of revenue chiefly on such duties. In most parts of it, excises must be confined within a narrow compass. The genius of the people will ill brook the inquisitive and peremptory spirit of excise laws. The pockets of the farmers, on the other hand, will reluctantly yield but scanty supplies, in the unwelcome shape of impositions on their houses and lands; and personal property is too precarious and invisible a fund to be laid hold of in any other way than by the inperceptible agency of taxes on consumption.

If these remarks have any foundation, that state of things which will best enable us to improve and extend so valuable a resource must be best adapted to our political welfare. And it cannot admit of a serious doubt, that this state of things must rest on the basis of a general Union. As far as this would be conducive to the interests of commerce, so far it must tend to the extension of the revenue to be drawn from that source. As far as it would contribute to rendering regulations for the collection of the duties more simple and efficacious, so far it must serve to answer the purposes of making the same rate of duties more productive, and of putting it into the power of the government to increase the rate without prejudice to trade.

The relative situation of these States; the number of rivers with which they are intersected, and of bays that wash there shores; the facility of communication in every direction; the affinity of language and manners; the familiar habits of intercourse; —all these are circumstances that would conspire to render an illicit trade between them a matter of little difficulty, and would insure frequent evasions of the commercial regulations of each other. The separate States or confederacies would be necessitated by mutual jealousy to avoid the temptations to that kind of trade by the lowness of their duties. The temper of our governments, for a long time to come, would not permit those rigorous precautions by which the European nations guard the avenues into their respective countries, as well by land as by water; and which, even there, are found insufficient obstacles to the adventurous stratagems of avarice.

In France, there is an army of patrols (as they are called) constantly employed to secure their fiscal regulations against the inroads of the dealers in contraband trade. Mr. Neckar computes the number of these patrols at upwards of twenty thousand. This shows the immense difficulty in preventing that species of traffic, where there is an inland communication, and places in a strong light the disadvantages with which the collection of duties in this country would be encumbered, if by disunion the States should be placed in a situation, with respect to each other, resembling that of France with respect to her neighbors. The arbitrary and vexatious powers with which the patrols are necessarily armed, would be intolerable in a free country.

If, on the contrary, there be but one government pervading all the States, there will be, as to the principal part of our commerce, but **ONE SIDE** to guard—the **ATLANTIC COAST**. Vessels arriving directly from foreign countries, laden with valuable cargoes, would rarely choose to hazard themselves to the complicated and critical perils which would attend attempts to unlade prior to their coming into port. They would have to dread both the dangers of the coast, and of detection, as well after as before their arrival at the places of their final destination. An ordinary degree of vigilance would be competent to the prevention of any material infractions upon the rights of the revenue. A few armed vessels, judiciously stationed at the entrances of our ports, might at a small expense be made useful sentinels of the laws. And the government having the same interest to provide against violations everywhere, the co-operation of its measures in each State would have a powerful tendency to render them effectual. Here also we should preserve by Union, an advantage which nature holds out to us, and which would be relinquished by separation. The United States lie at a great distance from Europe, and at a considerable distance from all other places with which they would have extensive connections of foreign trade. The passage from them to us, in a few hours, or in a single night, as between the coasts of France and Britain, and of other neighboring nations, would be impracticable. This is a prodigious security against a direct contraband with foreign countries; but a circuitous contraband to one State, through the medium of another, would be both easy and safe. The difference between a direct importation from abroad, and an indirect importation through the channel of a neighboring State, in small parcels, according to time and opportunity, with the additional facilities of inland communication, must be palpable to every man of discernment.

It is therefore evident, that one national government would be able, at much less expense, to extend the duties on imports, beyond comparison, further than would be practicable to the States separately, or to any partial confederacies. Hitherto, I believe, it may safely be asserted, that these duties have not upon an average exceeded in any State three per cent. In France they are estimated to be about fifteen per cent., and in Britain they exceed this proportion.1 There seems to be nothing to hinder their being increased in this country to at least treble their present amount. The single article of ardent spirits, under federal regulation, might be made to furnish a considerable revenue. Upon a ratio to the importation into this State, the whole quantity imported into the United States may be estimated at four millions of gallons; which, at a shilling per gallon, would produce two hundred thousand pounds. That article would well bear this rate of duty; and if it should tend to diminish the consumption of it, such an effect would be equally favorable to the agriculture, to the economy, to the morals, and to the health of the society. There is, perhaps, nothing so much a subject of national extravagance as these spirits.

What will be the consequence, if we are not able to avail ourselves of the resource in question in its full extent? A nation cannot long exist without revenues. Destitute of this essential support, it must resign its independence, and sink into the degraded condition of a province. This is an extremity to which no government will of choice accede. Revenue, therefore, must be had at all events. In this country, if the principal part be not drawn from commerce, it must fall with oppressive weight upon land. It has been already intimated that excises, in their true signification, are too little in unison with the feelings of the people, to admit of great use being made of that mode of taxation; nor, indeed, in the States where almost the sole employment is agriculture, are the objects proper for excise sufficiently numerous to permit very ample collections in that way. Personal estate (as has been before remarked), from the difficulty in tracing it, cannot be subjected to large contributions, by any other means than by taxes on consumption. In populous cities, it may be enough the subject of conjecture, to occasion the oppression of individuals, without much aggregate benefit to the

State; but beyond these circles, it must, in a great measure, escape the eye and the hand of the tax-gatherer. As the necessities of the State, nevertheless, must be satisfied in some mode or other, the defect of other resources must throw the principal weight of public burdens on the possessors of land. And as, on the other hand, the wants of the government can never obtain an adequate supply, unless all the sources of revenue are open to its demands, the finances of the community, under such embarrassments, cannot be put into a situation consistent with its respectability or its security. Thus we shall not even have the consolations of a full treasury, to atone for the oppression of that valuable class of the citizens who are employed in the cultivation of the soil. But public and private distress will keep pace with each other in gloomy concert; and unite in deploring the infatuation of those counsels which led to disunion.

Advantage of the Union in Respect to Economy in Government

For the Independent Journal.

HAMILTON

To the People of the State of New York:

As **CONNECTED** with the subject of revenue, we may with propriety consider that of economy. The money saved from one object may be usefully applied to another, and there will be so much the less to be drawn from the pockets of the people. If the States are united under one government, there will be but one national civil list to support; if they are divided into several confederacies, there will be as many different national civil lists to be provided for—and each of them, as to the principal departments, coextensive with that which would be necessary for a government of the whole. The entire separation of the States into thirteen unconnected sovereignties is a project too extravagant and too replete with danger to have many advocates. The ideas of men who speculate upon the dismemberment of the empire seem generally turned toward three confederacies—one consisting of the four Northern, another of the four Middle, and a third of the five Southern States. There is little probability that there would be a greater number. According to this distribution, each confederacy would comprise an extent of territory larger than that of the kingdom of Great Britain. No well-informed man will suppose that the affairs of such a confederacy can be properly regulated by a government less comprehensive in its organs or institutions than that which has been proposed by the convention. When the dimensions of a State attain to a certain magnitude, it requires the same energy of government and the same forms of administration which are requisite in one of much greater extent. This idea admits not of precise demonstration, because there is no rule by which we can measure the momentum of civil power necessary to the government of any given number of individuals; but when we consider that the island of Britain, nearly commensurate with each of the supposed confederacies, contains about eight millions of people, and when we reflect upon the degree of authority required to direct the passions of so large a society to the public good, we shall see no reason to doubt that the like portion of power would be sufficient to perform the same task in a society far more numerous. Civil power, properly organized and exerted, is capable of diffusing its force to a very great extent; and can, in a manner, reproduce itself in every part of a great empire by a judicious arrangement of subordinate institutions.

The supposition that each confederacy into which the States would be likely to be divided would require a government not less comprehensive than the one proposed, will be strengthened by another supposition, more probable than that which presents us with three confederacies as the alternative to a general Union. If we attend carefully to geographical and commercial considerations, in conjunction with the habits and prejudices of the different States, we shall be led to conclude that in case of disunion they will most naturally league themselves under two governments.

The four Eastern States, from all the causes that form the links of national sympathy and connection, may with certainty be expected to unite. New York, situated as she is, would never be unwise enough to oppose a feeble and unsupported flank to the weight of that confederacy. There are other obvious reasons that would facilitate her accession to it. New Jersey is too small a State to think of being a frontier, in opposition to this still more powerful combination; nor do there appear to be any obstacles to her admission into it. Even Pennsylvania would have strong inducements to join the Northern league. An active foreign commerce, on the basis of her own navigation, is her true policy, and coincides with the opinions and dispositions of her citizens.

The more Southern States, from various circumstances, may not think themselves much interested in the encouragement of navigation. They may prefer a system which would give unlimited scope to all nations to be the carriers as well as the purchasers of their commodities. Pennsylvania may not choose to confound her interests in a connection so adverse to her policy. As she must at all events be a frontier, she may deem it most consistent with her safety to have her exposed side turned towards the weaker power of the Southern, rather than towards the stronger power of the Northern, Confederacy. This would give her the fairest chance to avoid being the Flanders of America. Whatever may be the determination of Pennsylvania, if the Northern Confederacy includes New Jersey, there is no likelihood of more than one confederacy to the south of that State.

Nothing can be more evident than that the thirteen States will be able to support a national government better than one half, or one third, or any number less than the whole. This reflection must have great weight in obviating that objection to the proposed plan, which is founded on the principle of expense; an objection, however, which, when we come to take a nearer view of it, will appear in every light to stand on mistaken ground.

If, in addition to the consideration of a plurality of civil lists, we take into view the number of persons who must necessarily be employed to guard the inland communication between the different confederacies against illicit trade, and who in time will infallibly spring up out of the necessities of revenue; and if we also take into view the military establishments which it has been shown would unavoidably result from the jealousies and conflicts of the several nations into which the States would be divided, we shall clearly discover that a separation would be not less injurious to the economy, than to the tranquillity, commerce, revenue, and liberty of every part.

Objections to the Proposed Constitution From Extent of Territory Answered

From the New York Packet. Friday, November 30, 1787.

MADISON

To the People of the State of New York:

WE HAVE seen the necessity of the Union, as our bulwark against foreign danger, as the conservator of peace among ourselves, as the guardian of our commerce and other common interests, as the only substitute for those military establishments which have subverted the liberties of the Old World, and as the proper antidote for the diseases of faction, which have proved fatal to other popular governments, and of which alarming symptoms have been betrayed by our own. All that remains, within this branch of our inquiries, is to take notice of an objection that may be drawn from the great extent of country which the Union embraces. A few observations on this subject will be the more proper, as it is perceived that the adversaries of the new Constitution are availing themselves of the prevailing prejudice with regard to the practicable sphere of republican administration, in order to supply, by imaginary difficulties, the want of those solid objections which they endeavor in vain to find.

The error which limits republican government to a narrow district has been unfolded and refuted in preceding papers. I remark here only that it seems to owe its rise and prevalence chiefly to the confounding of a republic with a democracy, applying to the former reasonings drawn from the nature of the latter. The true distinction between these forms was also adverted to on a former occasion. It is, that in a democracy, the people meet and exercise the government in person; in a republic, they assemble and administer it by their representatives and agents. A democracy, consequently, will be confined to a small spot. A republic may be extended over a large region.

To this accidental source of the error may be added the artifice of some celebrated authors, whose writings have had a great share in forming the modern standard of political opinions. Being subjects either of an absolute or limited monarchy, they have endeavored to heighten the advantages, or palliate the evils of those forms, by placing in comparison the vices and defects of the republican, and by citing as specimens of the latter the turbulent democracies of ancient Greece and modern Italy. Under the confusion of names, it has been an easy task to transfer to a republic observations applicable to a democracy only; and among others, the observation that it can never be established but among a small number of people, living within a small compass of territory.

Such a fallacy may have been the less perceived, as most of the popular governments of antiquity were of the democratic species; and even in modern Europe, to which we owe the great principle of representation, no example is seen of a government wholly popular, and founded, at the same time, wholly on that principle. If Europe has the merit of discovering this great mechanical power in government, by the simple agency of which the will of the largest political body may be concentred, and its force directed to any object which the public good requires, America can claim the merit of making the discovery the basis of unmixed and extensive republics. It is only to be lamented that any of her citizens should wish to deprive her of the additional merit of displaying its full efficacy in the establishment of the comprehensive system now under her consideration.

As the natural limit of a democracy is that distance from the central point which will just permit the most remote citizens to assemble as often as their public functions demand, and will include no greater number than can join in those functions; so the natural limit of a republic is that distance from the centre which will barely allow the representatives to meet as often as may be necessary for the administration of public affairs. Can it be said that the limits of the United States exceed this distance? It will not be said by those who recollect that the Atlantic coast is the longest side of the Union, that during the term of thirteen years, the representatives of the States have been almost continually assembled, and that the members from the most distant States are not chargeable with greater intermissions of attendance than those from the States in the neighborhood of Congress.

That we may form a juster estimate with regard to this interesting subject, let us resort to the actual dimensions of the Union. The limits, as fixed by the treaty of peace, are: on the east the Atlantic, on the south the latitude of thirty-one degrees, on the west the Mississippi, and on the north an irregular line running in some instances beyond the forty-fifth degree, in others falling as low as the forty-second. The southern shore of Lake Erie lies below that latitude. Computing the distance between the thirty-first and forty-fifth degrees, it amounts to nine hundred and seventy-three common miles; computing it from thirty-one to forty-two degrees, to seven hundred and sixty-four miles and a half. Taking the mean for the distance, the amount will be eight hundred and sixty-eight miles and three-fourths. The mean distance from the Atlantic to the Mississippi does not probably exceed seven hundred and fifty miles. On a comparison of this extent with that of several countries in Europe, the practicability of rendering our system commensurate to it appears to be demonstrable. It is not a great deal larger than Germany, where a diet representing the whole empire is continually assembled; or than Poland before the late dismemberment, where another national diet was the depositary of the supreme power. Passing by France and Spain, we find that in Great Britain, inferior as it may be in size, the representatives of the northern extremity of the island have as far to travel to the national council as will be required of those of the most remote parts of the Union.

Favorable as this view of the subject may be, some observations remain which will place it in a light still more satisfactory.

In the first place it is to be remembered that the general government is not to be charged with the whole power of making and administering laws. Its jurisdiction is limited to certain enumerated objects, which concern all the members of the republic, but which are not to be attained by the separate provisions of any. The subordinate governments, which can extend their care to all those other subjects which can be separately provided for, will retain their due authority and activity. Were it proposed by the plan of the convention to abolish the governments of the particular States, its adversaries would have some ground for their objection; though it would not be difficult to show that if they were abolished the general government would be compelled, by the principle of self-preservation, to reinstate them in their proper jurisdiction.

A second observation to be made is that the immediate object of the federal Constitution is to secure the union of the thirteen primitive States, which we know to be practicable; and to add to them such other States as may arise in their own bosoms, or in their neighborhoods, which we cannot doubt to be equally practicable. The arrangements that may be necessary for those angles and fractions of our territory which lie on our northwestern frontier, must be left to those whom further discoveries and experience will render more equal to the task.

Let it be remarked, in the third place, that the intercourse throughout the Union will be facilitated by new improvements. Roads will everywhere be shortened, and kept in better order; accommodations for travelers will be multiplied and meliorated; an interior navigation on our eastern side will be opened throughout, or nearly throughout, the whole extent of the thirteen States. The communication between the Western and Atlantic districts, and between different parts of each, will be rendered more and more easy by those numerous canals with which the beneficence of nature has intersected our country, and which part finds it so little difficult to connect and complete.

A fourth and still more important consideration is, that as almost every State will, on one side or other, be a frontier, and will thus find, in regard to its safety, an inducement to make some sacrifices for the sake of the general protection; so the States which lie at the greatest distance from the heart of the Union, and which, of course, may partake least of the ordinary circulation of its benefits, will be at the same time immediately contiguous to foreign nations, and will consequently stand, on particular occasions, in greatest need of its strength and resources. It may be inconvenient for Georgia, or the States forming our western or northeastern borders, to send their representatives to the seat of government; but they would find it more so to struggle alone against an invading enemy, or even to support alone the whole expense of those precautions which may be dictated by the neighborhood of continual danger. If they should derive less benefit, therefore, from the Union in some respects than the less distant States, they will derive greater benefit from it in other respects, and thus the proper equilibrium will be maintained throughout.

I submit to you, my fellow-citizens, these considerations, in full confidence that the good sense which has so often marked your decisions will allow them their due weight and effect; and that you will never suffer difficulties, however formidable in appearance, or however fashionable the error on which they may be founded, to drive you into the gloomy and perilous scene into which the advocates for disunion would conduct you. Hearken not to the unnatural voice which tells you that the people of America, knit together as they are by so many cords of affection, can no longer live together as members of the same family; can no longer continue the mutual guardians of their mutual happiness; can no longer be fellowcitizens of one great, respectable, and flourishing empire. Hearken not to the voice which petulantly tells you that the form of government recommended for your adoption is a novelty in the political world; that it has never yet had a place in the theories of the wildest projectors; that it rashly attempts what it is impossible to accomplish. No, my countrymen, shut your ears against this unhallowed language. Shut your hearts against the poison which it conveys; the kindred blood which flows in the veins of American citizens, the mingled blood which they have shed in defense of their sacred rights, consecrate their Union, and excite horror at the idea of their becoming aliens, rivals, enemies. And if novelties are to be shunned, believe me, the most alarming of all novelties, the most wild of all projects, the most rash of all attempts, is that of rendering us in pieces, in order to preserve our liberties and promote our happiness. But why is the experiment of an extended republic to be rejected, merely because it may comprise what is new? Is it not the glory of the people of America, that, whilst they have paid a decent regard to the opinions of former times and other nations, they have not suffered a blind veneration for antiquity, for custom, or for names, to overrule the suggestions of their own good sense, the knowledge of their own situation, and the lessons of their own experience? To this manly spirit, posterity will be indebted for the possession, and the world for the example, of the numerous innovations displayed on the American theatre, in favor of private rights and public happiness. Had no important step been taken by the leaders of the Revolution for which a precedent could not be discovered, no government established of which an exact model did not present itself, the people of the United States might, at this moment have been numbered among the melancholy victims of misguided councils, must at best have been laboring under the weight of some of those forms which have crushed the liberties of the rest of mankind. Happily for America, happily, we trust, for the whole human race, they pursued a new and more noble course. They accomplished a revolution which has no parallel in the annals of human society. They reared the fabrics of governments which have no model on the face of the globe. They formed the design of a great Confederacy, which it is incumbent on their successors to improve and perpetuate. If their works betray imperfections, we wonder at the fewness of them. If they erred most in the structure of the Union, this was the work most difficult to be executed; this is the work which has been new modelled by the act of your convention, and it is that act on which you are now to deliberate and to decide.

The Insufficiency of the Present Confederation to Preserve the Union

To the People of the State of New York.

IN THE course of the preceding papers, I have endeavored, my fellow-citizens, to place before you, in a clear and convincing light, the importance of Union to your political safety and happiness. I have unfolded to you a complication of dangers to which you would be exposed, should you permit that sacred knot which binds the people of America together be severed or dissolved by ambition or by avarice, by jealousy or by misrepresentation. In the sequel of the inquiry through which I propose to accompany you, the truths intended to be inculcated will receive further confirmation from facts and arguments hitherto unnoticed. If the road over which you will still have to pass should in some places appear to you tedious or irksome, you will recollect that you are in quest of information on a subject the most momentous which can engage the attention of a free people, that the field through which you have to travel is in itself spacious, and that the difficulties of the journey have been unnecessarily increased by the mazes with which sophistry has beset the way. It will be my aim to remove the obstacles from your progress in as compendious a manner as it can be done, without sacrificing utility to despatch.

In pursuance of the plan which I have laid down for the discussion of the subject, the point next in order to be examined is the "insufficiency of the present Confederation to the preservation of the Union." It may perhaps be asked what need there is of reasoning or proof to illustrate a position which is not either controverted or doubted, to which the understandings and feelings of all classes of men assent, and which in substance is admitted by the opponents as well as by the friends of the new Constitution. It must in truth be acknowledged that, however these may differ in other respects, they in general appear to harmonize in this sentiment, at least, that there are material imperfections in our national system, and that something is necessary to be done to rescue us from impending anarchy. The facts that support this opinion are no longer objects of speculation. They have forced themselves upon the sensibility of the people at large, and have at length extorted from those, whose mistaken policy has had the principal share in precipitating the extremity at which we are arrived, a reluctant confession of the reality of those defects in the scheme of our federal government, which have been long pointed out and regretted by the intelligent friends of the Union.

We may indeed with propriety be said to have reached almost the last stage of national humiliation. There is scarcely anything that can wound the pride or degrade the character of an independent nation which we do not experience. Are there engag ·ments to the performance of which we are held by every tie respectable among men? These are the subjects of constant and unblushing violation. Do we owe debts to foreigners and to our own citizens contracted in a time of imminent peril for the preservation of our political existence? These remain without any proper or satisfactory provision for their discharge. Have we valuable territories and important posts in the possession of a foreign power which, by express stipulations, ought long since to have been surrendered? These are still retained, to the prejudice of our interests, not less than of our rights. Are we in a condition to resent or to repel the aggression? We have neither troops, nor treasury, nor government.

Are we even in a condition to remonstrate with dignity? The just imputations on our own faith, in respect to the same treaty, ought first to be removed. Are we entitled by nature and compact to a free participation in the navigation of the Mississippi? Spain excludes us from it. Is public credit an indispensable resource in time of public danger? We seem to have abandoned its cause as desperate and irretrievable. Is commerce of importance to national wealth? Ours is at the lowest point of declension. Is respectability in the eyes of foreign powers a safeguard against foreign encroachments? The imbecility of our government even forbids them to treat with us. Our ambassadors abroad are the mere pageants of mimic sovereignty. Is a violent and unnatural decrease in the value of land a symptom of national distress?

The price of improved land in most parts of the country is much lower than can be accounted for by the quantity of waste land at market, and can only be fully explained by that want of private and public confidence, which are so alarmingly prevalent among all ranks, and which have a direct tendency to depreciate property of every kind. Is private credit the friend and patron of industry? That most useful kind which relates to borrowing and lending is reduced within the narrowest limits, and this still more from an opinion of insecurity than from the scarcity of money. To shorten an enumeration of particulars which can afford neither pleasure nor instruction, it may in general be demanded, what indication is there of national disorder, poverty, and insignificance that could befall a community so peculiarly blessed with natural advantages as we are, which does not form a part of the dark catalogue of our public misfortunes?

This is the melancholy situation to which we have been brought by those very maxims and councils which would now deter us from adopting the proposed Constitution; and which, not content with having conducted us to the brink of a precipice, seem resolved to plunge us into the abyss that awaits us below. Here, my countrymen, impelled by every motive that ought to influence an enlightened people, let us make a firm stand for our safety, our tranquillity, our dignity, our reputation. Let us at last break the fatal charm which has too long seduced us from the paths of felicity and prosperity.

It is true, as has been before observed that facts, too stubborn to be resisted, have produced a species of general assent to the abstract proposition that there exist material defects in our national system; but the usefulness of the concession, on the part of the old adversaries of federal measures, is destroyed by a strenuous opposition to a remedy, upon the only principles that can give it a chance of success. While they admit that the government of the United States is destitute of energy, they contend against conferring upon it those powers which are requisite to supply that energy. They seem still to aim at things repugnant and irreconcilable; at an augmentation of federal authority, without a diminution of State authority; at sovereignty in the Union, and complete independence in the members. They still, in fine, seem to cherish with blind devotion the political monster of an imperium in imperio. This renders a full display of the principal defects of the Confederation necessary, in order to show that the evils we experience do not proceed from minute or partial imperfections, but from fundamental errors in the structure of the building, which cannot be amended otherwise than by an alteration in the first principles and main pillars of the fabric.

The great and radical vice in the construction of the existing Confederation is in the principle of **LEGISLATION** for **STATES** or **GOVERNMENTS**, in their **CORPORATE** or **COLLECTIVE CAPACITIES**, and as contradistinguished from the **INDIVIDUALS** of which they consist. Though this principle does not run through all the powers delegated to the Union, yet it pervades and governs those on which the efficacy of the rest depends. Except as to the rule of appointment, the United States has an indefinite discretion to make requisitions for men and money; but they have no authority to raise either, by regulations extending to the individual citizens of

America. The consequence of this is, that though in theory their resolutions concerning those objects are laws, constitutionally binding on the members of the Union, yet in practice they are mere recommendations which the States observe or disregard at their option.

It is a singular instance of the capriciousness of the human mind, that after all the admonitions we have had from experience on this head, there should still be found men who object to the new Constitution, for deviating from a principle which has been found the bane of the old, and which is in itself evidently incompatible with the idea of **GOVERNMENT**; a principle, in short, which, if it is to be executed at all, must substitute the violent and sanguinary agency of the sword to the mild influence of the magistracy.

There is nothing absurd or impracticable in the idea of a league or alliance between independent nations for certain defined purposes precisely stated in a treaty regulating all the details of time, place, circumstance, and quantity; leaving nothing to future discretion; and depending for its execution on the good faith of the parties. Compacts of this kind exist among all civilized nations, subject to the usual vicissitudes of peace and war, of observance and non-observance, as the interests or passions of the contracting powers dictate. In the early part of the present century there was an epidemical rage in Europe for this species of compacts, from which the politicians of the times fondly hoped for benefits which were never realized. With a view to establishing the equilibrium of power and the peace of that part of the world, all the resources of negotiation were exhausted, and triple and quadruple alliances were formed; but they were scarcely formed before they were broken, giving an instructive but afflicting lesson to mankind, how little dependence is to be placed on treaties which have no other sanction than the obligations of good faith, and which oppose general considerations of peace and justice to the impulse of any immediate interest or passion.

If the particular States in this country are disposed to stand in a similar relation to each other, and to drop the project of a general **DISCRETIONARY SUPERINTENDENCE**, the scheme would indeed be pernicious, and would entail upon us all the mischiefs which have been enumerated under the first head; but it would have the merit of being, at least, consistent and practicable Abandoning all views towards a confederate government, this would bring us to a simple alliance offensive and defensive; and would place us in a situation to be alternate friends and enemies of each other, as our mutual jealousies and rivalships, nourished by the intrigues of foreign nations, should prescribe to us.

But if we are unwilling to be placed in this perilous situation; if we still will adhere to the design of a national government, or, which is the same thing, of a superintending power, under the direction of a common council, we must resolve to incorporate into our plan those ingredients which may be considered as forming the characteristic difference between a league and a government; we must extend the authority of the Union to the persons of the citizens, —the only proper objects of government.

Government implies the power of making laws. It is essential to the idea of a law, that it be attended with a sanction; or, in other words, a penalty or punishment for disobedience. If there be no penalty annexed to disobedience, the resolutions or commands which pretend to be laws will, in fact, amount to nothing more than advice or recommendation. This penalty, whatever it may be, can only be inflicted in two ways: by the agency of the courts and ministers of justice, or by military force; by the **COERCION** of the magistracy, or by the **COERCION** of arms. The first kind can evidently apply only to men; the last kind must of necessity, be employed against bodies politic, or communities, or States. It is evident that there is no process of a court by which the observance of the laws can, in the last resort, be enforced. Sentences may be denounced against them for violations of their duty; but these sentences can only be carried into execution by the sword. In an association where the general authority is confined to the collective bodies of the communities, that compose it, every breach of the laws must involve a state of war; and military execution must become the only instrument of civil obedience. Such a state of things can certainly not deserve the name of government, nor would any prudent man choose to commit his happiness to it.

There was a time when we were told that breaches, by the States, of the regulations of the federal authority were not to be expected; that a sense of common interest would preside over the conduct of the respective members, and would beget a full compliance with all the constitutional requisitions of the Union. This language, at the present day, would appear as wild as a great part of what we now hear from the same quarter will be thought, when we shall have received further lessons from that best oracle of wisdom, experience. It at all times betrayed an ignorance of the true springs by which human conduct is actuated, and belied the original inducements to the establishment of civil power. Why has government been instituted at all? Because the passions of men will not conform to the dictates of reason and justice, without constraint. Has it been found that bodies of men act with more rectitude or greater disinterestedness than individuals? The contrary of this has been inferred by all accurate observers of the conduct of mankind; and the inference is founded upon obvious reasons. Regard to reputation has a less active influence, when the infamy of a bad action is to be divided among a number than when it is to fall singly upon one. A spirit of faction, which is apt to mingle its poison in the deliberations of all bodies of men, will often hurry the persons of whom they are composed into improprieties and excesses, for which they would blush in a private capacity.

In addition to all this, there is, in the nature of sovereign power, an impatience of control, that disposes those who are invested with the exercise of it, to look with an evil eye upon all external attempts to restrain or direct its operations. From this spirit it happens, that in every political association which is formed upon the principle of uniting in a common interest a number of lesser sovereignties, there will be found a kind of eccentric tendency in the subordinate or inferior orbs, by the operation of which there will be a perpetual effort in each to fly off from the common centre. This tendency is not difficult to be accounted for. It has its origin in the love of power. Power controlled or abridged is almost always the rival and enemy of that power by which it is controlled or abridged. This simple proposition will teach us how little reason there is to expect, that the persons intrusted with the administration of the affairs of the particular members of a confederacy will at all times be ready, with perfect good-humor, and an unbiased regard to the public weal, to execute the resolutions or decrees of the general authority. The reverse of this results from the constitution of human nature.

If, therefore, the measures of the Confederacy cannot be executed without the intervention of the particular administrations, there will be little prospect of their being executed at all. The rulers of the respective members, whether they have a constitutional right to do it or not, will undertake to judge of the propriety of the measures themselves. They will consider the conformity of the thing proposed or required to their immediate interests or aims; the momentary conveniences or inconveniences that would attend its adoption. All this will be done; and in a spirit of interested and suspicious scrutiny, without that knowledge of national circumstances and reasons of state, which is essential to a right judgment, and with that strong predilection in favor of local objects, which can hardly fail to mislead the decision. The same process must be repeated in every member of which the body is constituted; and the execution of the plans, framed by the councils of the whole, will always fluctuate on the discretion of the ill-informed and prejudiced opinion of every part. Those who have been conversant in the proceedings of popular assemblies; who have seen how difficult it often is, where there is no exterior pressure of circumstances, to bring them to harmonious resolutions on important points, will readily conceive how impossible it must be to induce a number of such assemblies, deliberating at a distance from each other, at different times, and under different impressions, long to co-operate in the same views and pursuits.

In our case, the concurrence of thirteen distinct sovereign wills is requisite, under the Confederation, to the complete execution of every important measure that proceeds from the Union. It has happened as was to have been foreseen. The measures of the Union have not been executed; the delinquencies of the States have, step by step, matured themselves to an extreme, which has, at length, arrested all the wheels of the national government, and brought them to an awful stand. Congress at this time scarcely possess the means of keeping up the forms of administration, till the States can have time to agree upon a more substantial substitute for the present shadow of a federal government. Things did not come to this desperate extremity at once. The causes which have been specified produced at first only unequal and disproportionate degrees of compliance with the requisitions of the Union. The greater deficiencies of some States furnished the pretext of example and the temptation of interest to the complying, or to the least delinquent States. Why should we do more in proportion than those who are embarked with us in the same political voyage? Why should we consent to bear more than our proper share of the common burden? These were suggestions which human selfishness could not withstand, and which even speculative men, who looked forward to remote consequences, could not, without hesitation, combat. Each State, yielding to the persuasive voice of immediate interest or convenience, has successively withdrawn its support, till the frail and tottering edifice seems ready to fall upon our heads, and to crush us beneath its ruins.

The Same Subject Continued: The Insufficiency of the Present Confederation to Preserve the Union

To the People of the State of New York:

THE tendency of the principle of legislation for States, or communities, in their political capacities, as it has been exemplified by the experiment we have made of it, is equally attested by the events which have befallen all other governments of the confederate kind, of which we have any account, in exact proportion to its prevalence in those systems. The confirmations of this fact will be worthy of a distinct and particular examination. I shall content myself with barely observing here, that of all the confederacies of antiquity, which history has handed down to us, the Lycian and Achaean leagues, as far as there remain vestiges of them, appear to have been most free from the fetters of that mistaken principle, and were accordingly those which have best deserved, and have most liberally received, the applauding suffrages of political writers.

This exceptionable principle may, as truly as emphatically, be styled the parent of anarchy: It has been seen that delinquencies in the members of the Union are its natural and necessary offspring; and that whenever they happen, the only constitutional remedy is force, and the immediate effect of the use of it, civil war.

It remains to inquire how far so odious an engine of government, in its application to us, would even be capable of answering its end. If there should not be a large army constantly at the disposal of the national government it would either not be able to employ force at all, or, when this could be done, it would amount to a war between parts of the Confederacy concerning the infractions of a league, in which the strongest combination would be most likely to prevail, whether it consisted of those who supported or of those who resisted the general authority. It would rarely happen that the delinquency to be redressed would be confined to a single member, and if there were more than one who had neglected their duty, similarity of situation would induce them to unite for common defense. Independent of this motive of sympathy, if a large and influential State should happen to be the aggressing member, it would commonly have weight enough with its neighbors to win over some of them as associates to its cause. Specious arguments of danger to the common liberty could easily be contrived; plausible excuses for the deficiencies of the party could, without difficulty, be invented to alarm the apprehensions, inflame the passions, and conciliate the good-will, even of those

States which were not chargeable with any violation or omission of duty. This would be the more likely to take place, as the delinquencies of the larger members might be expected sometimes to proceed from an ambitious premeditation in their rulers, with a view to getting rid of all external control upon their designs of personal aggrandizement; the better to effect which it is presumable they would tamper beforehand with leading individuals in the adjacent States. If associates could not be found at home, recourse would be had to the aid of foreign powers, who would seldom be disinclined to encouraging the dissensions of a Confederacy, from the firm union of which they had so much to fear. When the sword is once drawn, the passions of men observe no bounds of moderation. The suggestions of wounded pride, the instigations of irritated resentment, would be apt to carry the States against which the arms of the Union were exerted, to any extremes necessary to avenge the affront or to avoid the disgrace of submission. The first war of this kind would probably terminate in a dissolution of the Union.

This may be considered as the violent death of the Confederacy. Its more natural death is what we now seem to be on the point of experiencing, if the federal system be not speedily renovated in a more substantial form. It is not probable, considering the genius of this country, that the complying States would often be inclined to support the authority of the Union by engaging in a war against the non-complying States. They would always be more ready to pursue the milder course of putting themselves upon an equal footing with the delinquent members by an imitation of their example. And the guilt of all would thus become the security of all. Our past experience has exhibited the operation of this spirit in its full light. There would, in fact, be an insuperable difficulty in ascertaining when force could with propriety be employed. In the article of pecuniary contribution, which would be the most usual source of delinquency, it would often be impossible to decide whether it had proceeded from disinclination or inability. The pretense of the latter would always be at hand. And the case must be very flagrant in which its fallacy could be detected with sufficient certainty to justify the harsh expedient of compulsion. It is easy to see that this problem alone, as often as it should occur, would open a wide field for the exercise of factious views, of partiality, and of oppression, in the majority that happened to prevail in the national council.

It seems to require no pains to prove that the States ought not to prefer a national Constitution which could only be kept in motion by the instrumentality of a large army continually on foot to execute the ordinary requisitions or decrees of the government. And yet this is the plain alternative involved by those who wish to deny it the power of extending its operations to individuals. Such a scheme, if practicable at all, would instantly degenerate into a military despotism; but it will be found in every light impracticable.

The resources of the Union would not be equal to the maintenance of an army considerable enough to confine the larger States within the limits of their duty; nor would the means ever be furnished of forming such an army in the first instance. Whoever considers the populousness and strength of several of these States singly at the present juncture, and looks forward to what they will become, even at the distance of half a century, will at once dismiss as idle and visionary any scheme which aims at regulating their movements by laws to operate upon them in their collective capacities, and to be executed by a coercion applicable to them in the same capacities. A project of this kind is little less romantic than the monster-taming spirit which is attributed to the fabulous heroes and demi-gods of antiquity. Even in those confederacies which have been composed of members smaller than many of our counties, the principle of legislation for sovereign States, supported by military coercion, has never been found effectual. It has rarely been attempted to be employed, but against the weaker members; and in most instances attempts to coerce the refractory and disobedient have been the signals of bloody wars, in which one half of the confederacy has displayed its banners against the other half.

The result of these observations to an intelligent mind must be clearly this, that if it be possible at any rate to construct a federal government capable of regulating the common concerns and preserving the general tranquillity, it must be founded, as to the objects committed to its care, upon the reverse of the principle contended for by the opponents of the proposed Constitution. It must carry its agency to the persons of the citizens. It must stand in need of no intermediate legislations; but must itself be empowered to employ the arm of the ordinary magistrate to execute its own resolutions. The majesty of the national authority must be manifested through the medium of the courts of justice. The government of the Union, like that of each State, must be able to address itself immediately to the hopes and fears of individuals; and to attract to its support those passions which have the strongest influence upon the human heart. It must, in short, possess all the means, and have aright to resort to all the methods, of executing the powers with which it is intrusted, that are possessed and exercised by the government of the particular States. To this reasoning it may perhaps be objected, that if any State should be disaffected to the authority of the Union, it could at any time obstruct the execution of its laws, and bring the matter to the same issue of force, with the necessity of which the opposite scheme is reproached.

The pausibility of this objection will vanish the moment we advert to the essential difference between a mere **NON-COMPLIANCE** and a **DIRECT** and **ACTIVE RESISTANCE**. If the interposition of the State legislatures be necessary to give effect to a measure of the Union, they have only **NOT TO ACT**, or to **ACT EVASIVELY**, and the measure is defeated. This neglect of duty may be disguised under affected but unsubstantial provisions, so as not to appear, and of course not to excite any alarm in the people for the safety of the Constitution. The State leaders may even make a merit of their surreptitious invasions of it on the ground of some temporary convenience, exemption, or advantage.

But if the execution of the laws of the national government should not require the intervention of the State legislatures, if they were to pass into immediate operation upon the citizens themselves, the particular governments could not interrupt their progress without an open and violent exertion of an unconstitutional power. No omissions nor evasions would answer the end. They would be obliged to act, and in such a manner as would leave no doubt that they had encroached on the national rights. An experiment of this nature would always be hazardous in the face of a constitution in any degree competent to its own defense, and of a people enlightened enough to distinguish between a legal exercise and an illegal usurpation of authority.

The success of it would require not merely a factious majority in the legislature, but the concurrence of the courts of justice and of the body of the people. If the judges were not embarked in a conspiracy with the legislature, they would pronounce the resolutions of such a majority to be contrary to the supreme law of the land, unconstitutional, and void. If the people were not tainted with the spirit of their State representatives, they, as the natural guardians of the Constitution, would throw their weight into the national scale and give it a decided preponderancy in the contest. Attempts of this kind would not often be made with levity or rashness, because they could seldom be made without danger to the authors, unless in cases of a tyrannical exercise of the federal authority. If opposition to the national government should arise from the disorderly conduct of refractory or seditious individuals, it could be overcome by the same means which are daily employed against the same evil under the State governments.

The magistracy, being equally the ministers of the law of the land, from whatever source it might emanate, would doubtless be as ready to guard the national as the local regulations from the inroads of private licentiousness. As to those partial commotions and insurrections, which sometimes disquiet society, from the intrigues of an inconsiderable faction, or from sudden or occasional illhumors that do not infect the great body of the community the general government could command more extensive resources for the suppression of disturbances of that kind than would be in the power of any single member. And as to those mortal feuds which, in certain conjunctures, spread a conflagration through a whole nation, or through a very large proportion of it, proceeding either from weighty causes of discontent given by the government or from the contagion of some violent popular paroxysm, they do not fall within any ordinary rules of calculation. When they happen, they commonly amount to revolutions and dismemberments of empire. No form of government can always either avoid or control them. It is in vain to hope to guard against events too mighty for human foresight or precaution, and it would be idle to object to a government because it could not perform impossibilities.

The Same Subject Continued: The Insufficiency of the Present Confederation to Preserve the Union

To the People of the State of New York:

AN OBJECTION, of a nature different from that which has been stated and answered, in my last address, may perhaps be likewise urged against the principle of legislation for the individual citizens of America. It may be said that it would tend to render the government of the Union too powerful, and to enable it to absorb those residuary authorities, which it might be judged proper to leave with the States for local purposes.

Allowing the utmost latitude to the love of power which any reasonable man can require, I confess I am at a loss to discover what temptation the persons intrusted with the administration of the general government could ever feel to divest the States of the authorities of that description. The regulation of the mere domestic police of a State appears to me to hold out slender allurements to ambition. Commerce, finance, negotiation, and war seem to comprehend all the objects which have charms for minds governed by that passion; and all the powers necessary to those objects ought, in the first instance, to be lodged in the national depository. The administration of private justice between the citizens of the same State, the supervision of agriculture and of other concerns of a similar nature, all those things, in short, which are proper to be provided for by local legislation, can never be desirable cares of a general jurisdiction. It is therefore improbable that there should exist a disposition in the federal councils to usurp the powers with which they are connected; because the attempt to exercise those powers would be as troublesome as it would be nugatory; and the possession of them, for that reason, would contribute nothing to the dignity, to the importance, or to the splendor of the national government.

But let it be admitted, for argument's sake, that mere wantonness and lust of domination would be sufficient to beget that disposition; still it may be safely affirmed, that the sense of the constituent body of the national representatives, or, in other words, the people of the several States, would control the indulgence of so extravagant an appetite. It will always be far more easy for the State governments to encroach upon the national authorities than for the national government to encroach upon the State authorities. The proof of this proposition turns upon the greater degree of influence which the State governments if they administer their affairs with uprightness and prudence, will generally possess over the people; a circumstance which at the same time teaches us that there is an inherent and intrinsic weakness in all federal constitutions; and that too much pains cannot be taken in their organization, to give them all the force which is compatible with the principles of liberty.

The superiority of influence in favor of the particular governments would result partly from the diffusive construction of the national government, but chiefly from the nature of the objects to which the attention of the State administrations would be directed.

It is a known fact in human nature, that its affections are commonly weak in proportion to the distance or diffusiveness of the object. Upon the same principle that a man is more attached to his family than to his neighborhood, to his neighborhood than to the community at large, the people of each State would be apt to feel a stronger bias towards their local governments than towards the government of the Union; unless the force of that principle should be destroyed by a much better administration of the latter.

This strong propensity of the human heart would find powerful auxiliaries in the objects of State regulation.

The variety of more minute interests, which will necessarily fall under the superintendence of the local administrations, and which will form so many rivulets of influence, running through every part of the society, cannot be particularized, without involving a detail too tedious and uninteresting to compensate for the instruction it might afford.

There is one transcendant advantage belonging to the province of the State governments, which alone suffices to place the matter in a clear and satisfactory light,—I mean the ordinary administration of criminal and civil justice. This, of all others, is the most powerful, most universal, and most attractive source of popular obedience and attachment. It is that which, being the immediate and visible guardian of life and property, having its benefits and its terrors in constant activity before the public eye, regulating all those personal interests and familiar concerns to which the sensibility of individuals is more immediately awake, contributes, more than any other circumstance, to impressing upon the minds of the people, affection, esteem, and reverence towards the government. This great cement of society, which will diffuse itself almost wholly through the channels of the particular governments, independent of all other causes of influence, would insure them so decided an empire over their respective citizens as to render them at all times a complete counterpoise, and, not unfrequently, dangerous rivals to the power of the Union.

The operations of the national government, on the other hand, falling less immediately under the observation of the mass of the citizens, the benefits derived from it will chiefly be perceived and attended to by speculative men. Relating to more general interests, they will be less apt to come home to the feelings of the people; and, in proportion, less likely to inspire an habitual sense of obligation, and an active sentiment of attachment.

The reasoning on this head has been abundantly exemplified by the experience of all federal constitutions with which we are acquainted, and of all others which have borne the least analogy to them.

Though the ancient feudal systems were not, strictly speaking, confederacies, yet they partook of the nature of that species of association. There was a common head, chieftain, or sovereign, whose authority extended over the whole nation; and a number of subordinate vassals, or feudatories, who had large portions of land allotted to them, and numerous trains of **INFERIOR** vassals or retainers, who occupied and cultivated that land upon the tenure of fealty or obedience, to the persons of whom they held it. Each principal vassal was a kind of sovereign, within his particular demesnes. The consequences of this situation were a continual opposition to authority of the sovereign, and frequent wars between the great barons or chief feudatories themselves. The power of the head of the nation was commonly too weak, either to preserve the public peace, or to protect the people against the oppressions of their immediate lords. This period of European affairs is emphatically styled by historians, the times of feudal anarchy.

When the sovereign happened to be a man of vigorous and warlike temper and of superior abilities, he would acquire a personal weight and influence, which answered, for the time, the purpose of a more regular authority. But in general, the power of the barons triumphed over that of the prince; and in many instances his dominion was entirely thrown off, and the great fiefs were erected into independent principalities or States. In those instances in which the monarch finally prevailed over his vassals, his success was chiefly owing to the tyranny of those vassals over their dependents. The barons, or nobles, equally the enemies of the sovereign and the oppressors of the common people, were dreaded and detested by both; till mutual danger and mutual interest effected a union between them fatal to the power of the aristocracy. Had the nobles, by a conduct of clemency and justice, preserved the fidelity and devotion of their retainers and followers, the contests between them and the prince must almost always have ended in their favor, and in the abridgment or subversion of the royal authority.

This is not an assertion founded merely in speculation or conjecture. Among other illustrations of its truth which might be cited, Scotland will furnish a cogent example. The spirit of clanship which was, at an early day, introduced into that kingdom, uniting the nobles and their dependants by ties equivalent to those of kindred, rendered the aristocracy a constant overmatch for the power of the monarch, till the incorporation with England subdued its fierce and ungovernable spirit, and reduced it within those rules of subordination which a more rational and more energetic system of civil polity had previously established in the latter kingdom.

The separate governments in a confederacy may aptly be compared with the feudal baronies; with this advantage in their favor, that from the reasons already explained, they will generally possess the confidence and good-will of the people, and with so important a support, will be able effectually to oppose all encroachments of the national government. It will be well if they are not able to counteract its legitimate and necessary authority. The points of similitude consist in the rivalship of power, applicable to both, and in the **CONCENTRATION** of large portions of the strength of the community into particular **DEPOSITS**, in one case at the disposal of individuals, in the other case at the disposal of political bodies.

A concise review of the events that have attended confederate governments will further illustrate this important doctrine; an inattention to which has been the great source of our political mistakes, and has given our jealousy a direction to the wrong side. This review shall form the subject of some ensuing papers.

The Same Subject Continued: The Insufficiency of the Present Confederation to Preserve the Union

To the People of the State of New York:

AMONG the confederacies of antiquity, the most considerable was that of the Grecian republics, associated under the Amphictyonic council. From the best accounts transmitted of this celebrated institution, it bore a very instructive analogy to the present Confederation of the American States.

The members retained the character of independent and sovereign states, and had equal votes in the federal council. This council had a general authority to propose and resolve whatever it judged necessary for the common welfare of Greece; to declare and carry on war; to decide, in the last resort, all controversies between the members; to fine the aggressing party; to employ the whole force of the confederacy against the disobedient; to admit new members. The Amphictyons were the guardians of religion, and of the immense riches belonging to the temple of Delphos, where they had the right of jurisdiction in controversies between the inhabitants and those who came to consult the oracle. As a further provision for the efficacy of the federal powers, they took an oath mutually to defend and protect the united cities, to punish the violators of this oath, and to inflict vengeance on sacrilegious despoilers of the temple.

In theory, and upon paper, this apparatus of powers seems amply sufficient for all general purposes. In several material instances, they exceed the powers enumerated in the articles of confederation. The Amphictyons had in their hands the superstition of the times, one of the principal engines by which government was then maintained; they had a declared authority to use coercion against refractory cities, and were bound by oath to exert this authority on the necessary occasions.

Very different, nevertheless, was the experiment from the theory. The powers, like those of the present Congress, were administered by deputies appointed wholly by the cities in their political capacities; and exercised over them in the same capacities. Hence the weakness, the disorders, and finally the destruction of the confederacy. The more powerful members, instead of being kept in awe and subordination, tyrannized successively over all the rest. Athens, as we learn from Demosthenes, was the arbiter of Greece seventy-three years. The Lacedaemonians next governed it twenty-nine years; at a subsequent period, after the battle of Leuctra, the Thebans had their turn of domination.

It happened but too often, according to Plutarch, that the deputies of the strongest cities awed and corrupted those of the weaker; and that judgment went in favor of the most powerful party.

Even in the midst of defensive and dangerous wars with Persia and Macedon, the members never acted in concert, and were, more or fewer of them, eternally the dupes or the hirelings of the common enemy. The intervals of foreign war were filled up by domestic vicissitudes convulsions, and carnage.

After the conclusion of the war with Xerxes, it appears that the Lacedaemonians required that a number of the cities should be turned out of the confederacy for the unfaithful part they had acted. The Athenians, finding that the Lacedaemonians would lose fewer partisans by such a measure than themselves, and would become masters of the public deliberations, vigorously opposed and defeated the attempt. This piece of history proves at once the inefficiency of the union, the ambition and jealousy of its most powerful members, and the dependent and degraded condition of the rest. The smaller members, though entitled by the theory of their system to revolve in equal pride and majesty around the common center, had become, in fact, satellites of the orbs of primary magnitude.

Had the Greeks, says the Abbe Milot, been as wise as they were courageous, they would have been admonished by experience of the necessity of a closer union, and would have availed themselves of the peace which followed their success against the Persian arms, to establish such a reformation. Instead of this obvious policy, Athens and Sparta, inflated with the victories and the glory they had acquired, became first rivals and then enemies; and did each other infinitely more mischief than they had suffered from Xerxes. Their mutual jealousies, fears, hatreds, and injuries ended in the celebrated Peloponnesian war; which itself ended in the ruin and slavery of the Athenians who had begun it.

As a weak government, when not at war, is ever agitated by internal dissentions, so these never fail to bring on fresh calamities from abroad. The Phocians having ploughed up some consecrated ground belonging to the temple of Apollo, the Amphictyonic council, according to the superstition of the age, imposed a fine on the sacrilegious offenders. The Phocians, being abetted by Athens and Sparta, refused to submit to the decree. The Thebans, with others of the cities, undertook to maintain the authority of the Amphictyons, and to avenge the violated god. The latter, being the weaker party, invited the assistance of Philip of Macedon, who had secretly fostered the contest. Philip gladly seized the opportunity of executing the designs he had long planned against the liberties of Greece. By his intrigues and bribes he won over to his interests the popular leaders of several cities; by their influence and votes, gained admission into the Amphictyonic council; and by his arts and his arms, made himself master of the confederacy.

Such were the consequences of the fallacious principle on which this interesting establishment was founded. Had Greece, says a judicious observer on her fate, been united by a stricter confederation, and persevered in her union, she would never have worn the chains of Macedon; and might have proved a barrier to the vast projects of Rome.

The Achaean league, as it is called, was another society of Grecian republics, which supplies us with valuable instruction.

The Union here was far more intimate, and its organization much wiser, than in the preceding instance. It will accordingly appear, that though not exempt from a similar catastrophe, it by no means equally deserved it.

The cities composing this league retained their municipal jurisdiction, appointed their own officers, and enjoyed a perfect equality. The senate, in which they were represented, had the sole and exclusive right of peace and war; of sending and receiving ambassadors; of entering into treaties and alliances; of appointing a chief magistrate or praetor, as he was called, who commanded their armies, and who, with the advice and consent of ten of the senators, not only administered the government in the recess of the senate, but had a great share in its deliberations, when assembled. According to the primitive constitution, there were two praetors associated in the administration; but on trial a single one was preferred.

It appears that the cities had all the same laws and customs, the same weights and measures, and the same money. But how far this effect proceeded from the authority of the federal council is left in uncertainty.

It is said only that the cities were in a manner compelled to receive the same laws and usages. When Lacedaemon was brought into the league by Philopoemen, it was attended with an abolition of the institutions and laws of Lycurgus, and an adoption of those of the Achaeans. The Amphictyonic confederacy, of which she had been a member, left her in the full exercise of her government and her legislation. This circumstance alone proves a very material difference in the genius of the two systems.

It is much to be regretted that such imperfect monuments remain of this curious political fabric. Could its interior structure and regular operation be ascertained, it is probable that more light would be thrown by it on the science of federal government, than by any of the like experiments with which we are acquainted.

One important fact seems to be witnessed by all the historians who take notice of Achaean affairs. It is, that as well after the renovation of the league by Aratus, as before its dissolution by the arts of Macedon, there was infinitely more of moderation and justice in the administration of its government, and less of violence and sedition in the people, than were to be found in any of the cities exercising SINGLY all the prerogatives of sovereignty. The Abbe Mably, in his observations on Greece, says that the popular government, which was so tempestuous elsewhere, caused no disorders in the members of the Achaean republic, **BECAUSE IT WAS THERE TEMPERED BY THE GENERAL AUTHORITY AND LAWS OF THE CONFEDERACY.**

We are not to conclude too hastily, however, that faction did not, in a certain degree, agitate the particular cities; much less that a due subordination and harmony reigned in the general system. The contrary is sufficiently displayed in the vicissitudes and fate of the republic.

Whilst the Amphictyonic confederacy remained, that of the Achaeans, which comprehended the less important cities only, made little figure on the theatre of Greece. When the former became a victim to Macedon, the latter was spared by the policy of Philip and Alexander. Under the successors of these princes, however, a different policy prevailed. The arts of division were practiced among the Achaeans. Each city was seduced into a separate interest; the union was dissolved. Some of the cities fell under the tyranny of Macedonian garrisons; others under that of usurpers springing out of their own confusions. Shame and oppression erelong awaken their love of liberty.

A few cities reunited. Their example was followed by others, as opportunities were found of cutting off their tyrants. The league soon embraced almost the whole Peloponnesus. Macedon saw its progress; but was hindered by internal dissensions from stopping it. All Greece caught the enthusiasm and seemed ready to unite in one confederacy, when the jealousy and envy in Sparta and Athens, of the rising glory of the Achaeans, threw a fatal damp on the enterprise. The dread of the Macedonian power induced the league to court the alliance of the Kings of Egypt and Syria, who, as successors of Alexander, were rivals of the king of Macedon. This policy was defeated by Cleomenes, king of Sparta, who was led by his ambition to make an unprovoked attack on his neighbors, the Achaeans, and who, as an enemy to Macedon, had interest enough with the Egyptian and Syrian princes to effect a breach of their engagements with the league.

The Achaeans were now reduced to the dilemma of submitting to Cleomenes, or of supplicating the aid of Macedon, its former oppressor. The latter expedient was adopted. The contests of the

Greeks always afforded a pleasing opportunity to that powerful neighbor of intermeddling in their affairs. A Macedonian army quickly appeared. Cleomenes was vanquished. The Achaeans soon experienced, as often happens, that a victorious and powerful ally is but another name for a master.

All that their most abject compliances could obtain from him was a toleration of the exercise of their laws. Philip, who was now on the throne of Macedon, soon provoked by his tyrannies, fresh combinations among the Greeks. The Achaeans, though weakenened by internal dissensions and by the revolt of Messene, one of its members, being joined by the AEtolians and Athenians, erected the standard of opposition. Finding themselves, though thus supported, unequal to the undertaking, they once more had recourse to the dangerous expedient of introducing the succor of foreign arms.

The Romans, to whom the invitation was made, eagerly embraced it. Philip was conquered; Macedon subdued. A new crisis ensued to the league.

Dissensions broke out among it members. These the Romans fostered. Callicrates and other popular leaders became mercenary instruments for inveigling their countrymen. The more effectually to nourish discord and disorder the Romans had, to the astonishment of those who confided in their sincerity, already proclaimed universal liberty1 throughout Greece. With the same insidious views, they now seduced the members from the league, by representing to their pride the violation it committed on their sovereignty. By these arts this union, the last hope of Greece, the last hope of ancient liberty, was torn into pieces; and such imbecility and distraction introduced, that the arms of Rome found little difficulty in completing the ruin which their arts had commenced. The Achaeans were cut to pieces, and Achaia loaded with chains, under which it is groaning at this hour.

I have thought it not superfluous to give the outlines of this important portion of history; both because it teaches more than one lesson, and because, as a supplement to the outlines of the Achaean constitution, it emphatically illustrates the tendency of federal bodies rather to anarchy among the members, than to tyranny in the head.

The Insufficiency of the Present Confederation to Preserve the Union

To the People of the State of New York:

THE examples of ancient confederacies, cited in my last paper, have not exhausted the source of experimental instruction on this subject. There are existing institutions, founded on a similar principle, which merit particular consideration. The first which presents itself is the Germanic body.

In the early ages of Christianity, Germany was occupied by seven distinct nations, who had no common chief. The Franks, one of the number, having conquered the Gauls, established the kingdom which has taken its name from them.

In the ninth century Charlemagne, its warlike monarch, carried his victorious arms in every direction; and Germany became a part of his vast dominions. On the dismemberment, which took place under his sons, this part was erected into a separate and independent empire. Charlemagne and his immediate descendants possessed the reality, as well as the ensigns and dignity of imperial power.

But the principal vassals, whose fiefs had become hereditary, and who composed the national diets which Charlemagne had not abolished, gradually threw off the yoke and advanced to sovereign jurisdiction and independence.

The force of imperial sovereignty was insufficient to restrain such powerful dependants; or to preserve the unity and tranquillity of the empire. The most furious private wars, accompanied with every species of calamity, were carried on between the different princes and states.

The imperial authority, unable to maintain the public order, declined by degrees till it was almost extinct in the anarchy, which agitated the long interval between the death of the last emperor of the Suabian, and the accession of the first emperor of the Austrian lines. In the eleventh century the emperors enjoyed full sovereignty: In the fifteenth they had little more than the symbols and decorations of power.

Out of this feudal system, which has itself many of the important features of a confederacy, has grown the federal system which constitutes the Germanic empire. Its powers are vested in a diet representing the component members of the confederacy; in the emperor, who is the executive magistrate, with a negative on the decrees of the diet; and in the imperial chamber and the aulic council, two judiciary tribunals having supreme jurisdiction in controversies which concern the empire, or which happen among its members.

The diet possesses the general power of legislating for the empire; of making war and peace; contracting alliances; assessing quotas of troops and money; constructing fortresses; regulating coin; admitting new members; and subjecting disobedient members to the ban of the empire, by which the party is degraded from his sovereign rights and his possessions forfeited.

The members of the confederacy are expressly restricted from entering into compacts prejudicial to the empire; from imposing tolls and duties on their mutual intercourse, without the consent of the emperor and diet; from altering the value of money; from doing injustice to one another; or from affording assistance or retreat to disturbers of the public peace. And the ban is denounced against such as shall violate any of these restrictions. The members of the diet, as such, are subject in all cases to be judged by the emperor and diet, and in their private capacities by the aulic council and imperial chamber.

The prerogatives of the emperor are numerous. The most important of them are: his exclusive right to make propositions to the diet; to negative its resolutions; to name ambassadors; to confer dignities and titles; to fill vacant electorates; to found universities; to grant privileges not injurious to the states of the empire; to receive and apply the public revenues; and generally to watch over the public safety. In certain cases, the electors form a council to him. In quality of emperor, he possesses no territory within the empire, nor receives any revenue for his support. But his revenue and dominions, in other qualities, constitute him one of the most powerful princes in Europe.

From such a parade of constitutional powers, in the representatives and head of this confederacy, the natural supposition would be, that it must form an exception to the general character which belongs to its kindred systems. Nothing would be further from the reality. The fundamental principle on which it rests, that the empire is a community of sovereigns, that the diet is a representation of sovereigns and that the laws are addressed to sovereigns, renders the empire a nerveless body, incapable of regulating its own members, insecure against external dangers, and agitated with unceasing fermentations in its own bowels.

The history of Germany is a history of wars between the emperor and the princes and states; of wars among the princes and states themselves; of the licentiousness of the strong, and the oppression of the weak; of foreign intrusions, and foreign intrigues; of requisitions of men and money disregarded, or partially complied with; of attempts to enforce them, altogether abortive, or attended with slaughter and desolation, involving the innocent with the guilty; of general inbecility, confusion, and misery.

In the sixteenth century, the emperor, with one part of the empire on his side, was seen engaged against the other princes and states. In one of the conflicts, the emperor himself was put to flight, and very near being made prisoner by the elector of Saxony. The late king of Prussia was more than once pitted against his imperial sovereign; and commonly proved an overmatch for him. Controversies and wars among the members themselves have been so common, that the German annals are crowded with the bloody pages which describe them. Previous to the peace of Westphalia, Germany was desolated by a war of thirty years, in which the emperor, with one half of the empire, was on one side, and Sweden, with the other half, on the opposite side. Peace was at length negotiated, and dictated by foreign powers; and the articles of it, to which foreign powers are parties, made a fundamental part of the Germanic constitution.

If the nation happens, on any emergency, to be more united by the necessity of self-defense, its situation is still deplorable. Military preparations must be preceded by so many tedious discussions, arising from the jealousies, pride, separate views, and clashing pretensions of sovereign bodies, that before the diet can settle the arrangements, the enemy are in the field; and before the federal troops are ready to take it, are retiring into winter quarters.

The small body of national troops, which has been judged necessary in time of peace, is defectively kept up, badly paid, infected with local prejudices, and supported by irregular and disproportionate contributions to the treasury.

The impossibility of maintaining order and dispensing justice among these sovereign subjects, produced the experiment of dividing the empire into nine or ten circles or districts; of giving them an interior organization, and of charging them with the military execution of the laws against delinquent and contumacious members. This experiment has only served to demonstrate more fully the radical vice of the constitution. Each circle is the miniature picture of the deformities of this political monster.

They either fail to execute their commissions, or they do it with all the devastation and carnage of civil war. Sometimes whole circles are defaulters; and then they increase the mischief which they were instituted to remedy.

We may form some judgment of this scheme of military coercion from a sample given by Thuanus. In Donawerth, a free and imperial city of the circle of Suabia, the Abb 300 de St. Croix enjoyed certain immunities which had been reserved to him. In the exercise of these, on some public occasions, outrages were committed on him by the people of the city. The consequence was that the city was put under the ban of the empire, and the Duke of Bavaria, though director of another circle, obtained an appointment to enforce it. He soon appeared before the city with a corps of ten thousand troops, and finding it a fit occasion, as he had secretly intended from the beginning, to revive an antiquated claim, on the pretext that his ancestors had suffered the place to be dismembered from his territory,1 he took possession of it in his own name, disarmed, and punished the inhabitants, and reannexed the city to his domains.

It may be asked, perhaps, what has so long kept this disjointed machine from falling entirely to pieces?

The answer is obvious: The weakness of most of the members, who are unwilling to expose themselves to the mercy of foreign powers; the weakness of most of the principal members, compared with the formidable powers all around them; the vast weight and influence which the emperor derives from his separate and heriditary dominions; and the interest he feels in preserving a system with which his family pride is connected, and which constitutes him the first prince in Europe; —these causes support a feeble and precarious Union; whilst the repellant quality, incident to the nature of sovereignty, and which time continually strengthens, prevents any reform whatever, founded on a proper consolidation. Nor is it to be imagined, if this obstacle could be surmounted, that the neighboring powers would suffer a revolution to take place which would give to the empire the force and preeminence to which it is entitled. Foreign nations have long considered themselves as interested in the changes made by events in this constitution; and have, on various occasions, betrayed their policy of perpetuating its anarchy and weakness.

If more direct examples were wanting, Poland, as a government over local sovereigns, might not improperly be taken notice of. Nor could any proof more striking be given of the calamities flowing from such institutions. Equally unfit for self-government and self-defense, it has long been at the mercy of its powerful neighbors; who have lately had the mercy to disburden it of one third of its people and territories.

The connection among the Swiss cantons scarcely amounts to a confederacy; though it is sometimes cited as an instance of the stability of such institutions.

They have no common treasury; no common troops even in war; no common coin; no common judicatory; nor any other common mark of sovereignty.

They are kept together by the peculiarity of their topographical position; by their individual weakness and insignificancy; by the fear of powerful neighbors, to one of which they were formerly subject; by the few sources of contention among a people of such simple and homogeneous manners; by their joint interest in their dependent possessions; by the mutual aid they stand in need of, for suppressing insurrections and rebellions, an aid expressly stipulated and often required and afforded; and by the necessity of some regular and permanent provision for accomodating disputes among the cantons. The provision is, that the parties at variance shall each choose four judges out of the neutral cantons, who, in case of disagreement, choose an umpire.

This tribunal, under an oath of impartiality, pronounces definitive sentence, which all the cantons are bound to enforce. The competency of this regulation may be estimated by a clause in their treaty of 1683, with Victor Amadeus of Savoy; in which he obliges himself to interpose as mediator in disputes between the cantons, and to employ force, if necessary, against the contumacious party.

So far as the peculiarity of their case will admit of comparison with that of the United States, it serves to confirm the principle intended to be established. Whatever efficacy the union may have had in ordinary cases, it appears that the moment a cause of difference sprang up, capable of trying its strength, it failed.

The controversies on the subject of religion, which in three instances have kindled violent and bloody contests, may be said, in fact, to have severed the league. The Protestant and Catholic cantons have since had their separate diets, where all the most important concerns are adjusted, and which have left the general diet little other business than to take care of the common bailages. That separation had another consequence, which merits attention. It produced opposite alliances with foreign powers: of Berne, at the head of the Protestant association, with the United Provinces; and of Luzerne, at the head of the Catholic association, with France.

THE United Netherlands are a confederacy of republics, or rather of aristocracies of a very remarkable texture, yet confirming all the lessons derived from those which we have already reviewed.

The union is composed of seven coequal and sovereign states, and each state or province is a composition of equal and independent cities. In all important cases, not only the provinces but the cities must be unanimous.

The sovereignty of the Union is represented by the States-General, consisting usually of about fifty deputies appointed by the provinces. They hold their seats, some for life, some for six, three, and one years; from two provinces they continue in appointment during pleasure.

The States-General have authority to enter into treaties and alliances; to make war and peace; to raise armies and equip fleets; to ascertain quotas and demand contributions. In all these cases, however, unanimity and the sanction of their constituents are requisite. They have authority to appoint and receive ambassadors; to execute treaties and alliances already formed; to provide for the collection of duties on imports and exports; to regulate the mint, with a saving to the provincial rights; to govern as sovereigns the dependent territories. The provinces are restrained, unless with the general consent, from entering into foreign treaties; from establishing imposts injurious to others, or charging their neighbors with higher duties than their own subjects. A council of state, a chamber of accounts, with five colleges of admiralty, aid and fortify the federal administration.

The executive magistrate of the union is the stadtholder, who is now an hereditary prince. His principal weight and influence in the republic are derived from this independent title; from his great patrimonial estates; from his family connections with some of the chief potentates of Europe; and, more than all, perhaps, from his being stadtholder in the several provinces, as well as for the union; in which provincial quality he has the appointment of town magistrates under certain regulations, executes provincial decrees, presides when he pleases in the provincial tribunals, and has throughout the power of pardon.

As stadtholder of the union, he has, however, considerable prerogatives.

In his political capacity he has authority to settle disputes between the provinces, when other methods fail; to assist at the deliberations of the States-General, and at their particular conferences; to give audiences to foreign ambassadors, and to keep agents for his particular affairs at foreign courts.

In his military capacity he commands the federal troops, provides for garrisons, and in general regulates military affairs; disposes of all appointments, from colonels to ensigns, and of the governments and posts of fortified towns.

In his marine capacity he is admiral-general, and superintends and directs every thing relative to naval forces and other naval affairs; presides in the admiralties in person or by proxy; appoints lieutenant-admirals and other officers; and establishes councils of war, whose sentences are not executed till he approves them.

His revenue, exclusive of his private income, amounts to three hundred thousand florins. The standing army which he commands consists of about forty thousand men.

Such is the nature of the celebrated Belgic confederacy, as delineated on parchment. What are the characters which practice has stamped upon it? Imbecility in the government; discord among the provinces; foreign influence and indignities; a precarious existence in peace, and peculiar calamities from war.

It was long ago remarked by Grotius, that nothing but the hatred of his countrymen to the house of Austria kept them from being ruined by the vices of their constitution.

The union of Utrecht, says another respectable writer, reposes an authority in the States-General, seemingly sufficient to secure harmony, but the jealousy in each province renders the practice very different from the theory.

The same instrument, says another, obliges each province to levy certain contributions; but this article never could, and probably never will, be executed; because the inland provinces, who have little commerce, cannot pay an equal quota.

In matters of contribution, it is the practice to waive the articles of the constitution. The danger of delay obliges the consenting provinces to furnish their quotas, without waiting for the others; and then to obtain reimbursement from the others, by deputations, which are frequent, or otherwise, as they can. The great wealth and influence of the province of Holland enable her to effect both these purposes.

It has more than once happened, that the deficiencies had to be ultimately collected at the point of the bayonet; a thing practicable, though dreadful, in a confedracy where one of the members exceeds in force all the rest, and where several of them are too small to meditate resistance; but utterly impracticable in one composed of members, several of which are equal to each other in strength and resources, and equal singly to a vigorous and persevering defense.

Foreign ministers, says Sir William Temple, who was himself a foreign minister, elude matters taken ad referendum, by tampering with the provinces and cities. In 1726, the treaty of Hanover was delayed by these means a whole year. Instances of a like nature are numerous and notorious.

In critical emergencies, the States-General are often compelled to overleap their constitutional bounds. In 1688, they concluded a treaty of themselves at the risk of their heads. The treaty of Westphalia, in 1648, by which their independence was formerly and finally recognized, was concluded without the consent of Zealand. Even as recently as the last treaty of peace with Great Britain, the constitutional principle of unanimity was departed from. A weak constitution must necessarily terminate in dissolution, for want of proper powers, or the usurpation of powers requisite for the public safety. Whether the usurpation, when once begun, will stop at the salutary point, or go forward to the dangerous extreme, must depend on the contingencies of the moment. Tyranny has perhaps oftener grown out of the assumptions of power, called for, on pressing exigencies, by a defective constitution, than out of the full exercise of the largest constitutional authorities.

Notwithstanding the calamities produced by the stadtholdership, it has been supposed that without his influence in the individual provinces, the causes of anarchy manifest in the confederacy would long ago have dissolved it. "Under such a government," says the Abbe Mably, "the Union could never have subsisted, if the provinces had not a spring within themselves, capable of quickening their tardiness, and compelling them to the same way of thinking. This spring is the stadtholder." It is remarked by Sir William Temple, "that in the intermissions of the stadtholdership, Holland, by her riches and her authority, which drew the others into a sort of dependence, supplied the place."

These are not the only circumstances which have controlled the tendency to anarchy and dissolution. The surrounding powers impose an absolute necessity of union to a certain degree, at the same time that they nourish by their intrigues the constitutional vices which keep the republic in some degree always at their mercy.

The true patriots have long bewailed the fatal tendency of these vices, and have made no less than four regular experiments by **EXTRAORDINARY ASSEMBLIES**, convened for the special purpose, to apply a remedy. As many times has their laudable zeal found it impossible to **UNITE THE PUBLIC COUNCILS** in reforming the known, the acknowledged, the fatal evils of the existing constitution. Let us pause, my fellow-citizens, for one moment, over this melancholy and monitory lesson of history; and with the tear that drops for the calamities brought on mankind by their adverse opinions and selfish passions, let our gratitude mingle an ejaculation to Heaven, for the propitious concord which has distinguished the consultations for our political happiness.

A design was also conceived of establishing a general tax to be administered by the federal authority. This also had its adversaries and failed.

This unhappy people seem to be now suffering from popular convulsions, from dissensions among the states, and from the actual invasion of foreign arms, the crisis of their distiny. All nations have their eyes fixed on the awful spectacle. The first wish prompted by humanity is, that this severe trial may issue in such a revolution of their government as will establish their union, and render it the parent of tranquillity, freedom and happiness: The next, that the asylum under which, we trust, the enjoyment of these blessings will speedily be secured in this country, may receive and console them for the catastrophe of their own.

I make no apology for having dwelt so long on the contemplation of these federal precedents. Experience is the oracle of truth; and where its responses are unequivocal, they ought to be conclusive and sacred. The important truth, which it unequivocally pronounces in the present case, is that a sovereignty over sovereigns, a government over governments, a legislation for communities, as contradistinguished from individuals, as it is a solecism in theory, so in practice it is subversive of the order and ends of civil polity, by substituting **VIOLENCE** in place of **LAW**, or the destructive **COERCION** of the **SWORD** in place of the mild and salutary **COERCION** of the **MAGISTRACY**.

8

Defects of the Confederation

To the People of the State of New York:

HAVING in the three last numbers taken a summary review of the principal circumstances and events which have depicted the genius and fate of other confederate governments, I shall now proceed in the enumeration of the most important of those defects which have hitherto disappointed our hopes from the system established among ourselves. To form a safe and satisfactory judgment of the proper remedy, it is absolutely necessary that we should be well acquainted with the extent and malignity of the disease.

The next most palpable defect of the subsisting Confederation, is the total want of a SANCTION to its laws. The United States, as now composed, have no powers to exact obedience, or punish disobedience to their resolutions, either by pecuniary mulcts, by a suspension or divestiture of privileges, or by any other constitutional mode. There is no express delegation of authority to them to use force against delinquent members; and if such a right should be ascribed to the federal head, as resulting from the nature of the social compact between the States, it must be by inference and construction, in the face of that part of the second article, by which it is declared, "that each State shall retain every power, jurisdiction, and right, not EXPRESSLY delegated to the United States in Congress assembled." There is, doubtless, a striking absurdity in supposing that a right of this kind does not exist, but we are reduced to the dilemma either of embracing that supposition, preposterous as it may seem, or of contravening or explaining away a provision, which has been of late a repeated theme of the eulogies of those who oppose the new Constitution; and the want of which, in that plan, has been the subject of much plausible animadversion, and severe criticism. If we are unwilling to impair the force of this applauded provision, we shall be obliged to conclude, that the United States afford the extraordinary spectacle of a government destitute even of the shadow of constitutional power to enforce the execution of its own laws. It will appear, from the specimens which have been cited, that the American Confederacy, in this particular, stands discriminated from every other institution of a similar kind, and exhibits a new and unexampled phenomenon in the political world.

The want of a mutual guaranty of the State governments is another capital imperfection in the federal plan. There is nothing of this kind declared in the articles that compose it; and to imply a tacit guaranty from considerations of utility, would be a still more flagrant departure from the clause which has been mentioned, than to imply a tacit power of coercion from the like considerations. The want of a guaranty, though it might in its consequences endanger the Union, does not so immediately attack its existence as the want of a constitutional sanction to its laws.

Without a guaranty the assistance to be derived from the Union in repelling those domestic dangers which may sometimes threaten the existence of the State constitutions, must be renounced. Usurpation may rear its crest in each State, and trample upon the liberties of the people, while the national government could legally do nothing more than behold its encroachments with indignation and regret. A successful faction may erect a tyranny on the ruins of order and law, while no succor could constitutionally be afforded by the Union to the friends and supporters of the government. The tempestuous situation from which Massachusetts has scarcely emerged, evinces that dangers of this kind are not merely speculative. Who can determine what might have been the issue of her late convulsions, if the malcontents had been headed by a Caesar or by a Cromwell? Who can predict what effect a despotism, established in Massachusetts, would have upon the liberties of New Hampshire or Rhode Island, of Connecticut or New York?

The inordinate pride of State importance has suggested to some minds an objection to the principle of a guaranty in the federal government, as involving an officious interference in the domestic concerns of the members. A scruple of this kind would deprive us of one of the principal advantages to be expected from union, and can only flow from a misapprehension of the nature of the provision itself. It could be no impediment to reforms of the State constitution by a majority of the people in a legal and peaceable mode. This right would remain undiminished. The guaranty could only operate against changes to be effected by violence. Towards the preventions of calamities of this kind, too many checks cannot be provided. The peace of society and the stability of government depend absolutely on the efficacy of the precautions adopted on this head. Where the whole power of the government is in the hands of the people, there is the less pretense for the use of violent remedies in partial or occasional distempers of the State. The natural cure for an ill-administration, in a popular or representative constitution, is a change of men. A guaranty by the national authority would be as much levelled against the usurpations of rulers as against the ferments and outrages of faction and sedition in the community.

The principle of regulating the contributions of the States to the common treasury by QUOTAS is another fundamental error in the Confederation. Its repugnancy to an adequate supply of the national exigencies has been already pointed out, and has sufficiently appeared from the trial which has been made of it. I speak of it now solely with a view to equality among the States. Those who have been accustomed to contemplate the circumstances which produce and constitute national wealth, must be satisfied that there is no common standard or barometer by which the degrees of it can be ascertained. Neither the value of lands, nor the numbers of the people, which have been successively proposed as the rule of State contributions, has any pretension to being a just representative.

If we compare the wealth of the United Netherlands with that of Russia or Germany, or even of France, and if we at the same time compare the total value of the lands and the aggregate population of that contracted district with the total value of the lands and the aggregate population of the immense regions of either of the three last-mentioned countries, we shall at once discover that there is no comparison between the proportion of either of these two objects and that of the relative wealth of those nations. If the like parallel were to be run between several of the American States, it would furnish a like result. Let Virginia be contrasted with North Carolina, Pennsylvania with Connecticut, or Maryland with New Jersey, and we shall be convinced that the respective abilities of those States, in relation to revenue, bear little or no analogy to their comparative stock in lands or to their comparative population. The position may be equally illustrated by a similar process between the counties of the same State. No man who is acquainted with the State of New York will doubt that the active wealth of King's County bears a much greater proportion to that of Montgomery than it would appear to be if we should take either the total value of the lands or the total number of the people as a criterion!

The wealth of nations depends upon an infinite variety of causes. Situation, soil, climate, the nature of the productions, the nature of the government, the genius of the citizens, the degree of information they possess, the state of commerce, of arts, of industry, these circumstances and many more, too complex, minute, or adventitious to admit of a particular specification, occasion differences hardly conceivable in the relative opulence and riches of different countries. The consequence clearly is that there can be no common measure of national wealth, and, of course, no general or stationary rule by which the ability of a state to pay taxes can be determined. The attempt, therefore, to regulate the contributions of the members of a confederacy by any such rule, cannot fail to be productive of glaring inequality and extreme oppression.

This inequality would of itself be sufficient in America to work the eventual destruction of the Union, if any mode of enforcing a compliance with its requisitions could be devised. The suffering States would not long consent to remain associated upon a principle which distributes the public burdens with so unequal a hand, and which was calculated to impoverish and oppress the citizens of some States, while those of others would scarcely be conscious of the small proportion of the weight they were required to sustain. This, however, is an evil inseparable from the principle of quotas and requisitions.

There is no method of steering clear of this inconvenience, but by authorizing the national government to raise its own revenues in its own way. Imposts, excises, and, in general, all duties upon articles of consumption, may be compared to a fluid, which will, in time, find its level with the means of paying them. The amount to be contributed by each citizen will in a degree be at his own option, and can be regulated by an attention to his resources. The rich may be extravagant, the poor can be frugal; and private oppression may always be avoided by a judicious selection of objects proper for such impositions. If inequalities should arise in some States from duties on particular objects, these will, in all probability, be counterbalanced by proportional inequalities in other States, from the duties on other objects. In the course of time and things, an equilibrium, as far as it is attainable in so complicated a subject, will be established everywhere. Or, if inequalities should still exist, they would neither be so great in their degree, so uniform in their operation, nor so odious in their appearance, as those which would necessarily spring from quotas, upon any scale that can possibly be devised.

It is a signal advantage of taxes on articles of consumption, that they contain in their own nature a security against excess. They prescribe their own limit; which cannot be exceeded without defeating the end proposed, that is, an extension of the revenue. When applied to this object, the saying is as just as it is witty, that, "in political arithmetic, two and two do not always make four." If duties are too high, they lessen the consumption; the collection is eluded; and the product to the treasury is not so great as when they are confined within proper and moderate bounds. This forms a complete barrier against any material oppression of the citizens by taxes of this class, and is itself a natural limitation of the power of imposing them.

Impositions of this kind usually fall under the denomination of indirect taxes, and must for a long time constitute the chief part of the revenue raised in this country. Those of the direct kind, which principally relate to land and buildings, may admit of a rule of apportionment. Either the value of land, or the number of the people, may serve as a standard. The state of agriculture and the populousness of a country have been considered as nearly connected with each other. And, as a rule, for the purpose intended, numbers, in the view of simplicity and certainty, are entitled to a preference. In every country it is a herculean task to obtain a valuation of the land; in a country imperfectly settled and progressive in improvement, the difficulties are increased almost to impracticability. The expense of an accurate valuation is, in all situations, a formidable objection. In a branch of taxation where no limits to the discretion of the government are to be found in the nature of things, the establishment of a fixed rule, not incompatible with the end, may be attended with fewer inconveniences than to leave that discretion altogether at large.

Other Defects of the Present Confederation
From the New York Packet. Friday, December 14, 1787.
HAMILTON

To the People of the State of New York:

IN ADDITION to the defects already enumerated in the existing federal system, there are others of not less importance, which concur in rendering it altogether unfit for the administration of the affairs of the Union.

The want of a power to regulate commerce is by all parties allowed to be of the number. The utility of such a power has been anticipated under the first head of our inquiries; and for this reason, as well as from the universal conviction entertained upon the subject, little need be added in this place. It is indeed evident, on the most superficial view, that there is no object, either as it respects the interests of trade or finance, that more strongly demands a federal superintendence. The want of it has already operated as a bar to the formation of beneficial treaties with foreign powers, and has given occasions of dissatisfaction between the States.

No nation acquainted with the nature of our political association would be unwise enough to enter into stipulations with the United States, by which they conceded privileges of any importance to them, while they were apprised that the engagements on the part of the Union might at any moment be violated by its members, and while they found from experience that they might enjoy every advantage they desired in our markets, without granting us any return but such as their momentary convenience might suggest. It is not, therefore, to be wondered at that Mr. Jenkinson, in ushering into the House of Commons a bill for regulating the temporary intercourse between the two countries, should preface its introduction by a declaration that similar provisions in former bills had been found to answer every purpose to the commerce of Great Britain, and that it would be prudent to persist in the plan until it should appear whether the American government was likely or not to acquire greater consistency.

Several States have endeavored, by separate prohibitions, restrictions, and exclusions, to influence the conduct of that kingdom in this particular, but the want of concert, arising from the want of a general authority and from clashing and dissimilar views in the State, has hitherto frustrated every experiment of the kind, and will continue to do so as long as the same obstacles to a uniformity of measures continue to exist.

The interfering and unneighborly regulations of some States, contrary to the true spirit of the Union, have, in different instances, given just cause of umbrage and complaint to others, and it is to be feared that examples of this nature, if not restrained by a national control, would be multiplied and extended till they became not less serious sources of animosity and discord than injurious impediments to the intercourse between the different parts of the Confederacy. "The commerce of the German empire is in continual trammels from the multiplicity of the duties which the several princes and states exact upon the merchandises passing through their territories, by means of which the fine streams and navigable rivers with which Germany is so happily watered are rendered almost useless." Though the genius of the people of this country might never permit this description to be strictly applicable to us, yet we may reasonably expect, from the gradual conflicts of State regulations, that the citizens of each would at length come to be considered and treated by the others in no better light than that of foreigners and aliens. The power of raising armies, by the most obvious construction of the articles of the Confederation, is merely a power of making requisitions upon the States for quotas of men. This practice in the course of the late war, was found replete with obstructions to a vigorous and to an economical system of defense. It gave birth to a competition between the States which created a kind of auction for men. In order to furnish the quotas required of them, they outbid each other till bounties grew to an enormous and insupportable size. The hope of a still further increase afforded an inducement to those who were disposed to serve to procrastinate their enlistment, and disinclined them from engaging for any considerable periods. Hence, slow and scanty levies of men, in the most critical emergencies of our affairs; short enlistments at an unparalleled expense; continual fluctuations in the troops, ruinous to their discipline and subjecting the public safety frequently to the perilous crisis of a disbanded army. Hence, also, those oppressive expedients for raising men which were upon several occasions practiced, and which nothing but the enthusiasm of liberty would have induced the people to endure.

This method of raising troops is not more unfriendly to economy and vigor than it is to an equal distribution of the burden. The States near the seat of war, influenced by motives of self-preservation, made efforts to furnish their quotas, which even exceeded their abilities; while those at a distance from danger were, for the most part, as remiss as the others were diligent, in their exertions. The immediate pressure of this inequality was not in this case, as in that of the contributions of money, alleviated by the hope of a final liquidation. The States which did not pay their proportions of money might at least be charged with their deficiencies; but no account could be formed of the deficiencies in the supplies of men. We shall not, however, see much reason to reget the want of this hope, when we consider how little prospect there is, that the most delinquent States will ever be able to make compensation for their pecuniary failures. The system of quotas and requisitions, whether it be applied to men or money, is, in every view, a system of imbecility in the Union, and of inequality and injustice among the members.

The right of equal suffrage among the States is another exceptionable part of the Confederation. Every idea of proportion and every rule of fair representation conspire to condemn a principle, which gives to Rhode Island an equal weight in the scale of power with Massachusetts, or Connecticut, or New York; and to Deleware an equal voice in the national deliberations with Pennsylvania, or Virginia, or North Carolina. Its operation contradicts the fundamental maxim of republican government, which requires that the sense of the majority should prevail.

Sophistry may reply, that sovereigns are equal, and that a majority of the votes of the States will be a majority of confederated America. But this kind of logical legerdemain will never counteract the plain suggestions of justice and common-sense. It may happen that this majority of States is a small minority of the people of America3; and two thirds of the people of America could not long be persuaded, upon the credit of artificial distinctions and syllogistic subtleties, to submit their interests to the management and disposal of one third. The larger States would after a while revolt from the idea of receiving the law from the smaller. To acquiesce in such a privation of their due importance in the political scale, would be not merely to be insensible to the love of power, but even to sacrifice the desire of equality. It is neither rational to expect the first, nor just to require the last. The smaller States, considering how peculiarly their safety and welfare depend on union, ought readily to renounce a pretension which, if not relinquished, would prove fatal to its duration.

It may be objected to this, that not seven but nine States, or two thirds of the whole number, must consent to the most important resolutions; and it may be thence inferred that nine States would always comprehend a majority of the Union. But this does not obviate the impropriety of an equal vote between States of the most unequal dimensions and populousness; nor is the inference accurate in point of fact; for we can enumerate nine States which contain less than a majority of the people4; and it is constitutionally possible that these nine may give the vote. Besides, there are matters of considerable moment determinable by a bare majority; and there are others, concerning which doubts have been entertained, which, if interpreted in favor of the sufficiency of a vote of seven States, would extend its operation to interests of the first magnitude. In addition to this, it is to be observed that there is a probability of an increase in the number of States, and no provision for a proportional augmentation of the ratio of votes.

But this is not all: what at first sight may seem a remedy, is, in reality, a poison. To give a minority a negative upon the majority (which is always the case where more than a majority is requisite to a decision), is, in its tendency, to subject the sense of the greater number to that of the lesser. Congress, from the nonattendance of a few States, have been frequently in the situation of a Polish diet, where a single **VOTE** has been sufficient to put a stop to all their movements. A sixtieth part of the Union, which is about the proportion of Delaware and Rhode Island, has several times been able to oppose an entire bar to its operations. This is one of those refinements which, in practice, has an effect the reverse of what is expected from it in theory.

The necessity of unanimity in public bodies, or of something approaching towards it, has been founded upon a supposition that it would contribute to security. But its real operation is to embarrass the administration, to destroy the energy of the government, and to substitute the pleasure, caprice, or artifices of an insignificant, turbulent, or corrupt junto, to the regular deliberations and decisions of a respectable majority. In those emergencies of a nation, in which the goodness or badness, the weakness or strength of its government, is of the greatest importance, there is commonly a necessity for action. The public business must, in some way or other, go forward. If a pertinacious minority can control the opinion of a majority, respecting the best mode of conducting it, the majority, in order that something may be done, must conform to the views of the minority; and thus the sense of the smaller number will overrule that of the greater, and give a tone to the national proceedings. Hence, tedious delays; continual negotiation and intrigue; contemptible compromises of the public good.

And yet, in such a system, it is even happy when such compromises can take place: for upon some occasions things will not admit of accommodation; and then the measures of government must be injuriously suspended, or fatally defeated. It is often, by the impracticability of obtaining the concurrence of the necessary number of votes, kept in a state of inaction. Its situation must always savor of weakness, sometimes border upon anarchy.

It is not difficult to discover, that a principle of this kind gives greater scope to foreign corruption, as well as to domestic faction, than that which permits the sense of the majority to decide; though the contrary of this has been presumed. The mistake has proceeded from not attending with due care to the mischiefs that may be occasioned by obstructing the progress of government at certain critical seasons. When the concurrence of a large number is required by the Constitution to the doing of any national act, we are apt to rest satisfied that all is safe, because nothing improper will be likely **TO BE DONE**, but we forget how much good may be prevented, and how much ill may be produced, by the power of hindering the doing what may be necessary, and of keeping affairs in the same unfavorable posture in which they may happen to stand at particular periods.

Suppose, for instance, we were engaged in a war, in conjunction with one foreign nation, against another. Suppose the necessity of our situation demanded peace, and the interest or ambition of our ally led him to seek the prosecution of the war, with views that might justify us in making separate terms. In such a state of things, this ally of ours would evidently find it much easier, by his bribes and intrigues, to tie up the hands of government from making peace, where two thirds of all the votes were requisite to that object, than where a simple majority would suffice. In the first case, he would have to corrupt a smaller number; in the last, a greater number. Upon the same principle, it would be much easier for a foreign power with which we were at war to perplex our councils and embarrass our exertions. And, in a commercial view, we may be subjected to similar inconveniences. A nation, with which we might have a treaty of commerce, could with much greater facility prevent our forming a connection with her competitor in trade, though such a connection should be ever so beneficial to ourselves.

Evils of this description ought not to be regarded as imaginary. One of the weak sides of republics, among their numerous advantages, is that they afford too easy an inlet to foreign corruption. An hereditary monarch, though often disposed to sacrifice his subjects to his ambition, has so great a personal interest in the government and in the external glory of the nation, that it is not easy for a foreign power to give him an equivalent for what he would sacrifice by treachery to the state. The world has accordingly been witness to few examples of this species of royal prostitution, though there have been abundant specimens of every other kind.

In republics, persons elevated from the mass of the community, by the suffrages of their fellow-citizens, to stations of great pre-eminence and power, may find compensations for betraying their trust, which, to any but minds animated and guided by superior virtue, may appear to exceed the proportion of interest they have in the common stock, and to overbalance the obligations of duty. Hence it is that history furnishes us with so many mortifying examples of the prevalency of foreign corruption in republican governments. How much this contributed to the ruin of the ancient commonwealths has been already delineated. It is well known that the deputies of the United Provinces have, in various instances, been purchased by the emissaries of the neighboring kingdoms. The Earl of Chesterfield (if my memory serves me right), in a letter to his court, intimates that his success in an important negotiation must depend on his obtaining a major's commission for one of those deputies. And in Sweden the parties were alternately bought by France and England in so barefaced and notorious a manner that it excited universal disgust in the nation, and was a principal cause that the most limited monarch in Europe, in a single day, without tumult, violence, or opposition, became one of the most absolute and uncontrolled.

A circumstance which crowns the defects of the Confederation remains yet to be mentioned, the want of a judiciary power. Laws are a dead letter without courts to expound and define their true meaning and operation. The treaties of the United States, to have any force at all, must be considered as part of the law of the land. Their true import, as far as respects individuals, must, like all other laws, be ascertained by judicial determinations. To produce uniformity in these determinations, they ought to be submitted, in the last resort, to one **SUPREME TRIBUNAL**.

And this tribunal ought to be instituted under the same authority which forms the treaties themselves. These ingredients are both indispensable. If there is in each State a court of final jurisdiction, there may be as many different final determinations on the same point as there are courts. There are endless diversities in the opinions of men. We often see not only different courts but the judges of the came court differing from each other. To avoid the confusion which would unavoidably result from the contradictory decisions of a number of independent judicatories, all nations have found it necessary to establish one court paramount to the rest, possessing a general superintendence, and authorized to settle and declare in the last resort a uniform rule of civil justice.

This is the more necessary where the frame of the government is so compounded that the laws of the whole are in danger of being contravened by the laws of the parts. In this case, if the particular tribunals are invested with a right of ultimate jurisdiction, besides the contradictions to be expected from difference of opinion, there will be much to fear from the bias of local views and prejudices, and from the interference of local regulations. As often as such an interference was to happen, there would be reason to apprehend that the provisions of the particular laws might be preferred to those of the general laws; for nothing is more natural to men in office than to look with peculiar deference towards that authority to which they owe their official existence.

The treaties of the United States, under the present Constitution, are liable to the infractions of thirteen different legislatures, and as many different courts of final jurisdiction, acting under the authority of those legislatures. The faith, the reputation, the peace of the whole Union, are thus continually at the mercy of the prejudices, the passions, and the interests of every member of which it is composed. Is it possible that foreign nations can either respect or confide in such a government? Is it possible that the people of America will longer consent to trust their honor, their happiness, their safety, on so precarious a foundation? In this review of the Confederation, I have confined myself to the exhibition of its most material defects; passing over those imperfections in its details by which even a great part of the power intended to be conferred upon it has been in a great measure rendered abortive. It must be by this time evident to all men of reflection, who can divest themselves of the prepossessions of preconceived opinions, that it is a system so radically vicious and unsound, as to admit not of amendment but by an entire change in its leading features and characters.

The organization of Congress is itself utterly improper for the exercise of those powers which are necessary to be deposited in the Union. A single assembly may be a proper receptacle of those slender, or rather fettered, authorities, which have been heretofore delegated to the federal head; but it would be inconsistent with all the principles of good government, to intrust it with those additional powers which, even the moderate and more rational adversaries of the proposed Constitution admit, ought to reside in the United States. If that plan should not be adopted, and if the necessity of the Union should be able to withstand the ambitious aims of those men who may indulge magnificent schemes of personal aggrandizement from its dissolution, the probability would be, that we should run into the project of conferring supplementary powers upon Congress, as they are now constituted; and either the machine, from the intrinsic feebleness of its structure, will moulder into pieces, in spite of our ill-judged efforts to prop it; or, by successive augmentations of its force an energy, as necessity might prompt, we shall finally accumulate, in a single body, all the most important prerogatives of sovereignty, and thus entail upon our posterity one of the most execrable forms of government that human infatuation ever contrived. Thus, we should create in reality that very tyranny which the adversaries of the new Constitution either are, or affect to be, solicitous to avert.

It has not a little contributed to the infirmities of the existing federal system, that it never had a ratification by the **PEOPLE**. Resting on no better foundation than the consent of the several legislatures, it has been exposed to frequent and intricate questions concerning the validity of its powers, and has, in some instances, given birth to the enormous doctrine of a right of legislative repeal. Owing its ratification to the law of a State, it has been contended that the same authority might repeal the law by which it was ratified. However gross a heresy it may be to maintain that a **PARTY** to a **COMPACT** has a right to revoke that **COMPACT**, the doctrine itself has had respectable advocates. The possibility of a question of this nature proves the necessity of laying the foundations of our national government deeper than in the mere sanction of delegated authority. The fabric of American empire ought to rest on the solid basis of **THE CONSENT OF THE PEOPLE**. The streams of national power ought to flow immediately from that pure, original fountain of all legitimate authority.

The Necessity of a Government as Energetic as the One Proposed to the Preservation of the Union

From the New York Packet. Tuesday, December 18, 1787.

HAMILTON

To the People of the State of New York:

THE necessity of a Constitution, at least equally energetic with the one proposed, to the preservation of the Union, is the point at the examination of which we are now arrived.

This inquiry will naturally divide itself into three branches the objects to be provided for by the federal government, the quantity of power necessary to the accomplishment of those objects, the persons upon whom that power ought to operate. Its distribution and organization will more properly claim our attention under the succeeding head.

The principal purposes to be answered by union are these the common defense of the members; the preservation of the public peace as well against internal convulsions as external attacks; the regulation of commerce with other nations and between the States; the superintendence of our intercourse, political and commercial, with foreign countries.

The authorities essential to the common defense are these: to raise armies; to build and equip fleets; to prescribe rules for the government of both; to direct their operations; to provide for their support. These powers ought to exist without limitation, **BECAUSE IT IS IMPOSSIBLE TO FORESEE OR DEFINE THE EXTENT AND VARIETY OF NATIONAL EXIGENCIES, OR THE CORRESPONDENT EXTENT AND VARIETY OF THE MEANS WHICH MAY BE NECESSARY TO SATISFY THEM**. The circumstances that endanger the safety of nations are infinite, and for this reason no constitutional shackles can wisely be imposed on the power to which the care of it is committed. This power ought to be coextensive with all the possible combinations of such circumstances; and ought to be under the direction of the same councils which are appointed to preside over the common defense.

This is one of those truths which, to a correct and unprejudiced mind, carries its own evidence along with it; and may be obscured, but cannot be made plainer by argument or reasoning. It rests upon axioms as simple as they are universal; the **MEANS** ought to be proportioned to the **END**; the persons, from whose agency the attainment of any **END** is expected, ought to possess the **MEANS** by which it is to be attained.

Whether there ought to be a federal government intrusted with the care of the common defense, is a question in the first instance, open for discussion; but the moment it is decided in the affirmative, it will follow, that that government ought to be clothed with all the powers requisite to complete execution of its trust. And unless it can be shown that the circumstances which may affect the public safety are reducible within certain determinate limits; unless the contrary of this position can be fairly and rationally disputed, it must be admitted, as a necessary consequence, that there can be no limitation of that authority which is to provide for the defense and protection of the community, in any matter essential to its efficacy that is, in any matter essential to the **FORMATION**, **DIRECTION**, or **SUPPORT** of the **NATIONAL FORCES**.

Defective as the present Confederation has been proved to be, this principle appears to have been fully recognized by the framers of it; though they have not made proper or adequate provision for its exercise. Congress have an unlimited discretion to make requisitions of men and money; to govern the army and navy; to direct their operations. As their requisitions are made constitutionally binding upon the States, who are in fact under the most solemn obligations to furnish the supplies required of them, the intention evidently was that the United States should command whatever resources were by them judged requisite to the "common defense and general welfare." It was presumed that a sense of their true interests, and a regard to the dictates of good faith, would be found sufficient pledges for the punctual performance of the duty of the members to the federal head.

The experiment has, however, demonstrated that this expectation was ill-founded and illusory; and the observations, made under the last head, will, I imagine, have sufficed to convince the impartial and discerning, that there is an absolute necessity for an entire change in the first principles of the system; that if we are in earnest about giving the Union energy and duration, we must abandon the vain project of legislating upon the States in their collective capacities; we must extend the laws of the federal government to the individual citizens of America; we must discard the fallacious scheme of quotas and requisitions, as equally impracticable and unjust. The result from all this is that the Union ought to be invested with full power to levy troops; to build and equip fleets; and to raise the revenues which will be required for the formation and support of an army and navy, in the customary and ordinary modes practiced in other governments.

If the circumstances of our country are such as to demand a compound instead of a simple, a confederate instead of a sole, government, the essential point which will remain to be adjusted will be to discriminate the **OBJECTS**, as far as it can be done, which shall appertain to the different provinces or departments of power; allowing to each the most ample authority for fulfilling the objects committed to its charge. Shall the Union be constituted the guardian of the common safety? Are fleets and armies and revenues necessary to this purpose? The government of the Union must be empowered to pass all laws, and to make all regulations which have relation to them. The same must be the case in respect to commerce, and to every other matter to which its jurisdiction is permitted to extend. Is the administration of justice between the citizens of the same State the proper department of the local governments? These must possess all the authorities which are connected with this object, and with every other that may be allotted to their particular cognizance and direction. Not to confer in each case a degree of power commensurate to the end, would be to violate the most obvious rules of prudence and propriety, and improvidently to trust the great interests of the nation to hands which are disabled from managing them with vigor and success.

Who is likely to make suitable provisions for the public defense, as that body to which the guardianship of the public safety is confided; which, as the centre of information, will best understand the extent and urgency of the dangers that threaten; as the representative of the WHOLE, will feel itself most deeply interested in the preservation of every part; which, from the responsibility implied in the duty assigned to it, will be most sensibly impressed with the necessity of proper exertions; and which, by the extension of its authority throughout the States, can alone establish uniformity and concert in the plans and measures by which the common safety is to be secured? Is there not a manifest inconsistency in devolving upon the federal government the care of the general defense, and leaving in the State governments the **EFFECTIVE** powers by which it is to be provided for? Is not a want of co-operation the infallible consequence of such a system? And will not weakness, disorder, an undue distribution of the burdens and calamities of war, an unnecessary and intolerable increase of expense, be its natural and inevitable concomitants? Have we not had unequivocal experience of its effects in the course of the revolution which we have just accomplished?

Every view we may take of the subject, as candid inquirers after truth, will serve to convince us, that it is both unwise and dangerous to deny the federal government an unconfined authority, as to all those objects which are intrusted to its management. It will indeed deserve the most vigilant and careful attention of the people, to see that it be modeled in such a manner as to admit of its being safely vested with the requisite powers. If any plan which has been, or may be, offered to our consideration, should not, upon a dispassionate inspection, be found to answer this description, it ought to be rejected. A government, the constitution of which renders it unfit to be trusted with all the powers which a free people **OUGHT TO DELEGATE TO ANY GOVERNMENT**, would be an unsafe and improper depositary of the **NATIONAL INTERESTS**. Wherever THESE can with propriety be confided, the coincident powers may safely accompany them. This is the true result of all just reasoning upon the subject. And the adversaries of the plan promulgated by the convention ought to have confined themselves to showing, that the internal structure of the proposed government was such as to render it unworthy of the confidence of the people. They ought not to have wandered into inflammatory declamations and unmeaning cavils about the extent of the powers. The **POWERS** are not too extensive for the **OBJECTS** of federal administration, or, in other words, for the management of our **NATIONAL INTERESTS**; nor can any satisfactory argument be framed to show that they are chargeable with such an excess. If it be true, as has been insinuated by some of the writers on the other side, that the difficulty arises from the nature of the thing, and that the extent of the country will not permit us to form a government in which such ample powers can safely be reposed, it would prove that we ought to contract our views, and resort to the expedient of separate confederacies, which will move within more practicable spheres. For the absurdity must continually stare us in the face of confiding to a government the direction of the most essential national interests, without daring to trust it to the authorities which are indispensible to their proper and efficient management. Let us not attempt to reconcile contradictions, but firmly embrace a rational alternative.

I trust, however, that the impracticability of one general system cannot be shown. I am greatly mistaken, if any thing of weight has yet been advanced of this tendency; and I flatter myself, that the observations which have been made in the course of these papers have served to place the reverse of that position in as clear a light as any matter still in the womb of time and experience can be susceptible of.

This, at all events, must be evident, that the very difficulty itself, drawn from the extent of the country, is the strongest argument in favor of an energetic government; for any other can certainly never preserve the Union of so large an empire. If we embrace the tenets of those who oppose the adoption of the proposed Constitution, as the standard of our political creed, we cannot fail to verify the gloomy doctrines which predict the impracticability of a national system pervading entire limits of the present Confederacy.

The Powers Necessary to the Common Defense Further Considered

For the Independent Journal.

HAMILTON

To the People of the State of New York:

To THE powers proposed to be conferred upon the federal government, in respect to the creation and direction of the national forces, I have met with but one specific objection, which, if I understand it right, is this, that proper provision has not been made against the existence of standing armies in time of peace; an objection which, I shall now endeavor to show, rests on weak and unsubstantial foundations.

It has indeed been brought forward in the most vague and general form, supported only by bold assertions, without the appearance of argument; without even the sanction of theoretical opinions; in contradiction to the practice of other free nations, and to the general sense of America, as expressed in most of the existing constitutions.

The proprietory of this remark will appear, the moment it is recollected that the objection under consideration turns upon a supposed necessity of restraining the LEGISLATIVE authority of the nation, in the article of military establishments; a principle unheard of, except in one or two of our State constitutions, and rejected in all the rest.

A stranger to our politics, who was to read our newspapers at the present juncture, without having previously inspected the plan reported by the convention, would be naturally led to one of two conclusions: either that it contained a positive injunction, that standing armies should be kept up in time of peace; or that it vested in the EXECUTIVE the whole power of levying troops, without subjecting his discretion, in any shape, to the control of the legislature.

If he came afterwards to peruse the plan itself, he would be surprised to discover, that neither the one nor the other was the case; that the whole power of raising armies was lodged in the LEGISLATURE, not in the EXECUTIVE; that this legislature was to be a popular body, consisting of the representatives of the people periodically elected; and that instead of the provision he had supposed in favor of standing armies, there was to be found, in respect to this object, an important qualification even of the legislative discretion, in that clause which forbids the appropriation of money for the support of an army for any longer period than two years a precaution which, upon a nearer view of it, will appear to be a great and real security against the keeping up of troops without evident necessity.

Disappointed in his first surmise, the person I have supposed would be apt to pursue his conjectures a little further. He would naturally say to himself, it is impossible that all this vehement and pathetic declamation can be without some colorable pretext. It must needs be that this people, so jealous of their liberties, have, in all the preceding models of the constitutions which they have established, inserted the most precise and rigid precautions on this point, the omission of which, in the new plan, has given birth to all this apprehension and clamor.

If, under this impression, he proceeded to pass in review the several State constitutions, how great would be his disappointment to find that TWO ONLY of them1 contained an interdiction of standing armies in time of peace; that the other eleven had either observed a profound silence on the subject, or had in express terms admitted the right of the Legislature to authorize their existence. Still, however he would be persuaded that there must be some plausible foundation for the cry raised on this head.

He would never be able to imagine, while any source of information remained unexplored, that it was nothing more than an experiment upon the public credulity, dictated either by a deliberate intention to deceive, or by the overflowings of a zeal too intemperate to be ingenuous. It would probably occur to him, that he would be likely to find the precautions he was in search of in the primitive compact between the States. Here, at length, he would expect to meet with a solution of the enigma. No doubt, he would observe to himself, the existing Confederation must contain the most explicit provisions against military establishments in time of peace; and a departure from this model, in a favorite point, has occasioned the discontent which appears to influence these political champions.

If he should now apply himself to a careful and critical survey of the articles of Confederation, his astonishment would not only be increased, but would acquire a mixture of indignation, at the unexpected discovery, that these articles, instead of containing the prohibition he looked for, and though they had, with jealous circumspection, restricted the authority of the State legislatures in this particular, had not imposed a single restraint on that of the United States.

If he happened to be a man of quick sensibility, or ardent temper, he could now no longer refrain from regarding these clamors as the dishonest artifices of a sinister and unprincipled opposition to a plan which ought at least to receive a fair and candid examination from all sincere lovers of their country! How else, he would say, could the authors of them have been tempted to vent such loud censures upon that plan, about a point in which it seems to have conformed itself to the general sense of America as declared in its different forms of government, and in which it has even superadded a new and powerful guard unknown to any of them? If, on the contrary, he happened to be a man of calm and dispassionate feelings, he would indulge a sigh for the frailty of human nature, and would lament, that in a matter so interesting to the happiness of millions, the true merits of the question should be perplexed and entangled by expedients so unfriendly to an impartial and right determination. Even such a man could hardly forbear remarking, that a conduct of this kind has too much the appearance of an intention to mislead the people by alarming their passions, rather than to convince them by arguments addressed to their understandings.

But however little this objection may be countenanced, even by precedents among ourselves, it may be satisfactory to take a nearer view of its intrinsic merits. From a close examination it will appear that restraints upon the discretion of the legislature in respect to military establishments in time of peace, would be improper to be imposed, and if imposed, from the necessities of society, would be unlikely to be observed.

Though a wide ocean separates the United States from Europe, yet there are various considerations that warn us against an excess of confidence or security. On one side of us, and stretching far into our rear, are growing settlements subject to the dominion of Britain. On the other side, and extending to meet the British settlements, are colonies and establishments subject to the dominion of Spain. This situation and the vicinity of the West India Islands, belonging to these two powers create between them, in respect to their American possessions and in relation to us, a common interest.

The savage tribes on our Western frontier ought to be regarded as our natural enemies, their natural allies, because they have most to fear from us, and most to hope from them. The improvements in the art of navigation have, as to the facility of communication, rendered distant nations, in a great measure, neighbors. Britain and Spain are among the principal maritime powers of Europe. A future concert of views between these nations ought not to be regarded as improbable. The increasing remoteness of consanguinity is every day diminishing the force of the family compact between France and Spain. And politicians have ever with great reason considered the ties of blood as feeble and precarious links of political connection. These circumstances combined, admonish us not to be too sanguine in considering ourselves as entirely out of the reach of danger.

Previous to the Revolution, and ever since the peace, there has been a constant necessity for keeping small garrisons on our Western frontier. No person can doubt that these will continue to be indispensable, if it should only be against the ravages and depredations of the Indians.

These garrisons must either be furnished by occasional detachments from the militia, or by permanent corps in the pay of the government. The first is impracticable; and if practicable, would be pernicious. The militia would not long, if at all, submit to be dragged from their occupations and families to perform that most disagreeable duty in times of profound peace. And if they could be prevailed upon or compelled to do it, the increased expense of a frequent rotation of service, and the loss of labor and disconcertion of the industrious pursuits of individuals, would form conclusive objections to the scheme.

It would be as burdensome and injurious to the public as ruinous to private citizens. The latter resource of permanent corps in the pay of the government amounts to a standing army in time of peace; a small one, indeed, but not the less real for being small. Here is a simple view of the subject, that shows us at once the impropriety of a constitutional interdiction of such establishments, and the necessity of leaving the matter to the discretion and prudence of the legislature.

In proportion to our increase in strength, it is probable, nay, it may be said certain, that Britain and Spain would augment their military establishments in our neighborhood. If we should not be willing to be exposed, in a naked and defenseless condition, to their insults and encroachments, we should find it expedient to increase our frontier garrisons in some ratio to the force by which our Western settlements might be annoyed. There are, and will be, particular posts, the possession of which will include the command of large districts of territory, and facilitate future invasions of the remainder. It may be added that some of those posts will be keys to the trade with the Indian nations. Can any man think it would be wise to leave such posts in a situation to be at any instant seized by one or the other of two neighboring and formidable powers? To act this part would be to desert all the usual maxims of prudence and policy.

If we mean to be a commercial people, or even to be secure on our Atlantic side, we must endeavor, as soon as possible, to have a navy. To this purpose there must be dock-yards and arsenals; and for the defense of these, fortifications, and probably garrisons. When a nation has become so powerful by sea that it can protect its dock-yards by its fleets, this supersedes the necessity of garrisons for that purpose; but where naval establishments are in their infancy, moderate garrisons will, in all likelihood, be found an indispensable security against descents for the destruction of the arsenals and dock-yards, and sometimes of the fleet itself.

Bibliography

Ahmad, Imtiaz: *State and Foreign Policy: India's Role in South Asia*, New Delhi, Vikas, 1993.

Appleby, Paul H.: *Policy and Administration*, Birmingham, AL: University of Alabama Press, 1949.

Austin, Granville: *The Indian Constitution: Cornerstone of a Nation*, Oxford, Clarendon Press, 1966.

Barill, C.: *Social and Political Ideas of B.R. Ambedkar*, Jaipur, Aalekh Publishers, 1977.

Basu, Prahlad K.: *Governance and Public Administration for Poverty Reduction*, Salvador, Brazil, 1997.

Brecher, Michael: *The Politics of Succession in India*, Connecticut, Greenwood, 1976.

Carl J. Friedrich: *Constitutional Government and Democracy*, Boston, Ginn, 1950.

Chandel, M.P.S.: *A Social Force in Politics: Study of Scheduled Castes of UP*, New Delhi, Mittal, 1990.

Charles Howard McIlwain: *Constitutionalism: Ancient and Modern*, N.Y., Cornell University Press, 1958.

Dunner, Joseph: *Dictionary of Political Science*, New York, Philosophical Library, 1964.

Dwight Waldo: *Study of Public Administration*, New York, Random House, 1955.

Francis, E.: *Bureaucratic Power in National Politics*, Boston, Little Brown and Company, 1978.

Galanter, M.: *Competing Equalities: Law and the Backward Classes in India*, Berkeley, University of California Press, 1984.

Gargan, J.: *Handbook of Local Government Administration*, New York, Marcel Dekker, 1997.

Ghose, S.K.: *Politics of Violence: Dawn of a Dangerous Era*, Springfield, Nataraj, 1992.

Hazard, H.J.: *The Soviet System of Government*, Chicago, University of Chicago Press, 1960.

Heimanson, Rudolph: *Dictionary of Political Science and Law*, N.Y.: Oceana Publications, 1967.

Howard, McIlwain: *Constitutionalism: Ancient and Modern*, N.Y., Cornell University Press, 1958.

Jack Peltason: *Federal Courts in the Political Process*, New York, Random House, 1955.

Jalal, A.: *Nationalism, Democracy, and Development: State and Politics in India*, Delhi; New York: Oxford University Press, 1997.

Jenkins, Rob: *Democratic Politics and Economic Reform in India*, New York, Cambridge University Press, 1999.

Jones, W.H.: *The Government and Politics of India*, London, Hutchinson, 1971.

Joshi, B.: *A Democracy in Search of Equality: Untouchables, Politics and Indian Social Change*, New Delhi, Hindustan, 1982.

Joshi, Vijay: *India: Macroeconomics and Political Economy, 1964-1991*, Washington, World Bank, 1994.

Little, I.M.D.: *India: Macroeconomics and Political Economy, 1964-1991*, Washington, World Bank, 1994.

Mary, W.: *Asian Power and Politics: the Cultural Dimensions of Authority*, Cambridge, Belknap Press, 1985.

Max, Beloff: *Foreign Policy and the Democratic Process*, Baltimore, Johns Hopkins University Press, 1955.

Morris, W.H.: *The Government and Politics of India*, London, Hutchinson, 1971.

Paul, H.: *Policy and Administration*, Birmingham, AL: University of Alabama Press, 1949.

Prahlad, K.: *Governance and Public Administration for Poverty Reduction*, Salvador, Brazil, 1997.

Robert, W.: *Public Bureaucracy and the Incentive Problem*, Washington, D.C., World Bank, 1994.

Sharman, R.: *Aspects of Political Ideas and Institutions in Ancient India* Delhi, Motilal Banarsidass, 1968.

Srivastava, R.C.: *Judicial System in India*, Lucknow, Print House (India), 1992.

Sullivan, Ezra N.: *Bureaucrats and Policy Making*, New York, Holmes & Meier, 1984.

Victor G. : *Law as a Political Instrument*, New York, Random House, 1955.

Index

P

R

S

W